PACIFIC CENTURIES

T0271686

The increasing importance of the Pacific and Pacific Rim within the global economy places us on the brink of a "Pacific Century". While many hold that the concept of a Pacific region has only emerged in the twentieth century, this work demonstrates that such an economic region has existed for almost five hundred years.

Starting with the sixteenth century trade of Latin American silver for Chinese silk, leading researchers trace the economic, environmental and social history of the Pacific region. Chapters examine the trade of diverse commodities within the Pacific and analyse the ecological and social impacts of this increasing economic activity. The strong Chinese marketplace emerges as crucial to early Pacific development, and is compared with Japan's central role in the region's modern economy.

Pacific Centuries contributes to the understanding of a dynamic economic region. This valuable study also advances research into the economic histories of South and South East Asia, Australia and America, situating them within the wider Pacific context.

Dennis O. Flynn is Alexander R. Heron Professor of Economics at the University of the Pacific, California; **Lionel Frost** is Senior Lecturer in the School of Business at La Trobe University in Melbourne, Australia; and **A.J.H. Latham** is Senior Lecturer in International Economic History at University College, Swansea, UK.

ROUTLEDGE EXPLORATIONS IN ECONOMIC HISTORY

1 ECONOMIC IDEAS AND GOVERNMENT POLICY
Contributions to contemporary economic history
Sir Alec Cairncross

2 THE ORGANIZATION OF LABOUR MARKETS
Modernity, culture and governance in Germany, Sweden,
Britain and Japan
Bo Stråth

3 CURRENCY CONVERTIBILITY
The gold standard and beyond
Edited by Jorge Braga de Macedo, Barry Eichengreen and Jaime Reis

4 BRITAIN'S PLACE IN THE WORLD
A historical enquiry into import controls 1945–1960
Alan S. Milward and George Brennan

5 FRANCE AND THE INTERNATIONAL ECONOMY
From Vichy to the Treaty of Rome
Frances M.B. Lynch

6 MONETARY STANDARDS AND EXCHANGE RATES
M.C. Marcuzzo, L. Officer, A. Rosselli

7 PRODUCTION EFFICIENCY IN DOMESDAY
ENGLAND, 1086
John McDonald

8 FREE TRADE AND ITS RECEPTION 1815–1960
Freedom and trade: Volume 1
Edited by Andrew Marrison

9 CONCEIVING COMPANIES
Joint-stock politics in Victorian England
Timothy L. Alborn

10 THE BRITISH INDUSTRIAL DECLINE RECONSIDERED
Edited by Jean-Pierre Dormois and Michael Dintenfass

11 THE CONSERVATIVES AND INDUSTRIAL EFFICIENCY,
1951–1964
Thirteen Wasted Years?
Nick Tiratsoo and Jim Tomlinson

12 PACIFIC CENTURIES
Pacific and Pacific Rim History Since the Sixteenth Century
Edited by Dennis O. Flynn, Lionel Frost and A.J.H. Latham

PACIFIC CENTURIES

Pacific and Pacific Rim history
since the sixteenth century

*Edited by Dennis O. Flynn,
Lionel Frost and A.J.H. Latham*

Routledge
Taylor & Francis Group

LONDON AND NEW YORK

First published 1999
by Routledge
2 Park Square, Milton Park, Abingdon, Oxon OX14 4RN

Simultaneously published in the USA and Canada
by Routledge
711 Third Avenue, New York, NY 10017

Routledge is an imprint of the Taylor & Francis Group, an informa business

In editorial matter and selection © 1999 Dennis O. Flynn, Lionel Frost
and A.J.H. Latham, in individual chapters © the contributors

Typeset in Garamond by J&L Composition Ltd, Filey, North Yorkshire

British Library Cataloguing in Publication Data
A catalogue record for this book is available from the British Library

Library of Congress Cataloguing in Publication Data
Pacific centuries: Pacific and Pacific Rim history since the sixteenth
century/edited by Dennis O. Flynn, Lionel Frost and A.J.H. Latham.
p. cm.
Includes bibliographical references and index.
1. Pacific Area–Economic conditions. 2. Pacific Area–History.
I. Flynn, Dennis Owen, 1945– . II. Frost, Lionel. III. Latham
A.J.H.
HC681.P28295 1998
330.99–dc21 98–11844
CIP

ISBN 0–415–18431–2

CONTENTS

List of figures   vii
List of tables   viii
List of contributors   x

Introduction: Pacific centuries emerging   1
DENNIS O. FLYNN, LIONEL FROST AND A.J.H. LATHAM

1   **Spanish profitability in the Pacific: the**
    Philippines in the sixteenth and seventeenth
    centuries   23
    DENNIS O. FLYNN AND ARTURO GIRÁLDEZ

2   **The great silk exchange: how the world was**
    connected and developed   38
    DEBIN MA

3   **Islands in the rim: ecology and history in and**
    around the Pacific, 1521–1996   70
    JOHN R. MCNEILL

4   **Maritime trade and the agro-ecology of South**
    China, 1685–1850   85
    ROBERT B. MARKS

5   **Rice is a luxury, not a necessity: the sources of**
    Asian growth   110
    A.J.H. LATHAM

v

CONTENTS

6 Gold rushes and the trans-Pacific wheat trade:
California and Australia, 1848–57   125
JAMES GERBER

7 American trade dollars in nineteenth-century
China   152
DAVID J. ST. CLAIR

8 Alfred Crosby's *Ecological Imperialism*
reconsidered: a case study of European settlement
and environmental change on the Pacific Rim   171
WARWICK FROST

9 Economic motivations for China–United States
rapprochment in 1971   188
LORI WARNER

10 Migration and perceptions of identity: the case of
Singapore and Malaysian perceptions of the Australian
identity, 1966–96   224
KEVIN BLACKBURN

Index   251

FIGURES

2.1 Westward diffusion of sericultural knowledge   56
4.1 The South China Sea   88
4.2 Chinese maritime customs revenue, 1735–1812   93
4.3 Foreign trade at Guangzhou, 1723–39   98
4.4 Indian raw cotton imports, 1785–1833
(10-year averages)   99
4.5 China's foreign trade balances, 1760–1833
(5-year averages)   100
4.6 Silver flows at Guangzhou, 1800–33   101
4.7 Exports of Pearl River delta silk, 1723–1860   102
5.1 Chinese rice imports, 1867–1940   111
5.2 Income and rice consumption (belly-shaped curve)   119
5.3 Income and rice consumption (hypothesis)   120
6.1 Gold production in Australia and California at
U.S. Mint prices   129
6.2 Money wages, Northern California, 1849–57   134
6.3 Money wages, Melbourne, 1849–57   134
6.4 Wholesale prices, San Francisco, 1847–60   138
6.5 Prices of basic commodities, New South Wales and
Victoria, 1850–60   139
6.6 Australian wheat acreage, 1850–9   143
6.7 Wholesale wheat prices in three cities, 1849–57   145

TABLES

2.1	Chronology of silk development	42
5.1	Chinese rice imports 1867–1940	121
6.1	The spending and resource effects of a resource boom	133
6.2	The expansion of grain production during the gold rush	140
6.3	Exports of Californian wheat and flour, 1854–60	144
6.4	Gold production in California and Australia	147
7.1	Pure silver in various coins	160
7.2	Shipments of silver from San Francisco, 1873–5	164
9.1	China's trade with Communist and non-Communist countries, 1950–74	190
9.2	Phases in China's development and their reflections in technology acquisition, 1949–74	194–5
9.3(a)	Commodity composition of China's imports, 1966 and 1970	196
9.3(b)	The PRC's leading imports, 1969 and 1970	197
9.3(c)	The PRC's leading imports from the West, 1967	197
9.4	Commodity composition of U.S. exports, 1969 and 1970	198
9.5	Commodity composition of China's imports from the U.S., 1974	199
9.6	Commodity composition of China's exports to the U.S., 1974	200
9.7	PRC purchases of complete plants	201
9.8	Commodity composition of China's imports, 1970–4	202
9.9	Commodity composition of U.S. exports to China, 1973–4	204
9.10	China–U.S. trade, 1971–5	209

9.11   Commodity composition of China's exports by
        sector of origin, 1970–5   212
9.12   Growth of exports to China by selected nations,
        1962–9   213

CONTRIBUTORS

Kevin Blackburn is Lecturer in History at Nanyang Technological University, Singapore.

Dennis O. Flynn is Alexander R. Heron Professor of Economics at the University of the Pacific, California.

Lionel Frost is Senior Lecturer in the School of Business at La Trobe University in Melbourne.

Warwick Frost is Lecturer in Heritage, Environment and Culture at Royal Melbourne Institute of Technology University.

James Gerber is Associate Professor of Economics at San Diego State University, California.

Arturo Giráldez is Associate Professor of Modern Language and Literature at the University of the Pacific, California.

A.J.H. Latham is Senior Lecturer in International Economic History at University College, Swansea, U.K.

Debin Ma is a Researcher at the Institute of Economic Research, Hitotsubashi University, Japan.

John R. McNeill is Professor of History at Georgetown University, Washington DC.

Robert B. Marks is Professor of History at Whittier College, California.

David J. St. Clair is Professor of Economics at California State University at Hayward.

Lori Warner is Associate Professor of Economics at the University of the Pacific, California.

INTRODUCTION

Pacific centuries emerging

Dennis O. Flynn, Lionel Frost and A.J.H. Latham

During the last quarter of 1997, investor confidence around the world was being shaken by crises in the economies of East and Southeast Asia. Troubles had been brewing for months and currency and stock markets finally collapsed in Thailand, the Philippines, Malaysia, Indonesia, South Korea and Taiwan. Hong Kong and Singapore were also on shaky ground, the Japanese economy continues its struggle in the late-1990s; and while Chinese exports continue to boom, it is clear that further reforms to its inefficient state sector are needed. What was so unsettling about these developments was that they happened in a region which for some time had enjoyed rapid, seemingly limitless economic growth in the context of stock markets traditionally regarded as safe havens. How was it that Japanese, South Korean and other Asian "miracle" economies could falter so embarrassingly at this particular juncture? Whether these events prove a mere interruption to a stellar period of Asian economic growth from the mid-1960s, an upward trend bound to resume once economic restructuring is implemented, or whether they represent a serious turning point in the region's economic history, remains to be seen. But these developments clearly illustrate the Pacific region's growing influence in the global economy. International connections through trade, capital flows, and multinational companies mean that interruptions in Asian economic growth necessarily engender global repercussions.

Asia's economic achievements and problems are products of a matrix of complex interactions between humans and the environment, a matrix in turn shaped by past exchanges of commodities,

1

capital, ideas, and technologies among Asian countries themselves and between Asia and the rest of the world. When recently asked to advise students interested in careers in economics, Mr. Ian Macfarlane, Governor of the Reserve Bank of Australia, replied: "know your history." (*Mosaic* 1997: 21). Indeed, this injunction applies to those wishing to do business, not just in Asia, but anywhere in the world:

> "It is not a luxury for an investment manager to study the histories of the countries in which he or she invests. It is a vital and inherent part of the analytical task of assessing risk and assessing performance potential."
>
> (George 1992: 41)

With the economic importance of the Pacific region now obvious to a world generally acknowledged to be entering a new "Pacific Century", a deeper historical understanding of prior Pacific Centuries is essential.

Brief reflection upon the vastness of the Pacific, the diversity of its geography, cultures and institutions, and its long history of economic interaction, makes one realize that it would be difficult to write a comprehensive, general history of the Pacific region. There have been some useful attempts, ranging from a long-term view of history around the Pacific (Jones *et al.* 1993) to others decidedly oriented toward business practices and current concerns (Linder 1986; Segal 1990; Besher 1992; George 1992). These bold, sweeping works help provide context for a multitude of detailed studies focusing on specific concerns, but an adequate overview of Pacific history remains an abstract and distant aspiration at this moment.

Selected essays from the first Pacific Centuries conference (held 5–7 April 1994 at the University of the Pacific in Stockton, California) have recently been published (Miller *et al.* 1998). In the "Introduction: The Pacific Rim's Past Deserves a Future," Flynn and Giráldez state that: "substantial, continuous trade between Asia and the Americas did not exist prior to the founding of the city of Manila; Pacific Rim trade began in 1571, not earlier and not later." (1998: 1) The sudden eruption of substantial trade between Acapulco, Manila and mainland China depended primarily upon two industries: silver (produced in Spanish America and destined for end-market China) and silk (produced in China and destined for Spanish America).[1] Domestic monetary and fiscal events

2

led to China's "silverization" (see von Glahn 1996a; 1996b), which in turn generated the demand-side impetus leading to the birth of trans-Pacific and world trade in 1571. Indeed, the unifying thread connecting several essays in the initial Pacific Centuries volume revolves around the central role of China for centuries. Whether discussing Chinese silver imports from America up to 1850 (Wong 1998: 172–80), environmental history in the eighteenth and nineteenth centuries (McNeill 1998: 72–93), California's mercury exports in the second half of the nineteenth century (St. Clair 1998: 210–33), nineteenth- and twentieth-century U.S. policy on the Pacific (Dudden 1998: 94–106), Pacific rice trade between 1877 and World War I (Latham 1998: 155–71), or timber exports in the second half of the twentieth century (Daigle 1998: 234–43), scholars independently emphasize the crucial role of China in each case. Studies of diverse commodities and distinct centuries thus appear to support the contention (Frost 1998: 45–62) that today's Pacific Century indeed reflects a world economy which has come "full circle," in the sense that Asian economies are in the midst of a "return to prominence" on the global market landscape.

The metaphorical "economic-miracle" interpretation of late-twentieth century Asian economic growth is undergoing revision today in favor of a more balanced (i.e. less Eurocentric) world view which recognizes that global interdependence in economic terms entered its fifth century a generation ago. Whatever the century or product in question, Chinese demand and/or Chinese production usually played a central role; this was the lead story emerging from the initial 1994 Pacific Centuries conference. And this theme is compatible with several new studies which indicate that, despite the fact that Europeans and the U.S. achieved global economic and military hegemony between 1850 and 1950, the subsequent late-twentieth-century rise of Asian economies should be interpreted as a return to normality in the long-term context of global history (e.g. Frank 1998, Marks 1998, and Pomeranz forthcoming). Identification and exploration of key themes in Pacific Centuries history must form the next stage if our work is to remain coherent and relevant.

Approaching Pacific Centuries from this perspective opens a new range of possibilities for further work. As Sutcliffe (1993: 1) writes:

> Thematic history selects features of historical reality which persist from century to century or from place to place. It permits long continuities and comparisons from

area to area. It is often international in scope, and it can detect connections which might pass unperceived within unitary spatial and temporal formats.

Seen in this light, limitations of some previous writings and thinking about Pacific history are obvious. Foremost among modern misconceptions is the notion that the rise of today's Pacific Century as an arena of world trade is a recent phenomenon. Significant intercontinental trade between Asia, the Americas, Africa and Europe dates back much further than is commonly supposed, and studies which focus only on global trade from, say, 1945 necessarily overlook several centuries of earlier development which shaped the recent histories of all countries.

Chapters in this volume

Flynn and Giráldez (1995) have previously argued that the birth of Pacific and world trade can be dated to the founding of Manila by Spaniards in 1571. In Chapter 1 of this volume they explore the profitability of this trans-Pacific trade and conclude that it financed Imperial Spain's geo-military ambitions in Asian waters. In fact, the Manila galleons trade's influence reached well beyond Spain's protracted struggle with the Dutch for hegemony over non-Japanese/non-Chinese Pacific archipelagoes; it helped shape the histories of four continents: Europe (where Spain fought an 80-year battle for supremacy in the Low Countries), the Americas (primary silver source, where the local population was ravaged by disease and violence), Africa (where slaves were exported and bartered in exchange for silver along Latin America's Atlantic coast), Asia (end-market for the silver exchanged for silks, spices, and ceramics), and the Levant (gateway link between Asia and Europe) as well.

Flynn and Giráldez's work on Spain's effort to control the Pacific underlies one of the great continuities in Pacific Centuries: the influence of China. Profitability from Spain's only direct connection with Asia (via the Pacific) would have been impossible in the absence of silver demand on the part of Chinese customers. By the mid-fifteenth century, an increasing number of locations within China had come to adopt silver money in response to earlier over-issues of paper money. As a consequence, the world's largest economy gradually converted to silver monies for use in commerce and payment of taxes and tribute and the white metal's

4

value skyrocketed. Mines in the Andes and Japan, controlled by the Spanish monarchy and Tokugawa Shogunate respectively, yielded massive profits. The mines of Potosí became the richest, lowest-cost sources of silver in the Andes and in the world. The work of Flynn and Giráldez implies that without Chinese demand there would have been no extensive Spanish Empire; and that it was China, not Europe, which played a central role in the birth of global trade. Spaniards organized the production of silver in America, and Europeans acted as middlemen (Spaniards moved silver across the Atlantic and Pacific, numerous non-Spanish entities shipped silver via land and sea routes from Europe eastward, and Portuguese and Dutch were involved in the export of Japanese silver), but this activity would not have been undertaken in the absence of Chinese demand for silver. Economic theory teaches that the consumer, not the producer, is ultimately sovereign.

Silver history is indispensable for understanding the birth of Pacific and global trade, but silk production was just as prodigious (in value terms) during silver's heyday; moreover, silk's intercontinental significance spans millennia. In Chapter 2, Debin Ma highlights aspects of silk history since its initial production in China between 5,000 and 3,000 BC. Silk-weaving industries had spread to Byzantium and Persia between the fourth and sixth centuries AD and East–West trade flourished in the seventh and eighth centuries. Silk cultivation spread into Persia, Anatolia, and regions controlled by Byzantium, however, and the silk world bifurcated: Persia eventually became the primary source of silk for the Middle East, Europe and North Africa; China supplied raw silk and silk fabric exports to Japan, Southeast Asia, and parts of Central and South Asia. Only when the whole of Asia and Eastern Europe was later united under Mongol political authority did cheap Chinese raw silk inundate Europe between the 1260s and the 1350s. *Pax Mongolica* subsequently collapsed, however, and the silk world once again bifurcated: Chinese silk production dominated in East Asia, while Persian raw silk production dominated in the Middle East and Europe.

Ming China halted both tribute and private trade with Japan by the 1530s, but huge Japanese demand for Chinese silk and equally extensive Chinese demand for Japanese silver did not subside. Thus, immense profits via contraband trade were preordained. European merchants based on Macao and Taiwan became freight-forward specialists focusing on the illicit and lucrative Sino-Japanese exchange.

Technology was not about to stand still, however, and raw silk production was successfully transplanted onto Japanese soil in the seventeenth century. The Japanese market was lost to home-grown Japanese competitors, but Chinese silk interests were buoyed by exports to Spanish America once Spain founded the city of Manila in 1571. Peruvian silk prices were 10 times higher than in Manila in 1620–1 (Chuan 1972: 468), by which time Chinese silk imports had already destroyed the Mexican silk industry (itself a 1530s Spanish transplant).

> the opening-up of the Pacific route was a significant geographic break-through for the history of the silk trade. Chinese silk, for the first time, instead of going westward reversed its direction and went further east to be connected to the New Continent.
>
> (p. 52)

In the seventeenth and eighteenth centuries, Northern Italy and Southern France emerged as major producers and exporters of raw silk, probably surpassing China itself. By the early nineteenth century, London had become an important center for the silk trade. The outbreak of a silkworm disease in Europe and the Middle East in the 1850s and 1860s precipitated a drastic drop in European silk production, however, reviving silk production in East Asia. The mid-nineteenth century also witnessed the exportation of European silk-reeling technology and factory system back to China and Japan (from whence the original technology had been inherited).

The Suez Canal opened in 1869, at a time when Western powers were forcing Chinese and Japanese markets open to accommodate Western needs. Substantial amounts of raw silk began to cross the North Pacific from China and Japan to San Francisco once a regular shipping line had been established in 1867. Completion of the trans-continental railway system in 1869 permitted raw silk to be routed straight through to New York. Skilled British silk workers and entrepreneurs from Macclesfield had meanwhile migrated to Paterson, New Jersey after the U.S. Civil War; by the 1920s and 1930s the U.S. produced more finished silk than all European countries combined, and even double that of Japan. Japan overtook China in raw silk production by the mid-1910s and by the 1920s and 1930s Japan supplied 75 to 90 percent of total world raw silk exports, by which time "the

bulk of the global silk trade was carried through the Pacific route"
(p. 54). Once again, the silk trade had regained prominence
during the twentieth century, the fifth century during which
this product crossed the Pacific.

As explained above, the motivational force behind establishment
of trans-Pacific linkages was profit. Political consolidation was
required in order to secure profits; in turn, concentration of profits
furthered political and commercial goals. In Chapter 3, John R.
McNeill elucidates profound, yet unintended, consequences of the
European intrusion into the Pacific during what he describes as an
ecological "blip of time, the last 475 years." McNeill focuses on
two types of human impacts: (1) those derived from biological
invasions, and (2) others derived from the power of concentrated
demand (from peoples living around the Rim).

Pacific islands had remained remarkably isolated prior to
Magellan's crossing in 1521; their ecologies were therefore sus-
ceptible to violent disruptions when breached from outside.
Despite the fact that mid-seventeenth-century Manila contained
nearly 50,000 inhabitants – approximately the same population as
Barcelona, Valladolid, Danzig, Vienna, Marseille, and other major
trading centers with broader-based economies at that time
(deVries 1984: Appendix 1) – the vast Pacific was mostly unaf-
fected by the Rim-to-Rim exchange which heavily impacted the
rest of the world. After the Philippines, Guam was the first island
jolted with a biological invasion; 90 percent of the Chamorros
died shortly after Spaniards introduced foreign flora, fauna, and
germs. Sixty to 90 percent population declines typified island after
island, where numbers normally did not begin to recover for 90–150
years. Reduced human densities implied abandonment of fields
and gardens, of course, and newly introduced species quickly filled
gaps. Whalers later deposited goats on islands, whether inhabited
or not, just in case they might be needed later. The most devastating intruder was perhaps the Norway rat, inadvertently introduced by Cook (sailing the Pacific 1768–79) and his followers.

Prior to the time of Cook, concentrated demand from distant
lands had not yet rearranged oceanic island ecosystems, but late-
eighteenth century navigational advances made extraction of
island products profitable. Within a century of Cook's death,
oceanic islands had undergone booms and busts in mother-of-
pearl, beche-de-mer (sea cucumber), sealskins, tortoiseshell,
sandalwood and other commodities. All had direct ecological

effects, while some had indirect effects (for example, Fiji's forests were felled to fuel fires to dry sea cucumbers for export).

Sandalwood provides an interesting nineteenth-century example. Hawaiian kings put thousands to work burning forests in order to find sandalwood, which emits a distinctive smell when burned. Again, sandalwood was exported mainly to China, as were many other commodities:

> Aside from whale oil and whalebone, all the extractive Pacific trades before about 1860 were driven by Chinese demand. The opening of China to maritime trade from the 1780s onward, and the difficulty foreigners had in buying Chinese goods with anything but silver, created conditions in which it made economic sense to ransack the Pacific for specialty items that Chinese consumers cherished.
>
> (p. 76)

Phosphate – found as rock and in bird guano – provides another fascinating case study. West Australian wheat, pastures, and sheep populations depended upon superphosphates, while two tropical Pacific islands, Nauru and Banaba, happen to have been endowed with some of the richest guano in the world. These islands have been decimated, but the 5,000 Nauruans have become some of the richest people in the world since renegotiating mining leases in 1968 after independence from Australia.

After 1860, new technologies ushered in an age of plantations. Concentrated demand slowly shifted away from Chinese dominance. Due to the U.S. Civil War, France could not get enough American cotton, thereby motivating plantation development in French Polynesia. Sugar plantations were set up in Fiji, in Hawaii after 1890, and in the Marianas under Japanese rule (1920–44). Pineapples, bananas, coffee and copra were grown on these and other islands and the ecological effects were devastating. American, British, and Russian seal hunters scoured the Pacific between 1780 and 1850 to satisfy the demand for furs, mainly in China, Russia, and Europe. Growth in the economies of Japan, Australia and the U.S. reduced China's role as the environmental engine of change, but the overall impact grew nonetheless. In the late twentieth-century, it has been Japan, not China, which has been the main demand-side driving force behind the Pacific timber trade (and many others). Projected growth during the newest "Pacific Century" will no doubt engender environmental impacts which will attract the attention of environmentalists and future historians alike.

Analysis of coastal trade evidence has persuaded Robert Marks, in Chapter 4, to reject "the usual view of the place of China in the emerging world economy, from the passive object of European stimulation" in favor of interpreting China's domestic economy as "an active force in the shaping of the modern world economy" (p. 105). Marks' study begins in 1685 with the massive economic dislocation labeled the "Kangxi Depression." Between 1662 and 1685, the Qing government (which replaced the Ming Dynasty in 1644) forced China's coastal population to relocate inland and burned all ocean-going junks; these drastic actions were undertaken to deprive Ming-loyalist Koxinga of supplies. The capture of Taiwan in 1683 persuaded the emperor Kangxi to reopen coastal trade. Soon after 1684 thousands of new junks (most of which were small, non-ocean-going vessels) were constructed in the area around Guangzhou. By 1700, between 50 and 100 large ocean-going junks were already carrying 20,000 tons of goods back to Guangdong (compared with only 500 tons of European exports from Guangzhou). China's trade with the Nanyang (the Southern Ocean) exceeded Holland's (but was less than England's) Baltic trade. When China's domestic grain trade is included in the picture – which makes sense because the Chinese economy was bigger than that of all of Europe – the "total amount of grain entering long-distance trade in China . . . clearly outpaced that in [all of] Europe . . . " (p. 92) As late as 1735, only about 10–12 percent of coastal customs duties were attributable to European ships. (pp. 92–3)

Foshan's expanding cotton textile industry required the importation of raw cotton from India (brought by Indian, Muslim, or Portuguese traders) and from central and northern China. For some reason, cultivation of cotton died out in the Pearl River delta, an area which instead specialized in sugar cane exports which it swapped for imports of raw cotton. Sugar cane replaced rice production on roughly a one-to-one basis in Guangdong until by "the nineteenth century, entire villages specialized in only sugar cane" (p. 95). Since Guangdong itself, along with exports to the Nanyang, comprised the primary market for cotton thread and cloth production, the

"resumption of Chinese overseas and coastal trade in the late-seventeenth and early eighteenth centuries thus

provided the impetus not just to economic expansion following the mid-seventeenth century crisis, but also to the
commercialization and specialization of agriculture in
Guangdong."

(p. 96)

The European trade increased dramatically in the 1780s when the
British discovered the Chinese demand for raw cotton: "By the
end of the eighteenth century . . . European trade had eclipsed the
Chinese coastal and Nanyang trade, easily reaching four times the
Chinese trade" (p. 97). Indian raw cotton accounted for one-third
of English East India Company revenues in the late-eighteenth
century, from which level Chinese raw cotton imports doubled
during the first quarter of the nineteenth century (and increased
another 50 percent by the 1830s). About 50,000 people were
employed in 2,500 shops in the Foshan textile industry. It was
mainly domestic Chinese demand for cotton cloth which stimulated raw cotton imports, which in turn led to the conversion of
paddy fields to sugar cane fields. Other regions in China exported
rice to Guangdong.
 Silk exports led to a similar conversion of paddy fields to the
familiar "fish pond–mulberry tree" combination required for production of raw silk. Overseas exports of Guangdong silk increased
from about 25,000 piculs in 1723 to 1.1 million piculs in 1828,
doubling again from 1828 to 1834, and doubling yet again from
1850 to 1860. Add to this an increase in English demand for tea
throughout the eighteenth century, and China's foreign trade
picture clarifies: cotton textiles, raw silk, and tea were exported
in tremendous volumes in exchange for a number of imports,
prominent among which was – again – silver. Marks concludes:

In effect, until the early nineteenth century, China was *the*
industrialized country in the world . . . To be sure, Europeans introduced opium into the equation, but basically
the linking of China to the European world economy was
less a new phenomenon than a continuation of existing
patterns set deep within the functioning of the Chinese
economy.

(pp. 100, 105)

An international market in rice became established after 1800,
according to A.J.H. Latham in Chapter 5. It is clear why rice

flowed into countries such as Ceylon, Malaya, Indonesia, and the Philippines: it fed immigrant laborers working in mines and plantations in those countries. But why did China import rice? Conventional wisdom states that a Chinese economic crisis crippled domestic food production, and this crisis left no option to China's importation of rice. Latham argues the reverse: high and rising levels of Chinese income were spent on luxury food items, prominent among which was rice.

Rice culture in Southern China dates back 7,000 years, but low per capita incomes throughout Asia meant that peasants could not typically eat this preferred food on a regular basis. It was simply too expensive for daily consumption. Consumption of white rice spread amongst common people in Japan after 1400 and was widespread by the 1730s. Agricultural advances in Korea between 1400 and 1600 facilitated establishment of a market economy, resulting in the spread of rice cultivation: "To facilitate exchange, commodity monies were introduced, of which the two most important were rice itself, and cloth" (p. 115). By 1600 rice comprised 70 percent of Southern Chinese grain production, which reflected a high standard of living in that region of the country.

As explained in Marks' essay, sericulture (and to a lesser extent, sugar cane and tobacco later) replaced rice production in the Pearl River delta, but this occurred because of high rates of return in silk production in that region. High productivity implied regional prosperity, which in turn led to the importation of rice and stimulation of rice production elsewhere. Fertilizers were used and crop rotations introduced from the 1660s, so dry rice, yellow beans, wheat, barley, beans, and rapeseed became second crops to wet rice. From about 1700 in the lower Yangtze cotton was often grown in rotation with rice (with advantages in breaking the pest cycle):

> So the three major crops of the lower Yangtze area became rice, cotton, and mulberry leaves according to natural conditions, with other crops like wheat, rapeseed and beans as second crops. . . . That the region was increasingly turning to cash crops like cotton, silk, tobacco and sugar, and expensive food items such as fish, meat and fruit indicates rising living standards.
>
> (pp. 115–16)

11

Latham reports that the arrival of the American crops (introduced via Pacific trade routes) – maize, cassava, potatoes, and sweet potatoes – did not dethrone the preferred status of rice. The dry Northeast became an important grain producing area during the eighteenth century and the southward migration of northern crops enabled production on previously uncultivated dry land in the south: by "the 1930s half the land in cultivation in the Yangtze valley was dry, and more than that in Yunnan and the southwest" (p. 117). Although rice comprised 70 percent of Southern China's grain production in 1600, the spread of New World crops like maize and potatoes caused this proportion to fall to 36 percent by the 1930s. While the quantity of rice consumed has tended to stabilize during the last third of the twentieth century, expenditures on rice have risen because higher quality rice is being substituted.

A study by Rawski indicates that Chinese per capita output rose 10 percent during the period 1914/18 to 1931/36, while the most dynamic areas – the Lower Yangtze and the northeastern provinces – ran rice deficits with the Middle and Upper Yangtze provinces. This continuing pattern of rice importation by thriving regions within China supports Latham's contention that China's post-1800 importation of rice implied vigorous, not anemic, economic growth.

In Chapter 6 James Gerber investigates a phenomenon which contradicts received economic theory. Mid-nineteenth century gold discoveries propelled northern California into a period of demographic and economic boom, of course, but a less well-known fact is that California became one of the most important grain-producing areas of the U.S. during the second half of the nineteenth century. This development is surprising because it directly contradicts the "Dutch Disease" predictions for a major resource boom.

We encourage the reader to consult Gerber's brief and clear explanation of Dutch Disease logic. The essential idea is that a major resource boom like the California Gold Rush requires attraction of large volumes of productive inputs, including labor. There were about 15,000 non-Native Americans in California in 1848; by 1852 there were more than 250,000; numbers for the city of San Francisco were about 500 and 36,000 respectively. Immigrants streamed in from the East Coast, Europe, Mexico, Chile, Australia, and Hawaii. Attraction of scarce inputs requires the bidding up of wages and other input prices, which in fact happened in California. Since internationally-traded items like

12

wheat are characterized by prices determined in world – not local – markets, it was not possible to raise California wheat prices in order to cover rising input costs. Without some unusual outside influence, the non-gold export market should have crashed. Instead, California wheat exports boomed. Chilean millers even tried to corner the San Francisco market so as to stifle California grain production, but the plot failed. Already by 1854, combined wheat and flour exports totaled $538,000, nearly as much as California's second biggest export item, mercury. And the trend continued. California became the largest U.S. producer of barley by 1860 and the country's second largest producer of wheat by 1890 (9 percent of U.S. production).

Growing exports of surplus wheat were destined for Hawaii, Hong Kong, Russian North America, Mexico, Central America, Chile, Vancouver, Manila, Shanghai, New York, and Liverpool. But markets of the Pacific were far more important during the early phase of California's agricultural development than either European or U.S. markets:

> In effect, California's trade relations were those of a separate nation, rather than those of a U.S. region. Australia and New Zealand took more than 52 percent of California's combined wheat and flour exports during the first six years of export trade. Furthermore, . . . the trade led to premium prices for California producers who were struggling to become competitive on world markets.
>
> (pp. 144–5)

By 1860, this pattern would change and European markets, especially Liverpool, became the main market for Californian wheat. Throughout the second half of the nineteenth century, the anomalous explosion in exports of California grains is all the more striking in view of the fact that grains no longer figure prominently in Californian agriculture.

On the supply side, Gerber notes that Californian growers somehow maintained competitiveness internationally despite extraordinarily high labor costs. The key catalyst on the demand side was the discovery of gold in Australia, which was as large as (and almost simultaneous with) California's Gold Rush. The cities and regions of New South Wales and Victoria were far more populous and developed than was California in the mid-nineteenth century. Australian grain production could not keep pace with

Australian grain demand; thus, Australia was an important importer of grain during California agriculture's crucial early years. Both gold and grains traded heavily in the world market during the second half of the nineteenth century. Symbiosis between the two was both mysterious and fascinating around the Pacific.

Designed for circulation outside of the issuing jurisdiction, trade coins were not normally legal tender domestically. In Chapter 7, David J. St. Clair reinterprets U.S. Trade Dollars from their initial minting in 1873 until their demise later that decade. Nearly 36 million U.S. Trade Dollars were minted in just four years – consuming 23 percent of the Comstock Lode's silver – which more than quadrupled production of regular U.S. silver dollars in all years prior to 1873. Over 80 percent of these coins were shipped abroad, and 90 percent of the exported trade dollars reached China via San Francisco. But trade dollar production ended in 1879 and shortly thereafter earned the dubious distinction as America's only coin ever to be recalled. The trade dollar is generally considered an abject failure by historians and numismatists, who echo President Chester Arthur's 1883 description of the coin before Congress as "an embarrassment to our currency." Merchants came to hate the coin because its legal tender status was unclear. It was also dragged into the famous bimetallic controversy of that time and condemned as a disruptive element.

St. Clair instead pronounces the Trade Dollar a poorly understood success. China had been by far the world's most voracious importer of silver since the collapse of its paper money system in the fifteenth century. China did not mint silver coins, however, choosing instead to import silver coins from abroad. All over the world, confidence in the intrinsic value of Spanish money spread and Chinese customers also learned over time to trust the integrity of Spanish dollars. Worldwide confidence was advantageous to the Spanish Crown, which earned only a modest seigniorage profit on each coin, but issued prodigious quantities which were held throughout the world.

Because China's market was by far the world's most extensive, many mints desired to establish "brand loyalty" for their coin-products; tremendous profits awaited the few to succeed. Having been burned in innumerable (predictable) instances of debasement and other forms of deceit, however, the Chinese were reluctant to accept unfamiliar coins. The same was true elsewhere. Austria's famous Maria Theresa thaler circulated primarily in East Africa and the Middle East for two centuries, for example, maintaining the same appearance, content and even date (1780) irrespective of its date of issue. Even copies of the Maria Theresa thaler produced by Great Britain, Belgium, France, and Italy, featured the same likeness and 1780 date.

Great Britain tried to introduce a trade coin for use in China in 1778, but this Canton dollar was quickly debased and therefore repudiated by the Chinese. This episode led to private-sector innovation within China. Merchants "chopped" coins, which meant that the paying merchant guaranteed it purity and weight and would stand behind the coin. In 1863–4 Britain again minted a silver trade dollar in Hong Kong, but discontinued minting after only two years because of suspicion on the part of Chinese customers. A new Mexican silver dollar – the balance scale peso – was also introduced in 1869; it was smaller, had an unfamiliar design, and contained the designation "peso." Despite the fact that the balance scale peso contained the same silver content as before, unfamiliarity caused it to be rejected by the Chinese populace.

From the time the first American ship entered China in 1784 until 1833, Mexican silver dollars comprised 64 percent of American exports to China; U.S. silver production during that period was virtually zero. Silver exports to China totaled $10 million between 1856 and 1860, during which time only $400,000 in silver was mined in the U.S. Although crucial for U.S. trade with China, Mexican dollars commanded a premium in the marketplace:

> It should be noted that the failed scheme to produce Mexican dollars in San Francisco occurred in 1861, when American silver output was more than 38 times larger than the pre-Comstock level of 1858. In addition, American merchants had to contend with a 12 percent excise tax imposed by the Mexican government on the export of Mexican dollars in 1867.
>
> (Chapter 7, this volume: pp. 161-2)

Thus the American trade dollar – larger and a "superior brand" compared with the regular U.S. silver dollar – was introduced to compete with the Mexican dollar in the Chinese marketplace. Despite intial skepticism, the U.S. trade dollar enjoyed a 2 percent premium over the Mexican dollar in the China trade in 1877. In 1878 the U.S. trade dollar accounted for 82 percent of U.S. silver exports.

St. Clair endorses a technological explanation for abandonment of the U.S. trade dollar. Comstock bullion contained a higher gold content – a liability in Asian markets – than did Mexican ore. The high-capacity U.S. Mint was able to separate the metals for a cost of only 1.5 percent of value. Since the Mint could only process legal coins, however, the trade coin was given the status of a subsidiary coin. Unfortunately, its legal-tender status drug the coin into contentious domestic debates and led to abandonment of this promising coin. The history of the U.S. trade dollar offers interesting lessons both about monetary history and the importance of Chinese trade relations with the world during the second half of the nineteenth century.

While McNeill's essay in this volume is a bold, wide-ranging interpretation of the environmental impact of trade and settlements in the Pacific, Warwick Frost's work in Chapter 8 is a close-up study of the same theme. Crosby's argument about the superiority of the European biota of germs, plants, and animals, which together with advanced military power enabled European colonists to exert a major impact on the indigenous peoples and the environment, is modified here. Frost explains how in the high-rainfall, forested areas of Australia, plagues of native insects and animals, and vigorous plant re-growth, made it difficult for European settlers to clear the land for commercial farming. As a result, settlers used slash-and-burn clearance methods. This was supported and encouraged by colonial governments which wanted to bring as much land into production as possible. The destruction of nearly all of Australia's native forests created serious problems, as introduced animals and plants multiplied unchecked and became pests, and burning off brought with it the risk of forest fire (for instance, 71 people were killed by fires in Victoria on "Black Friday" in 1939). Deliberate environmental damage by humans, for what seemed at the time to be sensible reasons, is a recurring theme of Pacific history. Frost's analysis could be applied fruitfully to other parts of the Pacific, notably China and also Indonesia, where in late 1997 forest burning created a serious air pollution problem affecting much of Southeast Asia.

While there is truth in the conventional claim that U.S. trade restrictions during the Cold War (*economic* weapons) were used to apply *political* pressure upon Communist China, in Chapter 9 Lori Warner argues that rapprochement – from both Chinese and American perspectives – was also motivated by powerful economic considerations in their own right.

In the aftermath of World War II, the United States imposed severe restrictions on U.S.-produced exports to the Soviet Union and China. In 1949/50, thirteen NATO allies and Japan joined the U.S. in withholding an array of strategic goods from these Communist countries. The United Nations next charged China with aggression in Korea in 1951, causing the China embargo to expand throughout the free world. The "China differential" was expanding.

Despite these actions, Chinese foreign trade re-attained its pre-embargo level by 1954, but the trade share with other communist countries rose from 29 percent in 1950 to 66 percent by 1956. After the Korean Armistice, Japan and Western European economies rushed in to re-establish economic ties with China. The U.S. did not follow suit, of course, but free-world countries' share of China's foreign trade rose back up to 77 percent by 1967. The U.S. chose not to participate in trade with China despite the latter's favorable growth and growth prospects.

Sharp political ossillations between radical and moderate power blocks within China heavily influenced China's stance with respect to trade with foreigners. However, annual per capita GNP fell to $125 by 1968, more than 13 percent lower than a decade earlier, and the post-Cultural Revolution era was characterized by a clear ascendancy of pragmatic moderates. Provision of food became a higher priority. China's land mass approximately equals that of the continental United States, but only half as much can be cultivated (11 percent) compared with the U.S. (22 percent). China's huge population was growing and its agricultural sector could not keep pace. A net grain exporter (mostly rice) in 1960, China subsequently became a heavy grain importer (mostly wheat) during the 1960s. In the two years prior to Nixon's visit in 1971, grain imports comprised 13.5 percent of total Chinese imports; Canadian and Australian growers benefited on the supply side. U.S. grain exports to China boomed almost immediately after Nixon's visit; American grain lobbyists must have been pleased as U.S. shipments surged past 50 percent of total Chinese grain imports by 1974.

China's attempt to industrialize also required acquisition of capital goods. U.S. exports of "machinery and equipment" to China increased by 87 percent between 1973 and 1974. Thirty-nine percent of China's imports of aircraft and parts came from the U.S. in 1973. The U.S. became the fourth largest exporter of complete plants to China between 1972 and 1974. Many other areas of need could not be satisfied by U.S. producers, however, because they were not listed on Nixon's order relaxing trade

17

barriers. Japan and Western Europe therefore remained China's post-embargo sources of industrial plants and equipment.

China has been a great textile producer for centuries; textiles comprised 20–25 percent of total Chinese exports during the 1960s and 1970s. Silk was the main textile export worldwide, but U.S. imports were minimal because of a 60 percent *ad valorem* import duty. Chinese exports of finished cotton goods were also substantial. Since the U.S. produced about 20 percent of the world's raw cotton in 1969 (a quarter of which was already exported), 97 percent of China's cotton imports suddenly came from the United States by 1974. And Warner offers many other examples of matches between U.S. production and Chinese import needs. In a 1970 study, Robert Dernberger offered the much-quoted projection that U.S. exports to China could reach $900 million by 1980. Within two years of Nixon's trip, U.S. exports to China had already reached $819 million.

The United States ran its first merchandise trade deficit in half a century in 1970. It was clear to everyone that China would initially become a trade-surplus country (from the U.S. point of view), and this provided yet another rationale for liberalizing trade with China. Given the obvious advantages to both countries from opening trade, Warner concludes that economic motivations were an end in themselves.

Such is the diversity of cultures and historical experience around the Pacific that in some regions migrants have provided a major boost to economic development by providing much needed capital and cheap labor, while in other regions the contribution of migrants has been minimal. Thus, while California's Central Valley has drawn economic strength from the skills and sweat of generations of Asians, Hispanics, Africans, Europeans, and people from other parts of the U.S., in Japan, by contrast, society is racially homogeneous and permanent immigration is not allowed.

One of the few countries in the world still accepting large numbers of migrants is Australia. Historically this has not always been the case. Under the so-called "White Australia Policy" only migrants from Britain and northwest Europe were allowed. This immigration policy had its origins in the racial violence directed against the Chinese miners in the Australian goldfields in the mid-nineteenth century. After World War II, the Australian Federal Government permitted the entry of migrants from southern and eastern Europe to economically develop the country and turn

Australia into a "bastion" of European settlement in the Asia-Pacific region because if felt threatened by the large populations of Asian powers, Japan and China. However, during the 1960s the Australian government bowed to international pressure and relaxed the White Australian Policy, and then in 1973 formally abandoned it. A country which half a century ago was almost completely Anglo-Celtic in its ethnic composition and culture is today a far more multicultural and lively place as a result.

Nevertheless, as Kevin Blackburn observes in Chapter 10, a negative image persists in the media, and amongst some Asian politicians, of Australia as a place which discriminates against Asian immigrants. In this sense the effects of history have proved hard to shake off, leaving what one Singapore journalist called "negative psychological residues", in spite of increased business and educational contacts between Australia and Asian countries. Blackburn's essay is a reminder that around the diverse Pacific, even mutually-beneficial contacts may not always proceed smoothly. Again, a knowledge of history can help to provide understanding of the current situation.

The next step

Both this Routledge volume (which draws from the Melbourne Pacific Centuries conference, 5–7 July 1996) and its predecessor (based upon the Stockton Pacific Centuries conference, 5–7 April 1994) cover diverse topics touching specific areas of the Pacific over a span of five centuries. China's role in long-term Pacific (indeed, world) history has been emphasized by a number of independent authors thus far. The Pacific Centuries conference returned to the University of the Pacific in Stockton, California, 24–26 April 1998. In addition to presentations on China and Asia, there are sessions on Africans in the Pacific, the 1898 Philippines Revolution, Russia and the Pacific, Pacific Islands, Migrations to Mexico and the U.S., the French in California, Californian and Australian Gold Rushes, Canada and the Pacific, Galleons, Timber, Religion, Music, Visual Arts, and many others. Since the world is said to be entering *the* Pacific Century, it seems to us essential that scholars attempt to place the coming Pacific era into historical perspective. Why exactly is it that economic "dragons" or "tigers" spring forth exclusively from the western edge of the Asian Pacific? Americans perceive no threatening British, German, Dutch, French, Spanish, Portuguese, or Irish "dragons/tigers" arising along the eastern edge of the Atlantic. One answer might be that five centuries of Atlantic interaction among Europeans, Africans and peoples of the Americas seem to have yielded a heritage which, while not entirely pleasant, spans half a millennium and is understandable. There is comfort in the realization that a fairly clear outline exists for five centuries of Atlantic history.

The same cannot be said of the Pacific. Americans, for example, talk of Asian "miracles." And there is economic "warfare" (read: competitiveness) against Japan, China, and the emerging tigers. But what logic permits Americans to perceive (mostly) mutually beneficial trading relationships across the Atlantic, while simultaneously characterizing trade across the Pacific in war-like terms? Why isn't all trade conceptualized as plain trade, irrespective of which waterway connects participants? The pejorative American characterization of the Pacific seems to be based at least partly on fear of the unknown. To the extent that scholars are able to elucidate the rich historical legacy of the sixteenth through the twentieth Pacific Centuries – to create a Pacific heritage comparable with its Atlantic counterpart – then perhaps people around the world will be better prepared for a more sober, less hysterical assessment of new challenges as the next Pacific Century unfolds.

Note

1 Japan also played a key role on both sides of the silk-for-silver trade matrix. For an argument that silver and silk – from the same centers of production – were also crucial in determining trade pattens connecting Asia, Europe, the Levant, Africa, and across the Atlantic to America, see Flynn and Giráldez 1995; 1996; 1997.

References

Besher, A. (1992) *The Pacific Rim Almanac*. New York: Harper Perennial.
Chuan, Hang-shen (1969) "The Inflow of American Silver into China from the Lake Ming to the Mid-Ch'ing Period," *The Journal of the Institute of Chinese Studies of the Chinese University of Hong Kong*, 2: 61–75.
Daigle, Douglas (1998) "Environmental Impacts of the Pacific Rim Timber Trade: An Overview," in S.M. Miller, A.J.H. Latham and D.O. Flynn (eds), *Studies in the Economic History of the Pacific*. London and New York: Routledge, pp. 234–43.
Dudden, Arthur P. (1998) "The American Pacific: Where the West was also Won," in S.M. Miller, A.J.H. Latham and D.O. Flynn (eds),

Studies in the Economic History of the Pacific. London and New York: Routledge, pp. 94–103.

de Vries, Jan (1984) *European Urbanization 1500–1800*. Cambridge MA: Harvard University Press.

Flynn, Dennis O. and Giráldez, Arturo (1995) "Born with a 'Silver Spoon': The Origin of World Trade in 1571," *Journal of World History* 6: 201–21.

—— —— (1996) "Silk for Silver: Manila–Macao Trade in the 17th Century," *Philippine Studies* 44, 1: 52–68.

—— —— (1997) "Introduction: Monetary Substances in Global Perspective," in D.O. Flynn and A. Giráldez (eds), *Monies and Metals in an Emerging Global Economy*. Aldershot: Variorum.

—— —— (1998), "Introduction: The Pacific's Past Deserves a Future," in S.M. Miller, A.J.H. Latham and D.O. Flynn (eds), *Studies in the Economic History of the Pacific*. London and New York: Routledge, pp. 1–18.

Frank, Andre Gunder (1998) *ReOrient: Global Economy in the Asian Age*. Berkeley: University of California Press.

Frost, Lionel E. (1998) "Coming Full Circle: A Long-term Perspective on the Pacific Rim," in S.M. Miller, A.J.H. Latham and D.O. Flynn (eds), *Studies in the Economic History of the Pacific*. London and New York: Routledge, pp. 45–62.

George, Robert Lloyd (1992) *The East-West Pendulum*. London: Woodhead–Faulkner.

Jones, Eric, Frost, Lionel, and White, Colin (1993) *Coming Full Circle: An Economic History of the Pacific Rim*. Boulder: Westview Press.

Latham, A.J.H. (1998) "The Reconstruction of Hong Kong Nineteenth-Century Pacific Trade Statistics: The Emergence of Asian Dynamism," in S.M. Miller, A.J.H Latham and D.O. Flynn (eds), *Studies in the Economic History of the Pacific*. London and New York: Routledge, pp. 155–71.

Linder, Stefan (1986) *The Pacific Century: Economic and Political Consequences of Asian-Pacific Dynamism*. Stanford: Stanford University Press.

Marks, Robert (1998) *Tigers, Rice, Silk, and Silt: Environment and Economy in Late Imperial South China*. Cambridge and New York: Cambridge University Press.

McNeill, John R. (1998), "From Magellan to Miti: Pacific Rim Economies and Pacific Island Ecologies since 1521," in S.M. Miller, A.J.H. Latham and D.O. Flynn (eds), *Studies in the Economic History of the Pacific*. London and New York: Routledge, pp. 72–93.

Miller, Sally M., Latham, A.J.H., and Flynn, Dennis O. (1998) *Studies in the Economic History of the Pacific Rim*. London and New York: Routledge.

Mosaic (1997), Monash University Alumni.

Pomeranz, Kenneth (forthcoming) *Economy, Ecology, Comparison and*

D.O. FLYNN, L. FROST AND A.J.H. LATHAM

Connections: The Industrial Revolution from a Global Perspective. Princeton: Princeton University Press.

Segal, Gerald (1990) *Rethinking the Pacific.* Oxford: Clarendon Press.

St. Clair, David J. (1998), "California Quicksilver in the Pacific Rim Economy, 1850–90," in S.M. Miller, A.J.H. Latham and D.O. Flynn (eds), *Studies in the Economic History of the Pacific.* London and New York: Routledge, pp. 210–33.

Sutcliffe, Anthony (1993) "Introduction: The Giant City as a Historical Phenomenon," in Theo Barker and Anthony Sutcliffe (eds), *Megalopolis: The Giant City in History.* Basingstoke: Macmillan.

von Glahn, Richard (1996a), *Fountain of Fortune: Money and Monetary Policy in China, 1000–1700.* Berkeley, Los Angeles, London: University of California Press.

—— (1996b), "Myth and Reality of China's Seventeenth-Century Monetary Crisis," *Journal of Economic History* 56, (2): pp. 429–54.

Wong, R. Bin (1998), "Chinese Views of the Money Supply and Foreign Trade, 1400–1850," in S.M. Miller, A.J.H. Latham and D.O. Flynn (eds), *Studies in the Economic History of the Pacific.* London and New York: Routledge, pp. 172–80.

1

SPANISH PROFITABILITY IN THE PACIFIC

The Philippines in the sixteenth and seventeenth centuries

Dennis O. Flynn and Arturo Giráldez

The silver of Peru finds its way, not only to Europe, but from Europe to China. . . . In the cargoes, therefore of the greater part of European ships which sail to India, silver has generally been one of the most valuable articles. It is the most valuable article in the Acapulco ships which sail to Manila. The silver of the new continent seems in this manner to be one of the principal commodities by which the commerce between the extremities of the old one is carried on, and it is by means of it, in great measure, that those distant parts of the world are connected with one another.

(Adam Smith 1937 [1776]: 167–8, 207)

What Adam Smith characterized over two centuries ago as a fundamental feature of global trade history, we (Flynn and Giráldez 1995a) have re-emphasized in recent years: American silver, ultimately destined for China, was a prime impetus behind the birth of global trade. Having traversed the Atlantic Ocean, approximately three-quarters of the New World silver production continued on through a variety of European trade routes – via the Baltic and Russia and Persia, via caravans and waterways of the Middle East, around the Cape of Good Hope – and eventually on to China during three centuries. K.N. Chaudhuri (1978: 156) and others make clear why American (as well as Japanese) silver was attracted so relentlessly to China: the market value of silver was simply twice as high in China as it was elsewhere.

> So Italy stood at the cross roads where the south–north axis maintained by Spanish policy and the Genoese asientos met the east–west axis running to the Levant and the Far East, where the golden road from Genoa to Antwerp met the silver road to the east.
>
> On the eastern axis there were to be no surprises: silver was the favoured currency there, its value increasing once it reached the Levant . . . ; it increased even more the further east it travelled, crossing Persia and India finally to arrive perhaps in the Philippines or in China; Chinese gold was exchanged [against silver] . . . at 1 to 4, while the ratio in Europe was at least 1 to 12. This Italy–China axis, beginning in America and running right round the world either through the Mediterranean or round the Cape of Good Hope, can be considered a *structure*, a permanent and outstanding feature of the world economy which remained undisturbed until the twentieth century.[1]
>
> (Braudel 1972: 499–500)[2]

When Ming China's paper money system collapsed in the fifteenth century, its monetary and tax system gradually converted to a silver basis, culminating in the 1570s in the "single-whip tax reform." Conversion of both the monetary and fiscal systems of the world's largest economy to a silver standard naturally raised the price of silver in that region. Arbitrage profits – buying where a product is cheap and selling where it is dear – attracted innumerable European and Asian merchants (and their governments) engaged in fierce and deadly competition for access to profitable trade routes leading toward China.

Although controlling the richest silver mines in world history, Spaniards were locked out of trade routes connecting the markets of Europe and China. The Portuguese and Dutch had already established linkages in Asian waters, thereby blocking Spanish access. Spaniards were excluded from the lucrative spice trade, as well as the inter-Asiatic trade which was so crucial to the Portuguese and later the East India Companies of England and Holland. Under these circumstances, Spanish access to the world's largest market was only possible via the Pacific Ocean. The birth of Pacific Rim trade dates from 1571, the year the city of Manila was founded. Manila was the crucial entrepôt linking substantial, direct, and continuous trade between America and Asia for the first time in history. The profit motive was preeminent.

Fiscal nightmare in the Philippines: The traditional view

Historical consensus claims that the Philippines were a financial drain for Imperial Spain during the sixteenth and seventeenth centuries. Costs to mother-country Spain are alleged to have far outweighed Imperial benefits.[3] Religious and political goals must therefore have superseded financial considerations; otherwise, why would Spain have continued to subsidize these islands for centuries?

> The Philippines never provided Spain with the fabulous riches which it received from the gold and silver mines in America. But it was perhaps because Philip II of Spain was able to rely on a steady source of revenue from the Americas that he was willing to tolerate the losses sustained in the Philippines and magnanimously offer to make it "the arsenal and warehouse of the faith."
>
> (Andaya 1992, v.1: 357)

This chapter aims to challenge the conventional depiction of the Philippines as a "profitless archipelago" (Bauzon 1970: 172) during the sixteenth and seventeenth centuries.[4] Instead, we contend that the Spanish state enjoyed substantial net financial benefits from the Philippines. We estimate the Spanish Crown's net Philippine profit at some 218,415 pesos per year throughout the seventeenth century. Around 125,000 pesos (57.2 percent) in Philippine profit was collected inside of America prior to the loading of silver onto Manila galleons in Acapulco. We term this 125,000 pesos per year "indirect profit."

The methodology used to generate estimated yearly profits is explained below. It should be emphasized at the outset, however, that our 125,000 pesos per year Philippine "indirect profit" is described as *American mining* profit in the mainstream literature. At issue is whose methodology is most appropriate for allocation of overall Crown profit to specific geographical locations within Spain's global silver-trade network. Rather than attributing high profits solely to Spanish-American mines, we contend that a significant fraction of the profit normally attributed to Spanish-American mining should be viewed as "indirect profit" stemming from the Philippine trade. We feel that the silver-economy dichotomy between (a) silver mining, and (b) shipment of the white metal through Manila, is misleading. Mine activity and trade across the Pacific comprised aspects of a multi-faceted global marketplace. American mine profits were impossible without silver's dominant end-market customers in China.[5] Manila was the Pacific's linchpin, connecting silver's American supply-side (and silk's demand-side) with silver's dominant Chinese demand-side (and silk's supply-side). Therefore, assessment of the magnitude of Philippine profitability for the Spanish Crown requires a global perspective.

Profit from a global perspective

Debate over the rise and decline of the Spanish Empire has traditionally been restricted to "Western" (Spanish American, European, Spanish) issues. By contrast, we contend that Imperial Spain can be fully understood only within the context of an emerging, silver-centered *global* economy (Flynn and Giráldez 1996a). Spanish-American and Japanese silver mines dominated on the supply-side; China contained by far the most important customers on the demand-side. The sixteenth-century value of silver in China was double that of the rest of the world because China's enormous monetary and fiscal systems had gradually become "silverized" (von Glahn 1996a, b). High silver prices in China, in conjunction with low production costs in Japan and Spanish America, created enormous merchant profits throughout the world. And no entity profited more from the silver industry than did the Spanish Crown, which received up to 40 percent of the non-smuggled treasure shipped into Spain.[6] But we argue that, in the absence of Chinese demand for silver, there would have been no Spanish Empire; profit for every entity along silver's global mercantile chain – including Spain's central government – depended upon high silver prices offered by end-customers in China (Flynn and Giráldez 1996a).

The Pacific leg of the global silver trade

More than any other entity, the Spanish Crown controlled the Atlantic leg of silver's journey,[7] but Spain did not control subsequent legs of the continuum – vast networks of trade connecting European entrepôts with silver-hungry marketplaces in

Asia, especially China. The earliest Europeans to establish maritime-merchant empires in Asia were the Portuguese and Dutch; Spain was thereby blocked from the lucrative intra-Asian and Asia–Europe trade vectors. Thus, silver's Pacific route to China via Manila was Spain's only direct access to Asian marketplaces. Spaniards circumvented competing European middlemen by trading directly with (mostly) Asian merchants through Manila; the core Philippines trade bartered American silver for Chinese silks. Relatively direct access to the Chinese marketplace explains rates of Acapulco–Manila–China commercial profit which "probably ranged from one hundred to three hundred percent"[8] (Legarda 1955: 362). The goal of this essay is to assess Crown profits, however, not private profits. Analysis of Crown profits from the Philippines trade requires two steps: (1) establishment of a realistic estimate of the magnitude of trade passing through the Philippines, and (2) provision of a *global* perspective on Crown benefits and Crown costs stemming from trade via the Philippines.

The volume of Pacific trade

Most historians seem to accept, as fact, Chaunu's three-phased Manila trade: (1) continual increase until about 1620, (2) high plateau and slight decline after 1620, and (3) precipitous fall after 1640 (Chaunu 1960: 250). Chaunu's estimates were based upon *almojarifazgo* records, an *ad valorem* tax on legal imports/exports. Unfortunately, Chaunu's numbers misrepresent Philippine trade volumes. We know that an ever larger share of the merchandise traversing the Pacific was contraband over time; smuggled goods were not recorded in *almojarifazgo* tax documents, of course, so reliance upon *almojarifazgo* records led to serious underestimation of commodity values aboard the Manila galleons. Eschewing details of this debate (Flynn and Giráldez 1994; 1995b), suffice to say that Chaunu's estimates seriously understate the vitality of the Philippines trade. We find plausible, on the other hand, Chuan's (1969: 79) estimate of a two-million pesos annual Acapulco–Manila trade throughout the seventeenth century.[9] The Manila trade essentially boiled down to a barter of American silver for Chinese silks, so Flynn and Giráldez (1996b) investigated Mexican-bound Chinese silk exports via Manila and Macao; the silk-trade literature buttresses Chuan's contention that the annual Manila trade equalled at least 2 million pesos.[10] The trade did not drop off after 1620, nor precipitously after 1640, as mistakenly reported by Chaunu. Chuan (1975: 113) quotes a contemporary Jesuit's account of the situation in the Philippines in 1640: "All these goods [mostly Chinese silk goods] are exports to Mexico, where they are sold at great profit, and on the spot. I do not believe there is a richer traffic in the world than that."

Conceptualizing Crown benefits from the Manila trade

Based upon sustained silver imports into China via Manila at 2 million pesos/year throughout the seventeenth century, estimation of Spanish Crown benefits from this trade can be attempted. Most silver passing through Acapulco was contraband and therefore not fully taxed, however, so estimation of the Crown's percentage share of silver exported via the Pacific is bound to be tentative.

Rampant smuggling is a widely acknowledged characteristic of the Pacific trade (Schurz 1959; TePaske 1983: 437). Smuggling avoided payment of the *almojarifazgo*, a 15–17.5 percent customs duty on merchandise at Acapulco (Lynch 1969: 163), and circumvented quotas protecting Atlantic-trade interests from Chinese products offering intense competition through Manila.[11]

While Pacific smuggling permitted circumvention of *almojarifazgo* taxes, other Crown taxes collected in Spanish America prior to the export of silver via Acapulco were more difficult to avoid. There were severance taxes on mined silver, sometimes a *quinto* (20 percent), sometimes a *diezmo* (10 percent). There were profits from mercury mining (a Crown monopoly). There were also Indian tributes (6 pesos per capita), the *cruzada*, the *alcabala* (a sales tax raised to 4 percent in 1627), *donativos* ("gifts" to the Crown which were really payments in exchange for favors), sales of offices, "extraordinary taxes" like the 600,000 ducat annual assessment imposed on Peru and Mexico for 15 years by the Union of Arms in 1627, and so on. During truly desperate times, the Crown confiscated outright millions of ducats of private treasure on the Atlantic side (see Lynch 1969: 165). The threat of confiscation, of course, provided additional motivation to smuggle.

Even during years of crisis, Lynch (1969: 164–5) and Hamilton (1934: 34) have estimated the "surplus" generated for the Spanish Crown by America under Philip III and Philip IV – remaining Crown revenue, after subtracting American administration and defense costs – at roughly 1.15 million pesos per year. Since total annual American silver production has been estimated at 13.5

million pesos per year during the seventeenth century,[12] and since the Manila galleons trade carried an estimated 2 million pesos of this total, approximately 14.8 percent (a little over one-seventh) of estimated Spanish-American silver production passed through Manila. Since 14.8 percent of American silver production traversed the Pacific, perhaps we can assume that the Manila galleons were also responsible for 14.8 percent of the 1.15 million pesos annual Crown surplus estimated by Lynch and Hamilton. This would mean that the Manila galleons were responsible for 14.8 percent (170,200 pesos) of the 1.15 million annual Crown surplus from America. Since tax-avoiding smuggling was probably more pervasive in the Pacific than in the Atlantic, and since we wish to estimate only taxes collected prior to the exportation of silver from Acapulco, we arbitrarily reduce our estimate of the Manila-portion of Crown surplus from 170,200 pesos per year to 125,000 pesos per year. This 125,000 pesos annual Crown surplus from the Manila leg of the global silver trade implies an effective tax rate of 6.25 percent collected on the 2 million pesos Pacific commerce *prior to* silver's exportation via Acapulco.

Without claiming accounting accuracy, we simply wish to emphasize that any credible cost-benefit analysis must acknowledge *indirect* (i.e. not counting taxes collected at ports around the Pacific) Crown benefits from the Manila trade. Admitting that 125,000 pesos per year provides only a rough (but perhaps conservative) estimate of *indirect* Crown benefit from the Pacific trade-leg, we next suggest that *direct* costs of, and *direct* benefits for, the Acapulco–Manila trade-leg must also be re-conceptualized.

Attribution of costs to the Manila trade

The Philippines were administratively subordinate to the vice-royalty of New Spain. As a result, the Spanish accounting system categorized revenues and costs in a way which misleads modern historians. The Philippine *situado* – monies sent from Mexico to Manila to defray costs of administration in the Philippines and elsewhere in Asia – is a case in point. The *situado* is often portrayed as if it were a "subsidy," a drain upon the Mexican vice-royalty.[13] But the Philippine *situado* was at first only the returns from the *almojarifazgo* duties:

> collected at Acapulco . . . . In this context, the situado simply meant the income derived from the trading system

29

> . . . It was distinctly and unmistakably not intended to be
> a subsidy, as the word situado came to mean in later years
> . . . . the situado as income from the galleon trade [later]
> became half-subsidy and half-commercial income, with
> the Mexican treasury making up from its own financial
> resources what the galleon trade could not adequately
> produce.
>
> (Bauzon 1970: 129)

Regarding the 50 percent of the *situado* which Bauzon calls
"commercial income," it does not matter conceptually whether
almojarifazgo taxes were (a) collected in Mexico and then sent back
to Manila, or (b) collected and retained in Manila. The first case
involves a *situado*, however, and the second does not. Both have
exactly the same effect: receipts from tariffs on galleon commerce
cover a portion of operating and administrative expenses. In no
sense should these tax receipts be considered "subsidies"; rather,
they involve partial self-financing of the galleon trade. Irrespective
of whether the particular point of tax-collection happened to have
been in Mexico, half of the *situado* involved no subsidy. Collecting
almojarifazgo taxes at the Acapulco end of the commercial
exchange – prior to recycling back to Manila – did not alter
the fact that the "commercial" half of the *situado* involved a net
cost neither to the Crown, nor to New Spain.[14]

A distinction between "Philippine expenses" and "non-Philippine expenses"

The remaining half of the Philippine *situado* – the portion not
generated directly via galleon trade – might properly be classified
as a "subsidy". But the Philippines were not subsidized via the
"Philippines" *situado*. This *situado* financed Spain's battles with the
Dutch over hegemony in Asian waters.[15] What made the Philippines
"more insolvent than ever" over time was the "ambitious enterprise
undertaken by Spain, with the Philippines as the fitting-out point to
gain mastery over the remunerative spiceries of the Moluccas, a
concomitant of which was the prolonged Hispano-Dutch war"
(Bauzon 1970: 129). The so-called Philippine *situado* financed war
in the Moluccas; thus it should not be considered a "Philippine
subsidy":

In the Moluccas, while the Dutch continued to hem in

the Spanish forts on Ternate and Tidore and virtually monopolized the lucrative spice trade, little or no progress was made towards eliminating the unwelcome Spanish presence. Indeed, Dutch–Spanish friction in the Moluccas continued longer than in any other region of the world.

(Israel 1982: 336)

In 1621, according to Hernando de los Rios Coronel (former pro-curator-general) receipts at Manila's *real hacienda* totaled 255,541 pesos, compared with expenditures for the Moluccas of 218,372 pesos (Bauzon 1970: 158). In 1640, according to Grau y Monfalcon, procurator-general of the colony, total revenue was 256,000 pesos, while expenses for the Moluccas reached 230,000 pesos; thus, "only 26,000 pesos remained for the Philippines" (Bauzon 1970: 159). Receipts in these two years equalled 511,541 pesos combined, in other words, while 448,372 pesos were expenses for the Moluccas; this means that only 12.35 percent of receipts (a mere 31,585 pesos per year) was available for application to Philippine expenses in those two isolated years.

A rough sketch of Crown costs and benefits can now be attempted. We argued earlier that the Crown may have gained 125,000 pesos (6.25 percent) via taxes within America on the 2,000,000 pesos of mined silver before it entered the Pacific trade route. In addition, 50 percent (some 125,000 pesos per year) of the *situado* comprised taxes generated by the galleon trade itself; thus, this commercial-half of the *situado* should be viewed as a financial *benefit* from the government's point of view. While around 250,000 pesos per year were sent to Manila in the form

---

Benefits

Indirect Crown benefits	+125,000 pesos/year
Direct benefits (*almojarifazgo*)	+125,000 pesos/year

Costs

Portion of receipts retained in the Philippines (remaining 224,186 pesos passed through to Moluccas)	−31,585 pesos/year

Profit from Philippines

Benefits minus Costs	+218,415 pesos/year

---

of a *situado*, only about 31,000 pesos remained in the Philippines;[16] the rest financed expenditures in the Moluccas and elsewhere. A rough tally of the costs and benefits of the Manila trade indicates that the Philippines were a major profit center for the Spanish Crown.

While this Crown profit estimate is a crude approximation at best, it contrasts sharply with conventional views of a Philippine "financial nightmare" for the Spanish Crown; moreover, our position seems consistent with a contemporary's seventeenth-century testimony:

> Another reasoned defense of the Philippine Islands was offered in 1637 by the procurator-general of the colony, Grau y Monfalcon, who showed that if it were not for the Spanish desire to own the Moluccas, the [Philippine] islands actually contributed more than they cost, since, in reality what they were producing was being spent in Spain's behalf in the Moluccas and not for the development of the Philippines
>
> (quoted in Bauzon 1970: 159)

But given the tentative nature of our estimates, does it seem reasonable that the Crown could have secured 218,415 pesos in net profit per year (in the form of various taxes) on the basis of the production and export of 2,000,000 pesos in silver annually across the Pacific? It seems plausible to us that the Crown may have earned a 10.9 percent net profit rate, based upon all aspects of the silver business from below ground in America through the port of Manila. But even if the reader prefers a more conservative calculation, we cannot imagine a global interpretation capable of causing a metamorphosis of our "cash cow" Philippines back into the "financial alligator" portrayed in the current literature.

Conclusion

Phelan (1967: 112) describes Antonio de Morga as an imaginative and bold strategist when thinking about defense of the Spanish Pacific:

> Morga wrote Viceroy Esquilache at the latter's request a long memorandum in which he outlined . . . the Philippines as the anchor of the Spanish position in the whole Pacific basin.

The Spanish must retain control of the Philippines, not merely because of the Spanish colonists and the Catholic missions there. The loss of the islands would probably lead to the ouster [sic] of the Iberian powers from the Cape of Good Hope to the shores of Mexico. If the Dutch occupied the Philippines, not only would the Moluccas be lost, but also the key Portuguese enclaves of Goa on the Indian coast, Macao and Malacca could not long withstand the Dutch offensive. In 1615 Dr Morga correctly predicted that the Dutch would make a supreme effort, which they had not yet done, to take the Philippines.

The early-modern Philippines is best visualized against a backdrop of the Spanish Empire's global struggle for economic and political hegemony against the Dutch – in Europe, Angola, Brazil, the Caribbean, Manila, the Moluccas, Taiwan, and the American Pacific. Spain's 80-year war in the Low Countries was no doubt her greatest financial drain, but struggles against Dutch forces in America and Asia were also fierce and expensive. Battles in Asian waters siphoned off most of the so-called Philippines *situado*; costs on the Dutch side were no less daunting:

> Even during the truce, the cost of the [Dutch East India] Company's forts, garrisons, and battle fleet consumed most of the remittances sent from Holland as well as most of the profits of the Dutch inter-Asian trade. With the big offensive, the Company's costs inevitably had soared, rising in the three years 1620–2 to nearly 5 million guilders.
>
> (Israel 1982: 119)

The Dutch were perfectly aware that the exceptional harbors of Acapulco and Manila served as Spain's only direct gateways to China's lucrative, silver-hungry markets (and Spanish America's lucrative, silk-hungry markets). Why did the Dutch invest such prodigious sums to wrestle control of Manila – linchpin of the trans-Pacific economy – from Spain, if not for the prospect of immense trade profits? What motivated the Dutch to finance the attempted 1624 seizure of Acapulco itself? (Israel 1990: 293–4). Scholars will continue to argue endlessly over the primacy of religious versus economic motives under colonialism, but we can think of no reason to consider Spaniards less interested in galleon-trade profits than were the Dutch, Chinese, Portuguese, Japanese or others.

Notes

1 Even after the sixteenth and seventeenth century period under discussion here, silver continued to flow to East Asia in the eighteenth century. Isaac Newton (1717) stated "that in China and Japan the silver:gold ratio was 9 to 10 to 1 and in India 12 to 1, and this carries away the silver from all Europe" (quoted in Smith 1937 [1776]: 207).

2 While fundamentally sound in general, this quote from Braudel requires two modifications. First, the Philippines were not an end market for silver, as will become clear throughout the rest of this chapter. Second, bimetallic ratios in fact coverged around the world *c.* 1640, diverging again to a far lesser extent later in the seventeenth and through the eighteenth centuries.

3 See, for example, Zaide (1979, pp. 264, 324), Phelan (1959, pp. 93–94), and Legarda (1955, p. 371).

4 We focus only on Crown profitability in the sixteenth and seventeenth centuries. The eighteenth and nineteenth centuries deserve independent analysis. We also avoid discussion of private profitability (e.g. merchants, the church, bureaucrats, *obras pias* etc.).

5 See Flynn and Giráldez (1995b) for citations of the literature in this field.

6 In summarizing sixteenth-century Spanish finances, Steele (1986: 151–52) puts the King's portion of treasure landing in Seville at 40 percent, compared with Hamilton's (1934: 89–91) 27.5 percent.

7 For discussion of massive silver smuggling via America's "Back Door" to the Atlantic, however, see Moutoukias (1991).

8 Also see Chaun (1975: 114), Zaide (1979: 514), Legarda (1955: 352), Borah (1954: 122), Boxer (1963: 170), and Jara (1979: 67). The picture becomes clearer when looking at the Chinese silk side of the exchange. Chaun (1975: 106) points out that the price of silk in Manila was twice as high as in Hai-cheng in 1566 (the year after Spaniards arrived in the Philippines); subsequent competition with Japanese buyers in Manila increased this ratio to 4:1 or 5:1. And this was only the Manila–China leg of the trade! The price of silk was typically 300 percent higher in Acapulco than in Manila, and there are reported incidences of an 8:1 ratio. (Borah 1954: 122) Maintenance of silk prices in Acapulco at least six times higher than their Chinese counterparts is interesting because Chinese silk goods in Mexico – as late at 1640 – were only one-third of the price of comparable Spanish silk goods there (Chaun 1975: 116); this implies that silk goods in China were something like one-eighteenth of the price of similar silk goods in Spain.

9 See Reed (1967) for data on galleon passages and shipwrecks.

10 Caution is warranted in interpreting this figure of two million pesos per year. First, each million pesos of Chinese merchandise departing Manila became two million pesos of merchandise upon arrival in

Acapulco (see Zaide 1979: 514), so the port of measurement must be specified. Second, the value of the silver pesos declined steadily between the founding of Manila in 1571 and 1640; two million pesos in trade in 1571 was more valuable than two million pesos in trade in 1640.

11 Spanish silks in Peru were reportedly eight times more expensive than Chinese silks (Borah 1954: 122).

12 Barrett (1990: 225) estimates overall Spanish-American silver production at 34,000 metric tons for the entire seventeenth-century. Three hundred and forty metric tons per year equals approximately 13.5 million pesos in annual silver production.

13 The Philippine *situado* was not unique in any case:

> Peru was responsible for defense in the mar del Sur, and also subsidized Chile, Panama, and distant Cumana. New Spain provided the situados for the coasts and islands in the Caribbean from Florida to Paria, and also the Philippines. In 1664, for example, Lima was instructed to provide 105,150 pesos a year for the military defenses of Panama; in 1673 this was raised to 275,314 pesos. A subsidy of 212,000 ducats a year for the army in Chile was also charged on the viceroyalty.
>
> (Lynch 1969: 199–200)

14 Collection of taxes at the Mexican end of the trade may have been a matter of practicality. First, the value of Chinese merchandise in Acapulco was double the value of the same merchandise in Manila; therefore it was advantageous for the government to levy the *ad valorem almojarifazgo* in Mexico. Second, if smuggling Chinese products into Mexico was more difficult than exporting contraband silver, this offers yet another incentive for authorities to tax imports at the Mexican end of the voyage.

15 Also, "the Dutch wooed the support of the Muslim Malays of Mindanao and the Sulu Archipelago" (Abella 1974: 11) in an attack on Manila in 1616.

16 In a sense, the paltry 31,000 pesos per year may not even have "remained" in the Philippines, a colony which itself helped finance war against the Dutch. Forced "polo" Filipino laborers had to be subsidized by village treasuries; even their token wages were seldom paid. There was also compulsory sale of products to the government under the "vandala": "Between 1610 and 1616 the treasury owed Filipinos some 300,000 pesos. By 1616 the sum had climbed to 1,000,000 pesos. These sums include both labor services and enforced sale of goods" (Phelan 1959: 100).

References

Abella, Domingo (1974) *Spanish Philippines in the seventeenth Century: A Beleaguered outpost of the Empire.* Yogyakarta: 6th International Conference on Asian History.

Andaya, Leonard Y. (1992) "Interactions with the Outside World and Adaptation in Southeast Asian Society, 1500–1800," in Nicholas Tarling (ed.) *The Cambridge History of Southeast Asia vol. 1 From Early Times to c.1800*. Cambridge: Cambridge University Press, pp. 345–401.

Barrett, Ward (1990) "World Bullion Flows, 1450–1800," in James D. Tracy, (ed.) *The Rise of Merchant Empires: Long-Distance Trade in the Early Modern World, 1350–1750*. Cambridge: Cambridge University Press, pp. 224–54.

Bauzon, Leslie E. (1970) *Deficit Government: Mexico and the Philippine Situado (1606–1804)*. Duke University: Unpublished PhD dissertation.

Borah, Woodrow (1954) *Early Colonial Trade and Navigation between Mexico and Peru*. Berkeley: University of California Press.

Boxer, Charles R. (1963) *The Great Ship from Amacon: Annals of Macao and the Old Japan Trade*. Lisbon: Centro de Estudos Historicos Ultramarinos.

—— (1970) "Plata es Sangre: Sidelights on the Drain of Spanish-American Silver in the Far East, 1550–1700," *Philippine Studies*, vol. 18, (July): pp. 457–78.

Braudel, Fernand (1972) *The Mediterranean and the Mediterranean World in the Age of Philip II*. Vol 1. New York: Harper & Row.

Chaudhuri, K.N. (1978) *The Trading World of Asia and the English East India Company, 1660–1760*. Cambridge: Cambridge University Press.

Chaunu, Pierre (1960) *Les Philippines et le Pacifique des Iberiques (XVI, XVII,XVIII siécles)*. Paris: S.E.V.P.E.N.

Chuan, Hang-Sheng (1969) "The Inflow of American Silver into China from the Late Ming to the Mid-Ch'ing Period," *The Journal of the Institute of Chinese Studies of the Chinese University of Hong Kong*, vol. 2, pp. 61–75.

—— (1975) "The Chinese Silk Trade with Spanish America from the Late Ming to the Mid-Ch'ing Period," in Laurence G. Thompson (ed.), *Studia Asiatica Essays in Asian Studies in Felicitation of the Seventy-fifth Anniversary of Professor Ch'en Shou-yi*. San Francisco: Chinese Materials Center, pp. 99–117.

Flynn, Dennis O. and Giráldez, Arturo (1994) "China and the Manila Galleons," in A.J.H. Latham, and H. Kawakatsu, (eds.) *Japanese Industrialization and the Asian Economy*. London: Routledge.

—— (1995a) "Born with a 'Silver Spoon': The Origin of World Trade in 1571," *Journal of World History*, vol. 6, n.2, pp. 201–21.

—— (1995b) "Arbitrage, China, and World Trade in the Early Modern Period," *Journal of the Economic and Social History of the Orient*, vol. 38, n.4, pp. 429–48.

—— (1996a) "China and the Spanish Empire," *Revista de Historia Economica*, XIV, n.2, pp. 309–38.

—— (1996b) "Silk for Silver: Manila-Macao Trade in the seventeenth Century", *Philippine Studies*, vol. 44/First Quarter, pp. 52–68.

Hamilton, Earl J. (1934) *American Treasure and the Price Revolution in Spain, 1501–1650.* New York: Octogon Books.

Israel, Jonathan I. (1975) *Race, Class and Politics in Colonial Mexico 1610–1670.* Oxford: Oxford University Press.

—— (1982) *The Dutch Republic and the Hispanic World 1606–1661.* New York: Oxford University Press.

—— (1990) *Empires and Entrepots The Dutch, the Spanish Monarchy and the Jews 1585–1713.* London: The Hambledon Press.

Jara, Alvaro (1979) "Las conexiones e intercambios americanos con el Oriente bajo el marco imperial español (Siglos XVI-XVIII)," in Orrego Vicuña, F. (ed.) *La comunidad del Pacífico en perspectiva.* Santiago de Chile: Editorial Universitaria.

Legarda, Benito Jr. (1955) "Two and a Half Centuries of the Galleon Trade," *Philippine Studies,* vol. 3, (December), pp. 345–72.

Lynch, John (1969) *Spain under the Habsburgs Spain and America 1598–1700.* New York: Oxford University Press.

Moutoukias, Zacarias (1991) "Una forma de oposicion: el contrabando," in Massimo Ganci and Ruggiero Romano (eds.), *Governare il mondo. L'impero spagnolo dal XV al XIX secolo.* Palermo, pp. 333–368. [Reprinted in D.O. Flynn and A. Giráldez (eds), *Metals and Monies in an Emerging Global Economy.* Aldershot: Variorum, 1997, pp. 19–54.]

Phelan, John L. (1959) *The Hispanization of the Philippines Spanish Aims and Filipino Responses 1565–1700.* Madison: The University of Wisconsin Press.

—— (1967) *The Kingdom of Quito in the Seventeenth Century: Bureacratic Politics in the Spanish Empire.* Madison: University of Wisconsin Press.

Reed, Robert R. (1967) *Hispanic Urbanism in the Philippines: A study of the Impact of Church and State.* Manila: The University of Manila.

Schurz, Lyle W. (1959), *The Manila Galleon.* New York: E.P. Dutton.

Smith, Adam (1937 [1776]) *The Wealth of Nations.* New York: Modern Library.

Steele, Mark (1986) "La Hacienda Real," in V. Vázquez de Prada (ed.), *Historia General de España y América,* Tomo VI. Madrid: Ediciones Rialp.

TePaske, John J. (1983) "New World Silver, Castile, and the Philippines, 1590–1800," in J.F. Richards (ed.), *Precious Metals in the Later Medieval and Early Modern Worlds.* Durham, N.C.: Carolina Academic Press, pp. 425–46.

Von Glahn, Richard (1996a) *Fountain of Fortune: Money and Monetary Policy in China 100–1700.* Berkeley: University of California Press.

Von Glahn, Richard (1996b) "Myth and Reality of China's Seventeenth-Century Monetary Crisis." *Journal of Economic History* 56(2): 429–54.

Zaide, Gregorio F. (1979) *The Pageant of Philippines History, Political, Economic, and Socio-Cultural.* Manila: Philippine Education Company.

2

THE GREAT SILK EXCHANGE

How the world was connected and developed

Debin Ma

Students of the silk trade are blessed with the rare fortune to study an international trade that is almost as ancient and as continuous as the records of human civilization. Silk, with its appeal of lustrousness, elasticity and durability, has long been considered a symbol of luxury, elegance and sacredness, and was rightfully dubbed the queen of fabrics, the thread of gold. Even in the days of antiquity when transportation was primitive and treacherous, silk, with its high value and low volume and the ease with which it can be carried, stored and packed, could overcome what Braudel called the "tyranny of distance," which precluded long-distance trade of most commodities. Silk trade on a global scale has gone on for a recorded period of about 3,000 years.

The history of the silk trade evokes images of another well-known historical entity: the Silk Road, the famous overland route that traversed the heartland of the Eurasian continent. The term Silk Road (*die Seidenstrasse*) was coined by the nineteenth-century German explorer Baron Ferdinand von Richthofen. Although silk was perhaps the most important commodity that traveled along the Road, others such as precious metals and stones, spices, porcelain and textiles also passed through. However, the Silk Road was perhaps more significantly an avenue for the exchange of ideas. Some of the most fundamental ideas and technologies in the world – methods of making paper, printing, and manufacturing gunpowder, among many others – made their way across Asia via this highway. Migrants, merchants, explorers, pilgrims, refugees, and soldiers brought along with them religious and cultural ideas, domesticated animals, plants, flowers, vegetables, fruit, plagues and disease, as they joined this gigantic cross-continental exchange. The Silk Road, as so rightfully claimed, was the melting pot, the lifeline of the Eurasian Continent (Franck and Brownstone 1986: 2; Werblowsky 1988). In East Asia, the Silk Road has long been enshrined as a symbol of cross-cultural exchanges of religions, commodities and technology.

This chapter, motivated by the concept of the Silk Road as an avenue of exchange of goods and ideas, concerns the history of global trade and technological diffusion. The trading history of silk presents a classic case for studying the incremental and cumulative nature of growth of trade and the stock of knowledge made possible by the increasing human interactions and improved means of transportation. The chapter is divided into three parts: the first brings together a brief narrative of the long history of the silk trade and the technological diffusion on the overland route. The second focuses on the sea route and the third presents a discussion of the interactions among trade, technological and institutional progress and the transportation systems on the overland and sea routes.

Silk Road: the overland system

The Road: its beginning and consolidation

Sericulture and silk weaving had been established in the Yellow River and Yangtze River areas of China thousands of years before Christ. Production of silk started in China between perhaps 5000 and 3000 BC (Fan and Wen 1993: 2). This great Chinese invention began with the ingenious discovery of reeling silk threads off wild silkworm cocoons, followed by the conscious domestication of silkworms. The making of silk could be roughly divided into three main stages. Sericulture denotes the process of planting mulberry trees, feeding silkworms, and subsequently collecting cocoons spun by the silkworms. Then, from these cocoons, farmers could reel off long and continuous threads and wind them onto bobbins to form the so-called raw silk. Finally, raw silk (sometimes after an additional process of twisting or "throwing") was left to silk weavers (or knitters) to turn into silk cloth.[1]

Although Chinese silk was discovered in Europe as early as

500 BC, well-recorded trading only started in the Han dynasty (202 BC to AD 220). The aggressive sixth emperor of the Han dynasty, Wu-ti, in an imperial effort to expand Chinese territory and influence, sent out his militiaman Zhang Chien on a mission to explore China's western frontier in 138 BC. The knowledge of the environment and nomadic tribes and kingdoms brought back by Zhang Chien aided the Chinese conquest of Western Asia (currently the XinJiang province of China) around 120 BC. The long existing private silk trade saw its first boom when the western frontier came under the control of a single, central, consolidated power – the Western Han dynasty (202 BC to AD 9) (Li, M.W. 1991: 1–15). According to Joseph Needham (1954: 176, 181), the first recorded through caravans from China arrived in Persia around 106 BC and thereafter the trans-Asian silk trade was regularized.

The Road started out from the capital city of China, Chang-An (now Xian), and crossed into the newly acquired northwest frontier of China.[2] Beyond the sphere of Chinese influence, the route continued on westward, through the elaborate trading networks of the other major Eurasian civilization zones, under the control of the Kushans in Central Asia, the Parthians in Persia, and the Roman empire in Europe. Hudson divides the whole route into four sections: (1) as far west as the Pamirs, i.e. to the western boundaries of modern XinJiang (China's western frontier); (2) from the Pamirs to the Merv oasis, i.e. Bactria or Sogdiana (in current Northwest Afghanistan); (3) from Merv to Seleuceia in modern Iraq; (4) from Seleuceia to the Roman frontier.[3]

The collapses of the Han dynasty in AD 220, the Parthian empire in AD 227, and the end of the Kushan age in AD 330, along with the later disintegration of the Roman empire, brought severe disruptions and dislocation to this first great era of booming silk traffic opened up by the Silk Road. The fate of the silk trade on the eastern end of the Silk Road after the collapse of the Han dynasty was closely tied to the abilities of the various Chinese dynasties to control the Western frontier. Usually, trade benefited from the central protection and control of a powerful government such as the Sui dynasty in China (AD 581–618). Times of political disintegration left the trade at the mercy of various contentious local leaders. Close to the western end of the Silk Road, the Byzantine empire and the Sassanid empire in Persia survived the collapse of the so-called classical age of long-distance cross-cultural interactions between China under the Han dynasty and the

Roman empire (Bentley 1996: 763). Although long-distance trade became riskier and diminished as various Hunnish, Turkic and Mongol peoples divided and raided Central Asia, trade between Persia and Byzantium flourished.

One of the most important developments between the fourth and sixth centuries was that the growth of a large silk trade stimulated the establishment of silk-weaving industries both in Byzantium and Persia (Needham 1988: 418; Lopez 1945). The Byzantine and Persian importation of raw silk from China and Central Asia became much more important than that of the finished silk fabrics. Although the superior quality of silk material and the vigorous long-distance trade led to the early widespread diffusion of silk consumption on the Eurasian continent, diffusion of the knowledge of sericulture lagged far behind largely due to the difficulty of contacts between China and the outside world. The Romans, for example, with no clue to the origin of the silk materials, expended enormous amounts of treasure on importing Chinese silk, which was claimed to be worth more than its weight in gold in Rome (Boulnois 1966: 45–6; Fang, 1983: 165).

The high price of silk, due to worldwide demand and high transaction costs as well as constant disruptions in trade, were strong incentives for regions and states to acquire the knowledge of sericulture. Slowly, the knowledge of how to make silk threads began to unravel beyond the Chinese territory along the trade routes. Understandably, details regarding the timing and mechanism of the early technological diffusion of silk were largely lost in the long lapse of time, except perhaps in the form of legends. One such legend was the acquisition of the Chinese secret of sericulture by a Central Asian Kingdom located in Khotan, now Hotan in the Western part of China, the province of XinJiang. The legend had it that a Chinese princess married to the Central Asian King secretly brought silkworm eggs, hidden in her hair. Thereafter, sericulture took root and Khotan became a prosperous silk producing center. It is possible that Khotan might have been responsible for the further westward spread of Chinese sericulture knowledge to other parts of Central Asia, or even Persia and eventually Europe (see Table 2.1). The second legend presented more solid evidence on the spread of the knowledge of sericulture to Europe. Two monks were said to have smuggled silk cocoons in their canes out of the East and presented them to the court of the Byzantine Emperor Justinian in Constantinpole in AD 552 (see Table 2.1). However, large scale

Table 2.1 Chronology of silk development

Time	Diffusion of Sericulture	Development of Silk Manufacturing
c.3000 BC	Sericulture was discovered and utilized in China (Matsui 1930: 3; Fan and Wen 1993: 2)	
c.mid-100 BC	Sericulture brought to Khotan (West China) (Matsui 1930: 3; Fang 1983: 71–2) (AD 200, Li, M.W. 1991: 147) (AD 420–40, Boulnois 1966: 138)	
c.100 BC	Sericulture brought to Korea by Chinese immigrants (Needham 1988: 418)	
c.AD 100		Silk weaving in Syria and Palestine (Needham 1988: 418)
AD 282	Sericulture took root in Japan (Needham 1988: 418)	
c.AD 300	Sericulture introduced to Persia (Xu 1990: 43)	Silk weaving in Persia and Byzantium (Needham 1988: 418)
500–640		
AD 552	Sericulture introduced to Byzantium (Needham 1988: 419)	
c.8th century	Sericulture brought to Sicily (Edler 1930: 13)	Silk weaving brought to Spain by Arab conquest (Edler 1930: 12)
c.9th century		
c.10th century	Large scale production of raw silk export in Southern Spain (Edler 1930:12)	
Late 12th and early 13th centuries		Silk weaving took root in Northern Italy, esp. in Lucca (Edler 1930: chap. II)
14th century	Sericulture spread to North Italy (Edler 1930: 49)	Silk weaving in France, and Cologne, Zurich, Givet. (Edler 1930: 22)
15th century		Silk weaving started in England (Edler 1930: 22)
16th century	Large scale sericulture took root in France (Legget 1949: 250)	Silk industry also flourished
1530–80	Sericulture flourished in Mexico (Borah 1943: chap. II; Census, 1880)	
1623	Sericulture experimented in North America (Brockett 1876: 27)	

sericulture had to wait another two centuries to take firm root in the Middle East.[4]

Chinese scholars also emphasized a so-called southern Silk Road which started from Southwest China and passed through Sichuan and Yunan provinces in China, and Burma to reach India (Jiang 1995; Liu 1988: Ch. 1). Ancient Indian texts mentioned Chinese silk at least as early as 400 BC. Further, unlike the Romans and Greeks who had strange conjectures about the origin of silk, the ancient Indians seemed to be fully aware of the fact that silk derived from the cocoons spun by silkworms, and they learned how to reel silk from wild silkworms very early on (Ray 1995: 270–1). Trade in silk between China and India was quite substantial. In fact, as Liu Xinru argued, during the fourth and sixth centuries China's diminished exports of finished silk fabrics to Persia and Byzantium were made up for by increased sales to India (Liu 1988: 64–75).

The high age of overland trading in the era of Tang China and Abassaid Persia

The establishment of the powerful Tang dynasty in China (AD 618 to 960), which was to see the peak of classical Chinese civilization, heralded the second phase of the overland Silk Trade. The first two hundred years of the Tang dynasty (the seventh and eighth centuries) brought new prosperity to the silk trade, expanded China's western territory, and set up permanent government institutions in those regions. The prosperity of the area was indicated by the increased number of oasis towns and settlers along the road.[5]

The high age of the Tang dynasty in China also coincided with the rise and expansion of Islam in the Middle East and Central Asia. The eastward surge of the Islamic power in the seventh and eighth centuries led to its military show-down with the Tang military stationed in China's western frontier in AD 751. The victory of the Muslims over China on the Talas River (in northern Turkestan) was a major turning point for the history of the overland silk trade. First, it enabled the continuing eastward intrusion of the Islamic sphere of influence and led to the Tang dynasty's loss of control over China's western frontier. This, and the gradual internal weakening of the Tang government led to the partial closing of the overland Silk Road to China for almost four hundred years, until the era of the Mongol empire.[6] China's weakened control of its Northwestern territories, followed by frequent political and military turmoil were, in some way, responsible for the gradual southward migration of its economic, agricultural, industrial and population center from the Yellow River area towards the Yangtze River and the coastal regions. By the time of the Sung dynasty (AD 960–1279), the most productive silk centers found their home in the lower Yangtze River delta, far away from Xian, the starting point of the old Silk Road. This locational shift led to the increasing use of the sea route for silk exchange (Fan and Wen 1993: 58).

The other significant event, however, was that through the capture of Chinese prisoners in the Talas river, many of whom were skilled technicians, the Arabs obtained access to the rich technological knowledge base of China (Needham 1954: 236). The knowledge and the cultivation of silk were widely diffused from China to Persia, Anatolia, and regions controlled by Byzantium. In particular, the Chinese method of obtaining long and unbroken silk threads from the whole cocoons by killing the worm inside before it breaks out was widely adopted (Liu 1995: 43). The Islamic conquest of Sassanian Persia and parts of the Byzantine empire not only absorbed major silk-producing regions, but also eased the spread of sericulture and the silk industry to North Africa and Southern Spain.

If the closing of the first phase of the silk trade saw the rise of silk-weaving production centers in Persia and Byzantium, the second phase witnessed the effective end to the Chinese monopoly of sericulture and the successful adoption of raw silk production in the Islamic world. Persia, Anatolia, and the southern Mediterranean regions were to become primary production and export centers of raw silk and silk fabrics. The silk trade on the Eurasian continent was then partitioned into two rather self-contained trading circuits. While Chinese raw silk or silk fabrics largely went to Japan, Southeast Asia, parts of Central and South Asia, Persian silk (mostly raw silk) became the major supply source for the Middle East, Europe and North Africa.

The age of the Pax Mongolica and after

In the third phase of the silk trade, the entire overland route witnessed a vigorous revival when Mongol tribes, under Genghis Khan (1167–1227), broke out of the Karakorum steppe and built the largest empire across the Eurasian continent the world had ever seen. For the first time in history, the whole of Asia and Eastern Europe, from Shanhaikuan (in northeast China) to Budapest, and from Canton to Baghdad, was united under one political authority. The expansionary Mongol rulers were active in ensuring the safety of the trade routes, building effective post stations and rest stops, introducing the use of paper money and eliminating artificial trade barriers.[7] According to Robert Lopez, by 1257, Chinese raw silk appeared in the notarial records in the silk-producing area of Italy, Lucca (1952: 73). In the 1330s, a single merchant sold thousands of pounds of Chinese silk in Genoa (Reyerson 1982: 130). Between the 1260s and the 1350s, cheap Chinese raw silk was said to have arrived in Europe in "unlimited amounts."[8]

The over-extended Mongol empire began to collapse by the mid-fourteenth century. China was re-united under the native Chinese Ming dynasty (1368–1644). But the old problem of Northwestern territories which had haunted every Chinese emperor since the empire's founding was to surface again and again. Compared with the Mongol Yuan dynasty, Ming China's grip on this territory was much more tenuous. Silk trade between China, Central Asia and the Middle East went on intermittently, and at times, according to Morris Rossabi, became very active. It continued into the fifteenth and early sixteenth centuries. However, periodic warfare, shifting control of territories by different kingdoms in Central Asia, brought severe disruptions to the trade. The greatest menace came from local banditry and extortion, usually due to the absence of political and military protection from powerful empires. This point found reaffirmation from the revitalized overland trade between the Manchurian Qing China (1644–1911) that brought effective stability to China's western territories, and the Czarist Russia in the eighteenth and early nineteenth centuries. Silk fabrics produced in China's Lower Yangtze River area went northward and passed into southern Siberia and northern central Asia under Russian control (Fan and Wen 1993: Ch. 11). The success of the Russian–Chinese caravan commerce, as Rossabi argued, hinged on the relative safety on the northern trade routes. Banditry was virtually nonexistent, and custom duties were minimal, as the caravans merely traveled across one country instead of many disparate petty kingdoms and tribal units (Rossabi 1990: 368).

The fate of the Silk Road on the western end after the collapse of *Pax Mongolica* was more favorable, in contrast to the vicissitudes of its eastern end. The quick rise and expansion of the Ottoman empire in the fourteenth century filled the power vacuum left by the collapse of the Mongols and provided crucial protection for the trade. By this time, Persia had clearly emerged as the most important raw silk producer and exporter. The provinces to the south and west of the Caspian Sea – in particular, Shirvan, Karabagh and above all Gilan – sent out raw silk to important trading centers such as Tabriz, Bursa, Istanbul, Aleppo, Genoa, Venice and later Lyon (Inalcik 1994: 218–55). Although Mediterranean Europe and Syria were to develop a strong sericultural base in the next couple of centuries, they relied, to a significant degree, on Persian raw materials during this period. This trading pattern, with silk-production centers in southern Europe importing raw materials from Persia, through a largely overland caravan route (combined sometimes with the use of the Black Sea, the Persian Gulf and the Red Sea) lasted into the mid-eighteenth century, until the disintegration of the Safavid Persian state.[9]

The end of the Mongol age in the East coincided with the brewing Commercial Revolution in late medieval Europe, which marked the beginning of another epochal event in the history of the silk trade: the beginning of the western European silk-weaving industry. Important silk-manufacturing towns, such as Lucca in Northern Italy, began to establish themselves in the mid-thirteenth century and the industry and technology quickly diffused across the Continent (Edler 1930: Ch. II).

Although the western Europeans had most likely acquired sericultural and silk-making technology from the Arabs and East Romans through the crusaders' movement and warfare in the twelth and thirteenth centuries, contemporary scholars also emphasized the China connection. Both Dieter Kuhn and Claudier Zanier, in their comparative studies of pre-modern technology, unequivocally noted that the key elements of the early European silk-reeling and throwing equipment could find their origin in the earlier Chinese versions (Needham 1988: 418–33; Zanier 1994). Chinese sericulture and silk production had reached a peak in terms of both quality and productivity in the Song dynasty, immediately before the Mongol rule in China (Needham 1988: 384–90; Fan and Jin 1993: Ch. 4). The opening-up of the Eurasian continent by the Mongols marked the high stage of East–West exchange as symbolized by the famous travels of Marco Polo.

Silk Road: the sea route

Early maritime trade

The sea route, sometimes considered the second Silk Road, linked the South China Sea to the Indian Ocean, and through either the Persian Gulf or the Red Sea, connected to the Mediterranean. It brought out Chinese silk almost as early as the land route. In its early days, primitive ships and navigational tools and lack of geographical knowledge enabled the seafarers to cover only short distances, staying close to the shore lines. The sea route almost paralleled the overland route, and therefore, in the early days, served as an effective alternative (Needham 1954: 176–80).

The rise of Islam was as important for the development of the sea route as it was for the land route. During the eighth and nineth centuries the Islamic shipmasters penetrated into the Indian Ocean and Southeast Asia, China and even Korea and Japan (Needham 1954: 179; Hourani 1951: Ch. II). As illustrated earlier, pressure from Islamic and other forces on the Northwestern frontier had pushed China's external trade increasingly towards the sea route, to Japan, Southeast Asia and the Indian Ocean. (Chen and Wu 1981: 12; Li, M.-W. 1991: 135–51).

Towards the end of the twelfth century, Chinese outcompeted the Arabs in the Pacific waters. (Needham 1954, vol. 1, p. 180) The Mongol Yuan dynasty pursued an expansionary trade policy and greatly extended the Chinese overseas trading into the South China sea and the Indian Ocean. Chinese maritime supremacy culminated in the grandiose expedition led by the Muslim eunuch of the Ming Dynasty, Zheng Ho, during 1400–31, who sailed sea-going junks to Borneo, the Philippines, Ceylon, Malabar and even East Africa. While the Ming government was actively involved in the official tribute trade, its policy towards the burgeoning private trade was usually restrictive and inconsistent (Li, J.-M. 1990: 60–3). The rather abrupt withdrawal of Ming's naval presence in the Pacific waters at a time of rapidly growing private trade in the mid-fifteenth century opened the way for the arrival of the first European power: Portugal, which by 1488 found its way to East Asia, by bypassing the mighty Ottoman barrier and rounding the Cape of Good Hope.

The ascendancy of European technological leadership and the rise of European merchant empires

In Europe, silk-weaving technology continued its westward diffusion from the early silk-production centers in Northern Italy across the Continent. The technological diffusion was in many ways aided by the periodic migration of skilled artisans caused by the persecution of the Protestants. The seventeenth and eighteenth centuries saw the rise of important silk textile production centers such as Milan, Lyon, Zurich, Krefeld in Germany and Spitalfields in London.

While European silk weavers continued to rely on raw silk imports from Persia and Levant, Northern Italy and Southern France also emerged as principal producers and exporters of raw silk in the seventeenth and eighteenth centuries (Belfanti 1993: 269–71). More significantly, European silk-production technology had advanced rapidly from the seventeenth century. As argued by Claudier Zanier, European silk-reeling technology, with the Italian Tavelle and French Chambon system, and the rigid-axle transmission mechanism, probably surpassed that of China in the late seventeenth and early eighteenth centuries.[10]

Meanwhile, Italians also greatly improved the process of silk throwing although the idea of the twisting-frame – the arrangement and motion of dozens of parallel spindles – probably originated in China, but was rarely adopted after the Song and Yuan dynasties. In Italy, the twisting frame was developed into a big silk-throwing mill of higher capacity in the fourteenth and fifteenth centuries (Needham 1988: 420–33). In the early eighteenth century, the Lombe brothers in Britain smuggled this technology out of Italy and developed the famous Derby silk-throwing plant, a large-scale, water-powered, mechanized, manufacturing plant, the earliest institution that resembled a modern factory (Pacey 1990: 106).

During the seventeenth and eighteenth centuries, various experiments and improvements of the silk looms culminated in the invention of the so-called Jacquard loom by the Lyonese Joseph Jacquard in 1804. The Jacquard loom greatly improved upon the previously existing draw-loom – another Chinese invention – by attaching a punched-card system, which could handle complicated weaving patterns at greater efficiency. Towards the first part of the nineteenth century, steam power began to be applied to all the production processes, from reeling to throwing and weaving (Federico 1997: Ch. 7).

Southern European sericulture also benefited tremendously from advances made in European agronomic, biological and genetic science during this period. European scientists, guided by the methodology and tools of modern experimental science, enthusiastically studied the Chinese and Japanese sericultural texts acquired and translated in the eighteenth and nineteenth centuries (Foss 1986; Morris-Suzuki 1992; Zanier 1994: 71–94). Towards the latter part of the nineteenth century, European sericultural technology gained unquestionable leadership, aided by major discoveries, such as Pasteur's germ theory and Mendel's genetic law.

The rise of powerful merchant empires on the Iberian Peninsula and in Northwestern Europe marked the formation of a truly global trading system. However, the early intrusion of European navigation into the Pacific waters initially had limited impact on the pattern of the world silk trade. First, although some Chinese silk went directly to Europe on the sea route, Europe by then received its raw silk supply chiefly from Persia, which was delivered largely through the overland route. Second, as mentioned earlier, domestic substitution of raw silk production gradually took hold in Southern Europe. Europeans did continue to look eastward for raw silk supply – for diversification, and mostly for a cheaper and lower grade of raw silk.[11] With the establishment of the East India Companies, Britain and Holland began to explore ways of bringing raw silk directly through the Cape Route. In the early seventeenth century, they succeeded in partially diverting the raw silk exports of Iran from the caravan route to the sea route.[12] The search for cheaper raw silk brought the British further eastward along the sea route. After the mid-seventeenth century, the British East India Company started using large-scale imports of raw silk from Bengal. Towards the late seventeenth century, British and Dutch merchants sailed further eastward for direct purchase of raw silk for Europe. In the next two centuries, Britain succeeded in bringing out substantial amounts of Chinese raw silk through the Chinese government's restricted foreign trade port cities.

Silver for silks: the emergence of a global market

Although, by the time of the Cape Route breakthrough, Chinese silk had long lost its once exclusive appeal, Europeans still managed to play an important role by tapping into the pre-existing trading circuit in the Pacific. This was well-illustrated by Portugal's intermediary involvement in the ongoing silver for silk trade between Ming China and Tokugawa Japan. In the 1530s, Ming China ended its century-long official tribute trade with Japan due to unresolved disputes, and also banned private trade. During that time, the Japanese silk-weaving sector relied heavily on the imports of Chinese raw silk (Fan and Wen 1993: 262). This led to the booming smuggling trade between China and Japan. Using Macau, a base it seized from China in 1557, the Portuguese traders launched the so-called triangular trade of Nagasaki-Macau-Canton and acted as intermediary for this illicit trade of silver for silk.[13] Dutch as well as private Chinese merchants took over this transit trade in the early seventeenth century, using Taiwan as an intermediary base.

The persistent outflow of precious metals from Japan to China, in some way, prompted Tokugawa Shoguns' tight control of foreign trade and, in particular, the sweeping restrictions imposed in 1685 on imports of Chinese silk (Morris-Suzuki 1992: 106). These measures provided powerful incentives for creating a domestic supply of raw silk for Japan's growing silk-weaving sector. With the support of local domains, Japanese farmers responded vigorously and absorbed the supreme Chinese sericultural tradition through trans-lations of Chinese texts on agronomic and handicraft technology (Morris-Suzuki, 1994: 17; Ma 1997: 24–6). These efforts paid off as silkworm rearing was successfully acclimatized to the Japanese environment and raw silk production diffused widely throughout Japan in the next century. As domestic raw silk production increased, raw silk prices went down sharply towards the middle of the eighteenth century and the volume of transit trade of silk between China and Japan, started to decline towards the end of the eighteenth century (Fan and Wen 1993: 276).

While Chinese silk lost out in the face of successful domestic substitution in the Japanese market, it gained new ground across the Pacific, in the newly colonized South and Central American markets. The Andalusian regions in Southern Spain had a long and thriving history of sericulture and silk industry under the Islamic rule. The Christian take-over in 1477 infused refreshing Italian styles and designs into the industry (Legget 1949: 235). As part of the grand trans-oceanic transfer of animals and plants to the New Continent, the Spaniards successfully introduced sericulture and silk industry into Mexico in 1530. The culture and the industry were able to expand quickly (Borah 1943; Bazant 1964: 59–61).

However, the birth of a Mexican silk-sector, the fruit of successful trans-Atlantic migration of European agriculture and technology, turned out to be short-lived. The same forces that once landed silkworms in South America then crushed it, as Europeans continued westward and opened the Pacific for trade, which exposed the young Mexican silk industry to the onslaught of the world's oldest and most competitive silk industry, that of China. The year when the city of Manila was founded by the Spaniards, 1571, marked, as Flynn and Giráldez (1995) forcefully argue, the birth of Pacific trade and the emergence of global trade. The Canton–Manila–Acapulco triangular trade of silver for silks between China and New Spain could be viewed as a Pacific extension of the concurrent Nagasaki–Macau–Canton silver for silks exchange intermediated through the Portuguese and later the Dutch; but it was an extension of global proportion, as silk quickly found its way into the gigantic swirl of the global flows of precious metals in the wake of the discovery of gold and silver mines in the New World.

China's huge demand for silver resulted mainly from the Ming government's conversion to a silver standard, which provided significant arbitrage possibilities due to the gold/silver ratio discrepancies between Asia and Europe. China became a huge "suction pump," drawing silver first from Japan, then from Mexico and Peru. According to conservative estimates, 75 percent of the 400 million pesos of silver bound for the Philippines during the period 1565–1820 ended up in China. On average, roughly two million pesos of silver were shipped through Manila in the seventeenth century. However, it is important to note that the strength of the "suction power" from China was sustained by the silk threads – Chinese silk was the single most important export item to both Japan and Spanish America. In the high stage of the trade, China sent three- or even four-million pesos worth of silk goods a year to New Spain. For example, in 1727, China exported close to one million pounds of raw silk as well as a large proportion of finished silk products to New Spain (Fan and Wen 1993: 282).[14]

The success of Chinese silk products was not only due to their price competitiveness in comparison with the Spanish and Mexican products, but also the Chinese ability to adapt their products to Spanish fashion (Fan and Wen 1993: 279–80).

Chinese silk not only demolished the nascent Mexican sericulture, severely affected the young weaving industry there, but also effectively outcompeted the Spanish silk products in Spanish America. The burgeoning exports of raw silk also greatly stimulated the commercialization and specialization of the Chinese economy. In particular, they induced the rise of important silk producing, financing and trading towns in the coastal regions of Ming China (Chaun 1972: Ch 14; Fan and Wen 1993: 284). The Manila–Acapulco–Canton trade waned towards the early nineteenth century after the independence of Mexico. However, the opening-up of the Pacific route was a significant geographic breakthrough for the history of the silk trade. Chinese silk, for the first time, instead of going westward reversed its direction and went further east to be connected to the New Continent.

The modern Silk Road and the coming of a full circle: 1850–1930

The essence of the modern Silk Road era was the evolution of a single global market which unified all the extant regional trading circuits. The global silk trade also seemed to have come full circle as East Asia regained its predominant position and became the world's most important supplier of raw silk. Raw silk from China and Japan simultaneously went both ways, westward to Europe and eastward to North America. Except that at this time, East Asian predominance no longer rested on its long monopoly of technology but on the principle of comparative advantage.

The era started with the British engagement in the Opium War of 1842 which forcibly opened China to foreign trade with the establishment of the treaty ports, where traded commodities could enter and leave free from any restriction or tariff. After a sharp decline during the war period (1838–42), Chinese silk exports again recovered and reached close to two million pounds in 1845 (Shih 1976: 111; Fan and Wen 1993: 291). The treaty port system was extended to Japan in 1858. The Japanese raw silk industry, with more than one and a half centuries of successful import substitution experience, quickly became another important raw silk exporter. By the early nineteenth century, London had clearly emerged as a center for the silk trade. The age of *Pax Britannica*, like the previous *Pax Mongolica*, reunified the silk trade of the Eurasian continent. However, a fundamental change in this pattern of dual trading circuits between the East Asian bloc and the Euro-Middle-East bloc, had to await the coming of an internal crisis occurring within the world of the silk trade.

During the 1850s and 60s, the silkworm disease called pebrine broke out in Southern Europe and gradually spread to the Middle East. In its worst years, the sericultural crop in Europe declined by as much as 75 percent (Cayez 1979: 558–9). At this critical juncture, the British silk connection at the other end of the Eurasian continent rose to crucial importance. Between 1850 and 1860, Chinese and Japanese exports to Britain roughly quadrupled (Sugiyama 1988: 88).

In 1869, the Suez Canal was opened. Through the Red Sea route, French silk merchants could import directly from China and Japan. Between the 1880s and the 1930s, more than half of the raw silk used on the looms in Lyon, the world's silk-weaving capital, came from East Asia. Marseilles, Lyon and later Milan supplanted London and emerged as the world's most important trade centers of raw silk in the latter part of the nineteenth century. The maritime Silk Road thus ended its almost 300-year detour around the southern tip of the African continent. The long-cherished dream of Venetian merchants to obtain silk directly from China, the vision that sent the explorers of the fifteenth century out of the western end of the Mediterranean, had come true.

Meanwhile, Chinese and Japanese silk crossed the Pacific again, this time to North America. The British colonial government long encouraged the transfer of sericulture and the silk industry to North America. However, scarcity of labor (particularly, skilled labor) and lack of sericultural traditions severely impeded progress. On the eve of the Civil War, the U.S. silk-manufacturing industry remained small and produced unsophisticated products and its sericulture was next to non-existent. The erection of a tariff on the finished silk products for revenue purposes during the Civil War set the stage for the U.S. silk industry to take off. The U.S. industry benefited significantly from the almost simultaneous decline of the British silk industry, resulting mainly from the British government's abolition of the import tariff – a result of its free trade stand – against the more competitive European (particularly French) products. Significant numbers of skilled British silk workers and entrepreneurs, particularly from the town of Macclesfield, emigrated with European technology and machinery, which laid the foundation for America's leading silk town: Paterson in New Jersey. Behind the tariff wall, the U.S. silk industry grew quickly and by the twentieth century had become the world's largest importer of raw silk. By the 1920s and 30s, the production of the U.S. silk industry exceeded that of all European countries combined and doubled that of the Japanese silk industry. The U.S. silk industry developed a reputation for large-scale, capital intensive production of standardized silk products (Ma 1996).

The spectacular growth of the U.S. silk industry created an enormous demand for raw silk. Although imports of Chinese raw silk had begun as early as 1788 (Xu *et al.* 1990: 50), substantial amounts of raw silk crossed the North Pacific from China and Japan to San Francisco in 1867 after the establishment of a regular shipping line between China and the U.S. The raw silk was routed through the Continent to the silk manufacturing centers around New York city through the inter-continental railway system, completed in 1869 (Ma 1996: 338). The highly mechanized, large scale nature of the U.S. silk manufacturing placed exacting demands on the quality of imported raw silk. Japan succeeded in this competition and took an increasingly larger share in the U.S. market. By the mid-1910s, Japan, overtaking China, became the world's largest raw silk exporter, and by the 1920s and 30s, Japan supplied 75 to 90 percent of the total world raw silk exports (Ma 1996: 339). By then the bulk of the global silk trade was carried through the Pacific route.

Another distinguishing aspect of the modern silk road era was the massive reverse flow of technology from the West to the East, that is from Europe to Asia. The superior silk-reeling technology developed in Southern Europe in the eighteenth and nineteenth centuries went with the European merchants as they moved progressively eastward in their search for raw silk. The technology was brought to the Levant, Turkey, and India (Owen 1987; Quataert 1987; Bag 1989: Ch. IV). And most importantly, European silk-reeling technology and the factory system intruded into the traditional production system of China and Japan in the mid-nineteenth century. However, it was Japan after the Meiji Restoration that displayed the greatest receptivity to European technology and science. Within several decades after the initial arrival of European silk-reeling machines, the Japanese sericulture and silk-reeling industry had experienced a fundamental transformation through the successful borrowing and innovation of Western mechanical engineering and biological and genetic science. Japan also pioneered the introduction of the French Jacquard weaving loom in the early 1870s. As I have argued elsewhere, rapid techno-logical progress and productivity improvements, backed by Japan's successful concurrent industrialization experience, were the most essential factors accounting for Japan's rising share in the U.S. raw silk market, the world's largest by the early twentieth century. By the 1920s, Japanese sericultural and silk-reeling technology cap-tured global leadership. The direction of technological transfer again changed course, this time from Japan, first to China, its long-time teacher, then to Italy, its more recent teacher (Ma 1997). If the global silk trade finally made its circle around the globe in the modern era, so did the silk technology. Or to be more exact, technological leadership of raw silk production in the twentieth century converged back to the easternmost end of the Silk Road: Japan.

Trade, invention, institutions and the systems of transportation

The engine of growth: trade and invention

In close to two millennia, silk thread, starting from that treacher-ous, winding trail on the wild Western frontier of China, made its way around the globe. Sericulture and silk-making, based on a set of simple and ingenious ideas, landed on all the major continents of the world by the sixteenth century. Ernest Pariset, a nineteenth-century French scholar of silk, divided the long history of silk into four great ages: the age of the Chinese, the age of the Arabs (and Byzantines), the age of the Italians, and the age of the French. Not long after the publication of his book in 1862, Pariset began to call people's attention to the possible loss of Lyon's leadership in world silk production and trade to the rise of the mass-producing U.S. manufacturing (Allen 1904: 43). Both Table 2.1 and Figure 2.1 capture this progressive westward surge of silk trade and industry across time and space.

What could be the driving force behind this grand march of silk across time and space? The history of the Silk Road reveals that these "mysterious" and powerful forces may just lie within the process itself – specifically I mean the process of trading not only in goods, but also in knowledge. The silk exchange is nothing but part of the historical dynamics of human interaction. It is part of a process where trade induces diffusion of inventions

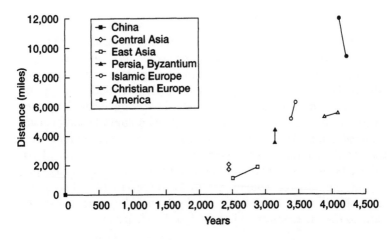

Figure 2.1 Westward diffusion of sericultural knowledge
Notes: 2600 BC has been set as the starting period (years = 0); Central Asia, Xian to Khotan = 1716 miles; India, Xian to Jammu, Kashmir = 1962 miles; East Asia, Xian to Seoul, Korea = 1063 miles and Xian to Tokyo, Japan = 1767 miles; Persia, Xian to Tabriz, Iran = 3429 miles; Byzantium, Xian to Istanbul = 4237 miles; Islamic Europe, Xian to Istanbul to Messina = 4237 + 756 miles and Messina to Seville = 1161 miles; Christian Europe, Messina to Milan = 598 miles and Milan to Lyon = 211 miles; America, Seville to Mexico City = 5591 miles and Milan to London to New York = 596 + 3434 miles

which induces further growth of trade – an accelerating spiral of growth of trade and technological exchange.

These ranged, to name just a few, from the technological progress made in the area of the domestication and management of animals for overland transportation; to the improvements in ship design and construction, the invention and diffusion of the lateen sail as well as the concurrent progress in navigation; to the inventions of the writing system, the paper, and printing, which made possible the recording of commercial transactions as well as taxes on the traded commodities; and to the development of standardized measurement systems and weighing instruments which eventually led to the use of carefully weighed and stamped metal coins as media of exchange, saving the transaction costs incurred in barter trade.[15] The following two sections make a comparative institutional analysis between the two major modes of transportation for the silk trade.

A caravan world

The modern English word *trade*, derives from an Old Saxon word, for footstep *trada*. It is a term appropriate to the long-distance trade of silk in the early age of the overland route, where the traces of footsteps led the caravans through deserts and mountains in the search of commercial profits. The geographical and environmental conditions were certainly no lure for the hapless merchants and travelers: vast and open deserts, along with lofty mountains and plateaus, and the constant threat of agressive nomadic tribespeople.

The greatest technological and institutional innovation in the means of transportation in the overland Silk Road was the adoption of camels and the subsequent rise of a camel-based caravan economy in Central Asia, North India, the Middle East and North Africa. The use of two-humped camels that could stand the extremes of heat and cold, and scent water from great distances, and warn of treacherous sandstorms, as well as the existence of oasis towns in between opened up the possibility of long-distance travel. In his classic study on the camels, Richard Bulliet argued that camels, in comparison to horses or oxen that pulled wheeled vehicles, were able to carry more, walk faster, had greater tenacity and endurance, greater powers of abstinence from food and water, and cost less to maintain (Bulliet 1975: 23; McNeill 1971: 1115). One of the greatest advantages of camel caravans was that they needed little in the way of a public infrastructure for long-distance trade. Camels did not need specially constructed roads or bridges, since they could traverse nearly any terrain and ford most streams without difficulty. Caravansaries, places to deposit goods safely while animals and men were resting and eating, were the only facilities caravans needed, and that type of rest place was just as important for wheeled transport. The capacity of camels enabled merchants to cross regions otherwise impenetrable. Improvements in the breeding and managing of camels and the making of saddles gradually reduced the costs for overland transportation. Bulliet (1975: 164) observed that the much heavier traffic on the Silk Road after about AD 100 was closely associated with the parallel rise in the diffusion of camels in Central Asia. After about AD 300, camels in Central Asia and the Middle East started to replace the wheel there, creating what William McNeill called a "caravan world."[16]

McNeill further argued that the smooth operation of the caravan transport network was also the result of the intimate symbiosis between the urban merchants and nomadic tribesmen in Middle Eastern society. The spread of the nomadic trading economy of caravans rode on the surging tide of the expansion of Islamic territories in the seventh and eighth centuries. After about AD 700 the caravan world and the world of Islam became almost co-terminous (McNeill 1971: 1118–9). Economic, social and legal institutions began to evolve around a caravan-based economy in Islamic societies. The increasing importance of nomadic tribes-people and urban merchants gradually created an environment generally favorable to the protection of caravan trade through the use of moderation of customs and taxation against that of one-time plundering.

Even compared with the rising importance of ocean transportation, early overland caravan-based transportation was competitive. McNeill (1971: 1122) argues convincingly that between AD 300 and 1300, the superior capacity of ships was not a decisive advantage, partly because shipping was seasonal, liable to shipwreck, and exposed to piracy, but also because economic production was not yet attuned to massive exchange of bulk commodities. As a result, for a thousand years and more, animal portage competed successfully with shipping in the movement of light-weight luxury goods between China, India, the Middle East, and Eastern Europe. Steensgaard made one calculation of transportation costs along the overland silk trade based upon an English merchant's records. He found that a journey of seventy-nine marching days between Northern Persia and Turkey in 1581–2 cost the merchant no more than three percent of the sales price of the silk transported. Thus Steensgaard concluded that, in terms of pure transportation costs (excluding the custom duties), silk transportation by camel was actually cheaper than by ship.[17]

The maritime system

Compared with other luxury commodities such as spices, porcelain, other textile materials and precious metals, silk was much more closely bound by the land route and was usually the last to switch to the extensive use of sea routes (Abu-Lughod 1989: 327; Li, M.-W. 1991: 46; Steensgaard 1973: 168). This was clearly due to its light weight, durability and ease for packing and storing. To understand the eventual waning of the overland route, we need to examine the most crucial feature distinguishing it from the maritime transportation system.

In nearly any terrain, camels could travel approximately 20 miles in six hours without difficulty. Still the entire trip from China to Europe was more than 5,000 miles and would take more than a year and a half (Rossabi 1990: 356). A single attendant could manage about six camels. Strings of camels, tied head to tail, were guided by one man in front and guarded by a second in the rear. Each camel could carry about 300–500 pounds of goods (McNeill 1971: 1115). As characterized by Steensgaard (1973: Ch. 1), it was the trade of peddlers, buying and selling small quantities on continuous travels from market to market. The trade was small, slow and characterized by the passing of goods through a chain of intermediaries. The peddling nature of the trade meant that, even when the volume of goods traded was considerable, the peddlers possessed little advance information concerning their targeted market. Since markets were isolated from one another, price differentials were often extraordinarily high, even between commercial centers located only moderate distances apart. High premiums were needed to compensate the merchants for the uncertainty and risk in trade.

Evidently, the concentration of so much wealth in a caravan plodding through territories under sometimes dubious political authorities was an invitation to robbery. Steensgaard (1973) emphasized the high protection costs incurred by the peddling trade because customs duties, risk of attack by robbers, and extortion on the part of local authorities constituted some of the most important entries among peddler expenses; and furthermore these expenses were more or less unpredictable. Using merchants' travel accounts and letters, Steensgaard concluded that the highly unpredictable protection costs contributed significantly to the irregularity of supply and therefore to violent short-term price fluctuations of raw silk in the seventeenth and eighteenth centuries' overland silk market (particularly in areas outside the political control of the Ottoman empire and the Safavid state). Protection costs also accounted for a much higher share than the pure transportation costs in the final value of goods. This can be seen in the long history of the silk trade. The rhythm of the various phases of silk trade echoed closely the rise and fall of political empires. Trade always thrived under the patronage of central powerful empires from Han and Tang China, to Rome, Mongols, Ottoman, Safavid Persia and Russia, which offered security against robbery and brigandage, maintained the roads, and levied predicable customs dues.[18]

Viewed from this perspective, the superiority of the sea route became clear. The sea wind that powered the ships was free and frequently traveled routes offered no problem, since one vessel's sails do not spoil the wind for another's. The problem of congestion and possible damage to the environment due to too many travels along the land route was not a problem on the wide and open sea. Protection costs for ships at sea were usually less troublesome than for caravans, if only because a ship traversed uninhabited expanses, whereas a caravan was seldom far from populated places, and caravans concentrated wealth in a way that tempted innumerable plunderers (McNeill 1971: 1119, 1123).

However, the early primitive ship-building and navigational technology, as well as limited geographical knowledge, initially prevented full exploitation of the non-rivalry and non-exclusive nature of the open sea. The early stages of ocean transportation shared many characteristics of a peddling trade over land routes: sailing short stages with little cargo and high crew costs (Curtin 1984: 119). However, according to Pierre Chaunu (1969), the pace of technological progress in marine transportation was rapidly overtaking that in land after the thirteenth century. Continuous progress in naval and nautical technology enabled ships to sail farther, faster and cheaper on the open sea; and with the discovery of an all-sea route from Europe to Asia and the crossing of the Pacific, it was only a matter of time before the sea route dominated global long-distance trade.

The "chains of markets" and all their associated problems which had long "shackled" the overland trade route began to dissolve on the vast open sea. The nature of the open sea meant that survival of long-distance trade no longer depended solely on the shifting political cycles of giant land-based empires. So long as traders had enough power to fend off seaborne piracy, they could bypass intermediaries and trade directly with destination port cities through all-sea routes. To a degree, this paved the way for the rise of European merchant empires such as Portugal, Spain, Holland and England, with small populations and limited natural resources, but strong naval power. The cost of keeping sea routes open and safe for lucrative long-distance trade – the suppression of seaborne piracy and the securing of strongholds at strategic trading ports – was much lower than that for controlling overland routes, which normally required military conquest and administration of alien territories.

This is Steensgaard's major point in explaining the success of sea routes in competing with land routes. Goods sailing along sea routes were no longer subject to various arbitrary taxes and extortion by local authorities and risks of attack by roving bandits on the overland route. In fact, the armed trading policies of the British and Dutch East India Companies internalized previously-unpredictable protection costs and risks of loss via land routes, and turned them into more well-defined entries of their internal military budgets. Reduction of the risk element in transportation costs brought greater certainty to trade, reduced price fluctuations, and enhanced the transparency of price formation (Steensgaard 1973). Further institutional (as well as technological) innovations such as the development of marine insurance, the gradual evolution of well-defined merchant law and its enhanced enforceability in Holland and England, brought further improvements to the marine transportation system (North 1991). If, as argued by McNeill, there existed a symbiotic relationship between the Islamic world and the Caravan world; clearly, the same was also true of the European expansion and the maritime transportation system (Chaunu 1969).

After the mid-nineteenth century, with the laying of intercontinental under-sea cable, the maritime transportation system ushered in a single, unified global market for raw silk, with standardization geared towards mass consumption and silk prices around the world moving in close unison. As the world knitted together, supply and demand shocks transmitted quickly from one region to another, sometimes within months, weeks, or even days (Ma 1996; Federico 1997: Ch. 8). By the twentieth century, a pound of raw silk sold in New York was only about one to five percent higher in price than a pound of raw silk of the same grade sold in Shanghai or Yokohama (Ma 1996). This contrasts sharply with the situation in 1620 and 1621 when prices of silk (both raw and finished fabrics) in Manila had risen almost tenfold upon reaching the port of Lima, Peru (Chuan 1972: 468). This huge drop in price difference over the Pacific reflected long-term improvements in marine transportation.

Conclusion: from luxury to mass consumption

Silk, with scarcity resulting from the high transportation and communication barriers, had long been the luxury product, having served gods, saints, emperors and aristocrats around the world. It became a symbol of political authority and social status; the code of silk dress once defined the political and religious hierarchy of the Tang China and the Islamic empires (Liu 1996). It was not just a symbol for wealth, it was wealth – silk was used as a medium of exchange in China and Central Asia. Wealth, unfortunately, was often associated with evil as it became the target of envy and the cause of much human warfare; yet silk had served for peace – it was usually the most important gift item in China's long history of tributary trade to appease the Central Asian kingdoms. In the modern age, silk became intimately linked with high fashion.

Luxuries are "goods whose principal use is rhetorical and social, goods that are simply incarnation signs, the necessity to which they respond is fundamentally political" (Liu 1996: 2). The welfare effects of early long-distance trade in luxury goods have always been dubious. But the exchange of the commodity such as silk (a private good) which brought forth the exchange of ideas (a public good) changed the nature of long-distance trade in luxury goods. The fundamental value of the silk exchange was its enduring testimony of the great cultural, religious and technological dialogue taking place across time along that legendary Road. The impact of the sharing, learning and accumulation of productive knowledge (a non-exhaustible public good) on human welfare far surpassed the mere trade of a luxury good.

The historical diffusion of the technologies of silk-making, transportation and communication, over time, brought down considerably the costs of both making and moving silk around the world and inadvertently set off a dynamic process which saw the gradual erosion of status of silk as a luxury good. Furthermore, this progressive democratization of silk started earlier than expected. For example even in the days of Byzantium and Tang China which had state monopoly of the production of high quality silks, the widespread diffusion of sericulture from Central Asia to the Mediterranean began to change people's attitudes towards this exquisite material. Easy accessibility of the silk materials and increased local production seriously weakened the royal monopolies in Byzantium and China. Silk textiles were gradually transferred into a common commodity, sometimes expensive and sometimes more reasonably priced (Liu 1996: 194).

This progressive "democratization" of silk accelerated over time. In the high age of the seventeenth century Pacific silver-for-silks trade between China and New Spain, Chinese silks could be found on the backs of even ordinary persons and on the altars of churches all over Spanish America (Li, L. 1981: 65). However, it was the twentieth-century U.S. silk-manufacturing industry that gave the most radical expression of silk "democratization." Large scale and mechanized factories in the U.S. used raw silk imported from thousands of miles away; they mass produced silk goods of a standardized quality and pattern, specifically geared towards the average consumers. By then, silk, the queen of fabrics, the thread of gold, served all echelons of a society, including the working classes.

Therefore, the full significance of silk as a commodity should be viewed in this context: silk was among the early products which broke the tyranny of distance, reduced the barriers to human exchange, promoted the spread of ideas, and ultimately led to the division of labor and expansion of the market – the so-called Smithian growth.

I would like to thank Peter Coclanis, William Darity, Miles Fletcher, Robert Gallman, Lenise Graber, Miguel Herce, Paul Rhode, and Ke Xu at University of North Carolina, Chapel Hill for comments and suggestions. My thanks also go to the participants of the Second Pacific Centuries Conference in Melbourne, Australia (July 1996), in particular, to Dennis Flynn, Lionel Frost and John McNeill. Of course, all errors are my sole responsibility.

Notes

1 Chinese scholar Zhao, Feng (1992: 218–21) distinguished three major historical regions of textile culture around the world. According to him, the Mediterranean textile circuit which included West Asia, Northern Africa and Europe developed technology in the utilization of wool and hemp. The India subcontinent, pioneered the use of cotton, whereas East Asia excelled in the use of silk. Distinct features of weaving and dying technology also characterized these three regions.
2 However, since the Silk Road also extended to Japan in the seventh and eighth centuries, the eastern terminus of the Road was in Japan (see Werblowsky 1988: 53).
3 For a description and mapping of the Silk Road see Boulnois 1966, Franck and Brownstone 1986, Needham 1954: 170–90.
4 As in so many other cases, knowledge and technology for commercially viable sericulture and silk production involved more than several pieces of information. Details on the type of mulberry trees suited to local soil conditions and temperature, the methods of pruning, propagating the trees, and the cutting of the leaves, the raising of silkworms as well as the construction and operation of reeling tools

were indispensable. This is why the diffusion of this technology was a cumulative and ongoing process requiring extensive human contact and repeated local experiments.

5 See Li, M.-W. 1991: 8. The well-known Chinese Buddhist monk and scholar, Shuang-Zhang, took advantage of the situation to travel along the Silk Road to India in AD 629. His translation and interpretation of the original Buddhist texts helped popularize Buddhism in East Asia, while his writings, based on his travels, greatly enhanced the Chinese understanding and knowledge of the geography and culture of these areas.

6 Needham 1954: 187. The road was opened and closed for silk trade several times depending on the political situation. See Boulnois 1966: 195.

7 See Fan and Wen 1993: 462–7, Li, M.-W. 1991: 153. Often cited as evidence for the safety of the Silk Road was a merchant's handbook of the fourteenth century which said: "The road which you travel from Tana (at the mouth of the Don) to Cathay is perfectly safe, whether by day or night, according to what the merchants say who have used it" (Needham 1954: 188) This is also the time the famous Polo brothers made their voyages to China between 1260–9 and 1271–96.

8 See Inalcik 1994: 218. However, the arrival of Chinese raw silk, although more competitive in price, did not outcompete the Persian and Turkestanian silk in the Italian market. One possible explanation, as argued by Lopez, was the deterioration of quality of Chinese raw silk resulting from the long distance traveled on the Silk Road (1952: 74–5).

9 In the sixteenth and seventeenth centuries, Russia also started purchasing Persian silk, shipped on the Volga river, and in sledges and carts, via Armenian merchants (see Curtin 1984: 188–92).

10 Both the Italian Tavelle and French Chambon systems involved wringing several silk threads dry and twisting them together to enhance the cohesiveness and evenness of the silk thread – features essential for high-quality raw silk (see Zanier 1994: 38–52).

11 Sericulture never found a home in Britain, which had a booming silk-weaving sector in the eighteenth and nineteenth centuries.

12 However, the project for such a diversion, with cooperation between Britain and Persia, met with only limited success. The British East India Company received only modest quantities up to the 1640s: proof that the silk trade was bound to the caravan route. By 1630, for example, the India spice traffic through the Ottoman-controlled caravan route was completely lost to the Cape route controlled by the British and the Dutch (see Chaudhuri 1978: 345; Inalcik 1994: 249; Steensgaard 1973: 168).

13 Precious Japanese metals, mainly silver, but also including gold and copper, exchanged for Chinese silk (see Flynn and Giráldez, 1995, 1996a, 1996b; von Glahn 1996; Fan and Wen 1993: 272).

14 For major literature on the subject of silver for silks exchange, see Chaudhuri, K.N. 1978, Chaun, Hang-Sheng 1971: vol. 1, Ch 12, 13 and 14, Fan and Wen 1993: 279–84, Flynn and Giráldez, 1995, 1996a, 1996b and von Glahn 1996: 434.

15 See Reid 1996: Ch. 2. Lius Rivera-Batiz and Paul Romer (1994) developed a growth model where output growth originated from the expansion of the world's total stock of productive knowledge. In their model, they defined the source of the growth of knowledge as coming from economic integration, more specifically, the concatenation of different nations' knowledge bases. Interestingly, the exchange through the Silk Road was cited as a supporting case for their model.

16 See McNeill 1971 and Bulliet 1975 for the different development paths of the use of camels and their combination with other domesticated animals and carts in North India, Persia, Arabia, Central Asia, and North Africa; and for animals other than camels used as power source and transportation tools.

17 The custom dues and protection costs totaled about twice that amount. See Steensgaard 1973: 32–3, 40. This unique symbiosis of the Caravan world and the Islamic world not only provided an important understanding of the persistence of the overland silk trade, but also gave an adequate explanation to the differential developments of the two ends of the Silk Road. Although the "caravan world" stretched through vast areas of the Eurasian continent, it stopped short of both China and Western Europe. The Chinese internal transportaion system was based largely on the canals, water-ways and the public road system, whereas Western Europe relied heavily on its natural riverways, and Mediterranean Europe on its numerous harbors and easily navigated waters. Neither transport system made much use of caravans. See McNeill 1971.

18 This is the central idea behind the game-theoretic model developed by Edi Karni and Subir Chakrabarti (1997). Their model shows that chains of markets under independent jurisdictions with non-cooperative tax policies (on traded goods going through the markets) entail externalities detrimental to trade; and that the monopolization of the chain markets (under, for example, a central political power) could internalize the costs associated with these externalities, increase the volume of trade and the tax revenues through the implementation of cooperative tax strategies.

References

Abu-Lughod, Janet L. (1989) *Before European Hegemony: The World System, AD 1250–1350.* New York: Oxford University Press.

Allen, Franklin (1904) *The Silk Industry of the World at the Opening of the Twentieth Century.* New York: Silk Association of America.

Bag, Sailendra Kumar (1989) *The Changing Fortunes of the Bengal Silk Industry 1757–1833.* Calcutta: Pradip Kumar Banerjee Manasi Press.

Bazant, Jan (1964) "Evolution of the Textile Industry of Puebla, 1544–1845" reprinted in Michael Adas (ed.) (1996) *Technology and European Overseas Enterprise.* Brookfield VT: Variorum.

Belfanti, Carlo Marco (1993) "Rural Manufactures and Rural Proto-industries in the 'Italy of the Cities' from the Sixteenth through the Eighteenth Century," *Continuity and Change* 8 (20): 253–80.

Bentley, Jerry H. (1996) "Cross-Cultural Interaction and Periodization in World History," *American Historical Review*, 101 (3): 749–70.

Borah, Woodrow (1943) *Silk Raising in Colonial Mexico*. Berkeley and Los Angeles: University of California Press.

Boulnois, L. (1966) *The Silk Road* (translated by Dennis Chamberlin). London: George Allen & Unwin Ltd.

Brockett, L.P. (1876) *The Silk Industry in America*. New York: The Silk Association of America.

Bulliet, Richard W. (1975) *The Camel and the Wheel*. Cambridge, MA: Harvard University Press.

Cayez, Pierre (1979) *L'industrialisation Lyonnaise au Xixeme Siécle, du Grand Commerce a la Grande Industrie*. Tome II. Thèse Presentée devant L'université de Lyon II. Service de Reproduction des Thèses Université de Lille III.

Chaudhuri, K.N. (1978) *The Trading World of Asia and the English East India Company 1660–1760*. Cambridge: Cambridge University Press.

—— (1991) "Reflections on the Organizing Principle of Premodern Trade," in James D. Tracy (ed.) *The Political Economy of Merchant Empires*. Cambridge: Cambridge University Press.

Chaun, Han-Shen (1972) *Zhong Guo Jin Ji Shi Ren Cong*. Vol.1 (Essays on Chinese Economic History). New Asia Research Institute Press.

Chaunu, Pierre (1969) "L'expansion europeene due XIIIe au Xv^e siécle," reprinted in Michael Adas (ed.) (1996) *Technology and European Overseas Enterprise*. Brookfield VT: Variorum.

Chen, Gao-Hua and Wu, Tai (1981) *Sun Yuan Shih Chi De Hai Wai Mao Yi* (The Overseas Trade in Sung and Yuan Dynasty). Tienjing: People's Publishing Co. of Tienjing.

Curtin, Philip D. (1984) *Cross-Cultural Trade in World History*. London: Cambridge University Press.

Edler, Florence M. (1930) *The Silk Trade of Lucca during the Thirteenth and Fourteenth Centuries*. PhD Dissertation submitted to the University of Chicago.

Fan, Jin-Ming and Jin, Wen (1993) *Jiang Nan Si Chou Shi Yen Jiu* (Study on the History of Chiang-Nan Silk). Beijing: Agricultural Publishing House.

Fang, Hao (1983) *Zhong Xi Jiao Tong Si* (History of Transportation and Communication between China and the West). Vols. I & II. Taipei: The Publishing Co. of Chinese Cultural University.

Federico, Giovanni (1997) *An Economic History of the Silk Industry, 1830–1930*. Cambridge: Cambridge University Press.

Foss, Theodore Nicholas (1986) "Chinese Silk Manufacture in Jean-Baptiste's Du Halde, *Description . . . de la Chine (1735)*," reprinted

in Michael Adas (ed.) (1996) *Technology and European Overseas Enterprise.*
Brookfield VT: Variorum.

Flynn, Dennis O. and Giráldez, Arturo (1995) "Born with a 'Silver
Spoon': The Origin of World Trade in 1571," *Journal of World History,*
6 (2): 201–19.

—— —— (1996a) "Silk for Silver: Manila–Macao Trade in the seventeenth Century," *Philippine Studies,* 44: 52–8.

—— —— (1996b) "Arbitrage, China and World Trade in the Early
Modern Period," *Journal of Economic and Social History of the Orient,* 38
(4): 429–48.

Franck, Irene M. and Brownstone, David M. (1986) *The Silk Road: A
History.* New York: Facts on File Publications.

Hourani, G.F. (1951) *Arab Seafaring in the Indian Ocean in Ancient and
Early Medieval Times.* London: Oxford University Press.

Inalcik, Halil (1994) "Bursa and the Silk Trade," pp. 218–255, in "Part
I The Ottoman State: Economy and Society, 1300–1600." in *An
Economic and Social History of the Ottoman Empire, 1300–1914.* Edited
by Inalcik, Halil with Quataert, Donald. Cambridge University Press.

Jiang, Yu-xiang (ed.) (1995) *Gu Dai Xi Nan Si Chou Zi Lu Yan Jiu*
(Studies of the Ancient Silk Road in Southwest China). Sichuan:
Sichuan University press.

Karni, Edi and Chakrabarti, K. Subir (1997) "Political Structure, Taxes,
and Trade," *Journal of Public Economics,* 64, (2) 241–58.

Leggett, William F. (1949) *The Story of Silk.* New York: Lifetime
Editions.

Liu, Xinru (1988) *Ancient India and Ancient China, Trade and Religious
Exchanges AD 1–600.* Delhi: Oxford University Press.

—— (1995) "Silks and Religions in Eurasia, *c.*AD 600–1200," *Journal of
World History,* 6: 25–48.

—— —— (1996) *Silk and Religion, an Exploration of Material Life and the
Thought of People, AD 600–1200.* Delhi: Oxford University Press.

Lopez, Robert (1945), "Silk Industry in the Byzantine Empire," *Speculum*
XX(1): 1–42.

—— —— (1952) "China Silk in Europe in the Yuan Period," *Journal of
the American Oriental Society,* 72: 72–6.

Li, Jin-Ming (1990) *Ming Dai Hai Wai Mao Yi Shi* (History of Overseas
Trade in the Ming Dynasty). Beijing: The Publishing Co. of Chinese
Social Science Academy.

Li, Lillian M. (1981) *China's Silk Trade: Traditional Industry in the Modern
World 1842–1937.* Harvard: Council on East Asian Studies, Harvard
University.

Li, Ming-wei (ed.) (1991) *Si Chou Zi Lu Mao I Shi* (Studies of the Trade
History of the Silk Road). LanZhou: People's Publishing House of
Gansu.

Ma, Debin (1996) "The Modern Silk Road: The Global Raw-Silk Market, 1850–1930" *Journal of Economic History*, 56(2): 330–55.

—— —— (1997) "Catching-up, Falling Behind and Catching-up – Chinese and Japanese Raw Silk Sectors: 1860s–1940s". Unpublished paper.

Matsui, Shichiro (1930) *The History of the Silk Industry in the United States*. New York: Howes Publishing Co.

McNeill, H. William (1971) "The Eccentricity of Wheels, or Eurasian Transportation in Historical Perspective," *American Historical Review*, 92: 1111–26.

Morris-Suzuki, Tessa (1992) "Sericulture and the Origins of Japanese Industrialization," *Technology and Culture* 33, (1): 101–21.

—— —— (1994) *The Technological Transformation of Japan, from the Seventeenth to the Twenty-first Century*. Cambridge: Cambridge University Press.

Needham, Joseph (1954) *Science and Civilization in China, Vol. I: Introductory Orientations*, Cambridge: Cambridge University Press.

—— —— (1986) *The Shorter Science and Civilization in China*, Vol. 3. London: Cambridge University Press.

—— —— (1988) *Science and Civilization in China, Vol. 5: Chemistry and Chemical Technology*. New York: Cambridge University Press.

North, Douglas (1991) "Institutions, Transaction Costs, and the Rise of Merchant Empires", in James D. Tracy (Ed.) *The Political Economy of Merchant Empires*, Cambridge: Cambridge University Press.

—— —— (1994) "Economic Performance Through Time" *American Economic Review*, 84 (3).

Owen, Roger (1987) "The Silk-reeling Industry of Mount Lebanon, 1840–1914: a Study of the Possibilities and Limitations of Factory Production in the Periphery." in *The Ottoman Empire and the World-Economy*. (ed.) Islamoglu-Inan, Huri, Cambridge: Cambridge University Press.

Pacey, Arnold (1990) *Technology in World Civilization*. Cambridge: MIT Press.

Quataert, Donald (1987) "The Silk Industry of Bursa, 1880–1914," in Huri Islamoglu-Inan (ed.) *The Ottoman Empire and the World-Economy*. Cambridge: Cambridge University Press.

Ray, Haraprasad (1995) "The Southern Silk Road from China to India – an Approach from India," in Jiang, Yu-Xiang (ed.) *Gu Dai Xi Nan Si Chou Zi Lu Yan Jiu* (Studies of the Ancient Silk Road in Southwest China). Sichuan: Sichuan University Press: 263–89.

Reid, Struan (1996) *Inventions and Trade, the Silk and Spice Routes*. New York: UNESCO Publishing.

Rivera-Batiz, Lius A. and Romer, Paul M. (1994). "Economic Integration and Endogenous Growth," in Gene M. Grossman (ed.) *Imperfect Competition and International Trade*. Cambridge: The MIT Press.

Reyerson, Kathryn (1982) "Medieval Silks in Montpellier: The Silk Market ca. 1250–ca. 1350" in *Journal of European Economic History*, 11(1): 117–40.

Rossabi, Morris (1990) "The 'Decline' of the Central Asian Caravan Trade" in James D. Tracy (ed.) *The Rise of Merchant Empires*. Cambridge: Cambridge University Press.

Shih, Min-hHsiung (1976) *Silk Industry in Ch'ing China*, (translated by E-tu Zen Sun), Ann Arbor: Center for Chinese Studies, the University of Michigan.

Steensgaard, Niels (1973) *The Asian Trade Revolution of the Seventeenth Century: the East India Companies and the Decline of the Caravan Trade*. Chicago: University of Chicago Press.

Sugiyama, Shinya (1988) *Japan's Industrialization in the World Economy 1859–1899, Export Trade and Overseas Competition*. London: The Athlone Press.

von Glahn, Richard (1996) "Myth and Reality of China's Seventeenth-Century Monetary Crisis." *The Journal of Economic History*, 56 (2): 429–54.

Werblowsky, R.J. Zwi (1988) "Contacts of Continents: The Silk Road," *Diogenes*, 144: 52–64.

Xu, Xin-wu (ed.) (1990) *Zhongguo Jindai Saosi Gongyeshi (Modern History of Chinese Silk-reeling Industry)*. Shanghai: People's Publishing House, 1990.

Zarier, Claudio (1994) *Where the Roads Meet, East and West in the Silk Production Process (seventeenth to nineteenth Century)*. Kyoto: Instituto Italiano di Cultura Sceiola di Studi Sull.

Zhao, Feng (1992) *Tang Dai Si Chou Yu Si Chou Zhi Lu* (Silk and the Silk Road in the Tang Dynasty). Xian, China: San-Qing Publishing House.

3

ISLANDS IN THE RIM

Ecology and history in and around the Pacific, 1521–1996

John R. McNeill

The largest ocean in the world is far from empty. It has several thousand islands, large and small, low and tall, rising above its surface. Hundreds of them have hosted human populations for centuries, and all of them (except those recently formed) have supported other life forms for longer still. For most of Pacific history, the oceanic islands (as opposed to inshore islands) have had little to do with the Pacific Rim. Their ecologies and economies evolved in unusual isolation. Since Magellan's voyages, however, the relative isolation of the Pacific islands has broken down. Increasingly reliable transport technology has brought these ecologies and economies into closer and closer touch with the wider world, and particularly with the vibrant economies of the Pacific Rim. This chapter considers the ecological consequences of this integration for the oceanic islands of the Pacific. They have been many and spectacular.

Environmental history of the Pacific Basin

While this chapter will only take up the fate of the oceanic islands, it is worth recognizing the degree to which these islands' environmental history is part of a larger whole. The entire Pacific Basin has elements of geological and climatic unity to it that affect both the islands and the Rim. The whole basin, for example, shares a considerable geological instability. Volcanoes ring the entire Ocean, from New Zealand clockwise around to Chile. Indonesian volcanic eruptions have deepened ice ages in prehistoric times, and more recently (AD 1815) have caused crops to fail around the world (Officer and Page 1993: 22).[1] Most of the oceanic islands result, in fact, from undersea volcanic eruptions. Pacific volcanoes continue to percolate, as Mount St. Helens (USA), Mount Pinatubo (Philippines), and Mount Ruahepa (New Zealand) attest. Earthquakes also abound around the Rim, where subduction zones create by far the most seismically active areas in the world. The northward march of Australia/New Guinea, which one day will crunch into southeast Asia, makes the southwest Pacific arguably the most geologically exciting place on the crust of the earth. All these geological vibrations (amongst other effects) create plenty of new rock, shatter old rock, and in general promote erosion from the slopes of the Rim and the islands down to the sea.

Particularly powerful storms also foment erosion around the Pacific. The western Pacific is subject to typhoons, high-energy maelstroms of wind and rain that can strip away almost anything in their paths. Most of the Pacific, islands and Rim, are affected by the irregular rhythms of ENSO (El Niño/Southern Oscillation) events. These bring drought to some places and torrential rains to others, often drenching the western coasts of the Americas, from Peru to California.[2] Drought and forest fire history in Australia and Indonesia danced to the rhythm tapped out by ENSO. Climate as well as geology plays an assertive and unpredictable role in the Pacific.

One final element that lends a certain unity to Pacific environmental history is the unusual richness of the Ocean's coastal fisheries. New Zealand, Japanese, Kamchatkan, Alaskan, Californian, British Columbian, Peruvian, and Antarctic coastal waters all teem (or until recently have teemed) with edible and otherwise useful fish. Wherever oxygen-rich cold water wells up near the surface it acquires a nutritious litter of organic material and thus accommodates large populations of fish. This happens especially in coastal waters that receive heavy injections of organic debris from rivers. Where rivers run down steep mountains and carry quantities of sediment, as all around the Pacific, they help create notably rich fishing grounds.

All this – vulcanism, earthquakes, rich fisheries – the Pacific Basin shares. The Rim does not have the same biogeographical unity as do some smaller littorals, such as the Mediterranean. It is much too big for that, with a full range of arctic, temperate and tropical ecosystems. But the histories of both the Rim and the islands unfold amid a particularly lively and violent Nature. This makes it especially difficult to disentangle human impact from non-human – which is rarely an easy task in environmental history, whatever the context (Nunn 1994b).

The human impacts that I will trace here are those derived from biological invasions and from the power of concentrated demand. Biological invasions occur when new species are somehow introduced into environments previously free of them. They succeed most readily when human beings (or some other disruptive forces) tear open the fabric of an ecosystem, more or less the way torn skin invites infection. They are frequent in the history of islands because island ecosystems have evolved in relative isolation from the main currents of terrestrial evolution. Islands tend to have many endemic species, and to have few of the species that co-exist most successfully with humanity. When people introduce such species – rats, horses, viruses – to islands they often prosper at the expense of the indigenous species and people.

Concentrated demand also works powerfully upon islands, but its effect is equally strong on any economically isolated zone. When new connections are forged between large or unusually affluent populations and small zones of supply, the environmental impact is often sudden and enormous. For example, in the 1880s German and British imperialism linked the large and affluent populations of Europe and (indirectly) North America to the savanna lands of East Africa. Suddenly, millions of people who wanted ivory combs, piano keys, and billiard balls could get them. Elephant-hunters could sell all the soft-ivory tusks they could collect. And, thus, by 1920 the elephant population of East Africa had declined by 90 percent or so.

The Rim and the islands

The ecological relationship between the Rim and the islands is a long one, stretching back millions of years. But here I will focus on a blip of time, the last 475 years. Concentrated demand, like biological invasions, affected Pacific island ecology with a remarkable intensity, especially after 1780, because the islands had been remarkably isolated, economically as well as ecologically, from the Rim and the wider world. That would change, first with the Portuguese captain Ferdinand Magellan, and then with the British navigator James Cook.

A few unknown sailors probably crossed the Pacific before Magellan sailed from Chile to Guam to the Philippines in

1520-1. If they did, they, like Columbus' predecessors in the Atlantic, had no discernible consequences – Magellan did. Within five decades of his death (in the Philippines in 1521), his successors forged links between Latin America, archipelagic southeast Asia, and East Asia. By 1565 the Spanish crown had established what would become the longest-running shipping line in world history, the Manila galleons. They regularly traversed the Pacific, from Acapulco to Manila and back again. By 1571, when Manila was founded, the Acapulco–Manila–Canton [Guangdong] axis formed one of the sinews of the nascent world economy. The Manila galleons after 1668 stopped in Guam, as Magellan had done, but other than that they had no impact on oceanic islands. Cook's successors did.

Cook first entered the Pacific in 1768 and died there (in Hawaii) in 1779. In the course of his three voyages he charted the Pacific using the latest scientific instruments, delineating continental coasts and pinpointing island locations. Within five decades of his death, by 1829, European and North-American sailors had forged links between most of the inhabited oceanic islands and the world beyond. Island ecosystems and economies henceforth felt the unsettling effect of contacts with the Rim.

Biological invasions

Biological invasion of oceanic islands involved all manner of species. Microbes and mammals carried the greatest consequences and Guam felt these first. Soon after 1668 the local population, known as Chamorros, began to succumb to alien diseases introduced inadvertently by Spanish soldiers, sailors, and Jesuit priests. Smallpox, influenza and violence reduced the Chamorro population by about 90 percent. Spaniards also introduced their favorite domesticated animals, goats, pigs, cattle and the like, which inevitably changed vegetation. Intentionally and accidentally, the Manila galleons also introduced new plants, many of which were well-adapted to life with grazing animals or to life on disturbed and abandoned patches of ground. By 1914, about one-fifth of Guam's plant species were exotic intruders from the Americas, brought in the hulls of the Manila galleons and by their successors (Merrill 1954: 230–7).

Guam's experience presaged that of many other oceanic islands after Cook. On dozens of islands, repeated contact with European or North-American whalers, traders, beachcombers, and missionaries brought a torrent of lethal pathogens. Pacific-islander immune systems had no experience of the majority of human diseases before 1768, and so the microbial baptism came at horrific cost. Population declines of 60–90 percent followed on one island after another.

The Marquesas appear to have suffered the harshest decline, about 95 percent, while New Zealand's Maori survived best (Rallu 1990; Pool 1991). Depopulation tended to last for three to five generations, maybe 90–150 years, before numbers began to climb again. The Marquesas have yet to exceed the population they (probably) carried in 1800.

The widespread destruction of human population meant abandonment of fields and gardens. Newly introduced species rushed to fill the gap. Exotic weeds and resurgent native bush made a succulent diet for grazing animals, which arrived in the wake of whalers and traders. Whalers made it a special practice to deposit goats of breeding age on every island they could, whether inhabited or not, so as to create a ready supply of fresh meat should they ever need it. Caprine population explosions usually followed, creating tremendous pressure on vegetation. Native plants, with no experience of grazing animals, and hence no spikes or toxins with which to defend against them, suffered under the attention of goats (and to a lesser extent cattle, pigs, and sheep). This spelled further opportunity for alien plants to colonize (see Crosby 1986).

Perhaps the most devastating intruder was the rat. Many Pacific islands had rats from the time of first settlement. These were so-called Polynesian rats, or *kiore*, part of the diet of many islanders. Cook and his followers accidentally introduced the Norway rat, *rattus norvegicus*, a magisterial opportunist and reproductive Stakhanovite. Two healthy Norway rats in three years can produce 20 million descendants. The appetites of millions of rats led quickly to the extinction of many Pacific-island birds, whose eggs appealed to rats, and to the marginalization of *kiore* and other small creatures whose *lebensraum* the Norway rat had seized. Rats succeeded so well that the Micronesian language of Marshallese developed a word, *kkijdikdik*, to mean "to be teeming with rats."

Altogether the maritime connections that followed Cook's navigations brought arkfuls of new creatures to the oceanic islands. Many failed to establish themselves, but a few succeeded spectacularly, changing flora and fauna forever. Most of the invaders were launched from the Pacific Rim, from Chile and Mexico, from China and Malaysia. But fundamentally, they came from all over the world, colonizing or passing through the Rim before moving on to the oceanic islands.

Concentrated demand

Prior to Cook's arrival, concentrated demand from distant quarters had not rearranged oceanic island ecosystems. Guam had provisioned the Manila galleons, but had scarcely exported anything and no other oceanic islands traded to the Rim or beyond. But, by the late eighteenth century, advances in navigation made it possible to build trade relations and businesses based on the extraction of island products. Within a century of Cook's death, oceanic islands had undergone booms and busts in mother-of-pearl, bêche-de-mer (sea cucumber), sealskins, tortoiseshell, sandalwood and a few other native products. Additionally, some introduced species, such as hogs in Tahiti, were extensively harvested for trade to the Rim (in this case Sydney). All of these trades had direct ecological effects. Some had considerable indirect consequences, such as the bêche-de-mer business in Fiji. Broad swathes of Fiji's forests were felled to fuel fires to dry sea cucumbers for export. Here I will provide only two examples of the impacts of concentrated demand, that of sandalwood in the nineteenth century and phosphate in the twentieth.

Sandalwood is an aromatic tree that grew widely throughout the tropical regions of the Indian and Pacific oceans. It made fine ornamental boxes, chests and furniture. Oil from its heartwood makes a heady incense especially popular in China, as well as prized perfumes. After 1804, European and American merchants learned of its value in China and began to cut it or buy it in Fiji (1804-16), the Marquesas (1815-20), Hawaii (1811–31) and the New Hebrides (1841-65). In Hawaii the monarchs sold sandalwood to merchants in exchange for the products of the outside world. Those products held such appeal that Hawaiian kings put thousands of commoners to work burning forests to make it easier to find sandalwood, which emits a distinctive smell when burned. As their own sandalwood stands thinned, the kings even tried to expand their business to Melanesia, thousands of kilometers away, outfitting two ships to exploit sandalwood on Vanuatu in 1829. (The ships vanished.) The demand of millions of Chinese consumers for comparatively trivial items had a lasting effect on Pacific-island forests. Sandalwood remains rare today (Shineberg 1967; Merlin and VanRavensway 1990).

Phosphate, found as rock and in bird guano, is a useful ingredient in fertilizers. Calcium phosphate, suitably treated with sulfuric acid, produces superphosphate, just the thing to enhance plant growth in the pastures of Australia and New Zealand. Two tropical Pacific islands, Nauru and Banaba, used to have some of the richest guano in the world. Millennia of seabird visits yielded deep deposits of fossilized guano, mixed helpfully with occasional bird feathers and bones for calcium. Beginning in 1905, Australian phosphateers organized the mining of phosphate on Nauru and Banaba. Miners stripped off vegetation and topsoil, and dug pits down to seven meters deep to extract the white gold. The surface of both islands is now pockmarked with pits amid limestone pillars, and little land suitable for agriculture or indeed anything is left. Banaba phosphate essentially ran out in 1979 and many Banabans now work for wages on Nauru, where the phosphate will run out shortly. Nauruans, of whom there are about 5,000, will not need to work at all when that happens: they will be rentiers, living off investments. They renegotiated the mining lease in 1968 after independence from Australia and have since become some of the richest people in the world. This may or may not compensate for the corroded condition of their island.

Unlike sandalwood on the China market, superphosphate supply to Australia and New Zealand is no trivial matter. The productivity of pastures, and indeed sheep populations, have in the twentieth century correlated closely with imports of superphosphates. (Soils in both countries generally lack adequate phosphorus). The large and buoyant pastoral economies of these two Rim countries required superphosphates, as did Western Australia's wheat. Tiny Nauru and Banaba offered the cheapest source, thanks to concessions that until 1968 paid islanders next to nothing for a multi-million dollar resource (Hein 1990; MacDonald and Williams 1985; Weeramantry 1992).[3]

The sandalwood trade was typical of nineteenth-century Pacific island exports in one important respect: it focused on China. Aside from whale oil and whalebone, all the extractive Pacific trades before about 1860 were driven by Chinese demand. The opening of China to maritime trade from the 1780s onward, and the difficulty foreigners had in buying Chinese goods with anything but silver, created conditions in which it made economic sense to ransack the Pacific for specialty items that Chinese consumers cherished. By the 1840s opium produced in Bengal filled the bill nicely, especially for British traders, so the incentive to hunt and gather every last exploitable species in the Pacific dwindled. Indian opium may conceivably have saved some Pacific-island species from extinction: commerce works in mysterious ways.

After 1860 the power of concentrated demand slowly shifted in the oceanic islands. New technologies and more capital ushered in an age of plantations on which indentured and wage-laborers raised crops to meet external demand. Hunting and gathering of the fruits of nature gave way to systematic production. Plantations developed in French Polynesia in the 1860s because French looms could not get enough American cotton due to the U.S. Civil War. Sugar plantations developed in Fiji, in Hawaii after 1890, and in the Marianas under Japanese rule (1920–44). These and other islands also raised pineapple, bananas, coffee and copra for the wider world. Plantation agriculture everywhere brings about thorough environmental change. Extant vegetation must be burned and cleared to make room for crops. Sugar plantations cut mountains of fuelwood to boil cane syrup. Row upon row of pineapple or sugarcane – monocropping – invites infestation with pests that had found poorer pickings in previous times, as Polynesians and other islanders had usually practiced polyculture. Plantation agriculture thus played a crucial role in changing the habitat and biota in many Pacific islands. In Hawaii, where 10 percent of the native flora has disappeared, it has been the main cause of species extinctions in the twentieth century (Cuddihy and Stone 1990: 41–44, 104).

Post-Magellan ecological impacts upon the Rim

The environmental history of the varied landscapes and myriad peoples around the Pacific Rim, while a worthy theme, is far too complex for full treatment here. I will offer a small handful of examples to show how the themes of biological invasion and con-centrated demand have operated in the context of ever-tightening economic integration of global markets and of the Rim.

Biological invasion

The Manila galleons that changed the biota of Guam no doubt introduced the same weeds, crops, pathogens and animals into the Philippines. Other ships transported elements of this immigrant biota to South China and elsewhere in East and Southeast Asia. But whereas biotic revolutions took place in Guam, and later in hundreds of oceanic islands, the Asian Rimlands saw much smaller changes.

The main reason for this is that most of the immigrant biota, so novel in the oceanic islands, already existed in the Asian Rimlands. East and Southeast Asia north of the Wallace line[4] was part of the same biological realm as Iberia, indeed all of Eurasia. The Philippines and China had long experience with smallpox and influenza. Goats and pigs already roamed (or were herded) in these lands. The only significant newcomers were food crops from the Americas, notably maize and potatoes. These proved popular, especially in hilly country, and played a major role in permitting population growth in China. Their cultivation also exacerbated Chinese erosion, sedimentation, and flooding difficulties (Elvin and Liu 1998). But, generally speaking, mainland Asia and most of archipelagic southeast Asia proved biologically stable and resistant in the face of trans-Pacific shipping.

Australia and New Zealand were another matter. Well beyond the Wallace line, their biotas prior to 1780 had evolved in long isolation from that of mainland Eurasia. Their populations had no prior experience of most human infections. In these respects they resembled oceanic islands. Their indigenous populations declined sharply when exposed to new diseases (and to brutality by people with more lethal weaponry). Their widowed landscapes proved vulnerable to biological invasion on a grand scale. With British and other European colonists came domestic animals, European crops, grasses, pests – the "portmanteau biota" (Crosby 1986) of European settler imperialism. A great deal of this process in Australia and New Zealand was the deliberate work of acclimatization societies which sought to recreate in the Antipodes the familiar biota of the British Isles. In Australia European settlement began in 1788; in New Zealand it began in a major way in 1840. By 1930, biological invasion had recast both lands (Clark 1949; Dodson 1992; Druett 1983; Flannery 1995; King 1984).

The west coast of the Americas also underwent biological changes in the centuries after Magellan. Most of the changes had nothing to do with pan-Pacific connections, however, and are part of the Columbian Exchange. The invasive species that remade California and Chile came mainly across the Atlantic from Europe and the Mediterranean, rather than across the Pacific. I will accordingly pass over this tale.

As a general rule, no great biotic revolutions followed from Magellan's linking of the coasts of the Pacific. It remained for

Cook to bring the Antipodes, as he did the oceanic islands, into the wider network of commercial and ecological exchange. When he did, and their biotas' long isolation came to an end, major biological invasions, ably assisted by settler society, resulted.

Concentrated demand

For millennia circuits of seaborne trade have united people and markets in segments of the Pacific Rim. These circuits were most elaborate in the inland seas between Borneo and Japan. Here reliable monsoon winds and the abundance of islands and bays create admirable sailing conditions that early on led to developed commerce in the archipelagoes of East and southeast Asia and between them and the Asian mainland. Elsewhere around the Pacific, trade circuits prior to Magellan were smaller and less significant. But the Siberian Chukchi and Alaskan Inuit found scope for trade, as did the Amerindians of the California coast. And in South America the Inca empire eventually organized considerable exchange along the Pacific coast. In several cases, distant demand focused on circumscribed zones of supply, and occasionally led to environmental changes. These were probably small, however, compared to what came later for the simple reason that the largest economy, that of China, imported so little from the Rim (other than Southeast Asian spices) prior to the sixteenth century.

After the foundation of Manila (1571), when the trading world of the South China Sea was linked to Spanish trans-Pacific routes, China's participation in the Pacific Rim economy spelled major environmental changes. Eventually, the tighter integration of the Rim and the economic growth of Japan, Australia, the U.S. and others, reduced China's role as an engine of environmental change, while raising the rate of change as a whole. Here I will touch briefly on three extractive trades that led to sharp ecological changes: seal-hunting, timber, and mining.[5]

Sealing in Pacific waters took off in the 1780s and remained a prosperous business until about 1850. By that time too few fur-bearing seals remained in reasonably accessible places to make it worth the trouble of finding and killing them. But for 60 or 70 years Europeans (mainly Britons and Russians) and Americans scoured the seals' breeding grounds around the Rim. They operated in New Zealand, Tasmania, the Kuriles, Kamchatka, the Aleutians and Alaska, British Columbia, California and Chile, as well as on remote island outcroppings in the Southern Ocean such as Macquarie Island. The market for all these sealskins lay in China, in Russia, and in Europe. The Juan Fernández Islands, off the Chilean coast, sent three million sealskins to China in seven years in the early nineteenth century. Until recently the fur seal was thought to be extinct there. Throughout the cooler shores of the Pacific, fur seal populations crashed sharply under this onslaught. The full ecological effects of the near elimination of a major predator are impossible to know, but it might have been good for the fish that fur seals prefer to eat – and perhaps for fishermen who might have gotten a larger share in the absence of fur seals' competition (Bonner 1982; Wester 1991).

Forests grow all around the Pacific Rim with only a few exceptions, such as the highest latitudes and the coastal desert of Peru and Chile. Until fairly recently, local supplies typically met local demand for timber. This has changed with the integration of the Rim economies in the late-twentieth century. In the timber market, Japan, not China, has driven matters. Japan's demand for timber has at times in the past proved environmentally costly to the home islands. But lately Japan has gone to great lengths to preserve its native forests and import timber from overseas (Marchak 1996; Totman 1989). It drew upon Manchuria in its imperial heyday, but more recently, with its spectacular economic growth since 1960, has imported timber from British Columbia and the Pacific Northwest of the U.S., from Malaysia and Indonesia, from the Solomons and Papua New Guinea. More recently still, Japanese demand has led to wood-chipping of Western Australia forests and felling of timber in the Russian Far East. The environmental effects of Japanese demand for timber range from the trivial to the catastrophic.

Mining perhaps exemplifies the effects of concentrated demand better than anything else. It is often ecologically devastating, as it can lead to deforestation, toxic pollution, flooding, siltation, and several other problems. But the lure and prices of precious and useful metals have long been sufficient to assure miners will persist, especially when the ecological costs can be shunted onto others. The geologically active character of the Pacific Rim has created plenty of valuable metal ores around the Pacific. The first major exploitations probably occurred in Chinese coal- and iron-mining, which flourished in the tenth and eleventh centuries. This had little effect beyond Chinese borders however. But China also played a central role in the first major long-distance trade in metals, that of silver. China's demand for silver spurred production in

Japanese mines from the 1540s. Control of its supply (especially on the island of Sado) helped concentrate power in Japan, laying foundations for political unification by 1603. China's appetite for silver quickened the pace of mining in Spanish America from the 1550s onward. In the nineteenth century, a series of gold rushes animated mining around the Pacific Rim. Miners flocked to California in 1849, to Victoria in 1853, to New Zealand in 1860, and to the Yukon and Klondike in 1896. These mining episodes, from Sado and Potosí to the Klondike, deforested surrounding lands to supply braces for mines and fuel for smelting ores. They produced mountains of slag. They spilled toxic heavy metals into local waterways. But these effects were small in scale compared to the impact of modern mining (Kobata 1965; Totman 1993: 69–70).

Since 1960, huge mechanized mines, extracting millions of tons of iron ore, copper, and other industrial metals, have shattered local environments in Australia, New Guinea, Chile, and elsewhere. Modern equipment makes it practical to crush tons of rock to get a gram of gold, and makes it worthwhile to level small mountains to remove a few tons of copper. Copper-mining in the last 25 years has thoroughly corroded sizeable regions of New Guinea (Hyndman 1994). Optic fiber and wireless communications, combined with local insurgency, have closed Panguna, formerly the world's largest copper mine. But the ecological effects of this and other New Guinean copper mines will last for a long time to come.

Conclusion

The environmental history of the Pacific islands and the Pacific Rim since Magellan has been a turbulent one. Looking only at the effects of biological invasion and concentrated demand emphasizes the importance of long isolation and the impact of sudden integration into larger ecosystems and economies. Other themes, say population growth, would generate different conclusions.

Whatever the theme, the connections among the Rim countries, and between the islands and the Rim, must loom large in environmental history. The low cost of seaborne transport helped make fragments of the Pacific world into epidemiological and commercial units long ago, driving ecological change. Steamship trade lowered per unit costs so drastically that it made sense to haul bulk goods over gargantuan distances by 1900. Furthermore, whatever the theme, the enormous inequalities in wealth and in power between small island societies (e.g. Nauru) and large Rim states (e.g. Australia or Japan), surely played a central role in determining environmental outcomes.

Large chunks of the Rim await careful investigation from the point of view of environmental history, really everywhere outside of Australia and California. Many, indeed most, islands outside of New Zealand, Fiji, and Hawaii would reward investigation richly. This chapter has only scratched the surface, like a Melanesian digging stick. An army of researchers equipped with the right tools might find a Potosí or a Panguna of information, ideas, and perspectives about the environmental history of the Pacific islands and Rim.

Notes

1 The prehistoric eruption was that of Toba, in Sumatra, about 75,000 years ago. In 1815 Tambora erupted.
2 According to Chinese and Californian data (Nunn 1994a: 11) the century AD 1250–1350 had four to five times as much rainfall as during periods before or after. This probably represents a transitional phase in world climate between the so-called medieval climatic optimum and the Little Ice Age. In any case, it could well have led to disruptions of economies and politics. Would not such heavy rains damage Chinese productivity and raise that of the nomads of the eastern steppe? Could this have played a role in preserving Mongol ascendancy? Similarly, would such rainfall not assist populations in the ordinarily dry zones of northern Mexico, from which the Aztecs soon after 1250 launched their infiltration of the richer lands of Central Mexico?
3 Pelau amd Makatea also supplied phosphates to Rim countries (and to Europe) in the twentieth century. The consumers of Pacific island phosphate were Australia (c. 66 percent), New Zealand (c. 25 percent), Japan, Malaysia, Britain and France.
4 In 1869 Alfred Russel Wallace first proposed that a line running south and east of Bali, Borneo and the Philippines, and north and west of Lombok, the Celebes, and New Guinea, divides an Australasian faunal region from an Asian one. The line has lesser validity for plants and human pathogens, and indeed modern zoogeographers find several exceptions to its validity for animals.
5 Concentrated demand also encouraged agricultural changes and in particular plantations around the Rim, in places such as Central America and Malaya. I will skip over this theme here.

References

Bonner, Nigel (1982) *Seals and Man*. Seattle: Washington Sea Grant.
Clark, A.H. (1949) *The Invasion of New Zealand by People, Plants and Animals*. New Brunswick, NJ: Rutgers University Press.

Crosby, A.W. (1986) *Ecological Imperialism*. New York: Cambridge University Press.

Cuddihy, Linda and Stone, Charles (1990) *Alteration of Native Hawaiian Vegetation: Effects of Humans, Their Activities, and Introductions*. Honolulu: University of Hawaii Cooperative National Park Resources Study Unit.

Dodson, John (ed.) (1992) *The Naive Lands*. Melbourne: Longman Cheshire.

Druett, Joan (1983) *Exotic Intruders*. Auckland: Heinemann.

Elvin, Mark and Liu, Ts'ui-jung (eds) (1998) *Sediments of Time: Environment and Society in Chinese History*. New York: Cambridge University Press.

Flannery, Tim (1995) *The Future Eaters*. New York: Braziller.

Hein, Philippe L. (1990) "Between Aldabra and Nauru," in W. Beller, P. D'Ayala and P. Hein (eds), *Sustainable Development and Environmental Management of Small Islands*. Paris: UNESCO.

Hyndman, David (1994) *Ancestral Rain Forests and the Mountain of Gold*. Boulder: Westview.

King, Carolyn (1984) *Immigrant Killers*. Auckland: Oxford University Press.

Kobata, A. (1965) "The Production and Uses of Gold and Silver in Sixteenth- and Seventeenth-Century Japan," *Economic History Review*, 18: 245–66.

MacDonald, Barrie and Williams, Maslyn (1985) *The Phosphateers*. Melbourne: Melbourne University Press.

Marchak, Patricia (1996) *Logging the Globe*. Kingston and Montreal: McGill-Queen's Press.

Merlin, Mark and VanRavensway, Dan (1990) "The History of the Genus *Santalum* in Hawai'i," in *Proceedings of the Symposium of Sandalwood in the Pacific*. Berkeley: US Forest Service Pacific Southwest Research Station.

Merrill, E.D. (1954) "The Botany of Cook's Voyages, and Its Unexpected Significance in Relation to Anthropology, Biogeography and History," *Chronica Botanica* 14: 161–384.

Nunn, Patrick (1994a) "Beyond the Naive Lands: Human History and Environmental Change in the Pacific Basin," in E. Waddell and P.D. Nunn (eds) *The Margin Fades: Geographical Itineraries in a World of Islands*. Suva, Fiji: Institute of Pacific Studies, University of the South Pacific.

—— (1994b) *Oceanic Islands*. Cambridge: Blackwell.

Officer, Charles and Page, Jake (1993) *Tales of the Earth*. New York: Oxford University Press.

Pool, Ian (1991) *Te iwi Maori*. Auckland: Auckland University Press.

Rallu, J.-L. (1990) *Les populations océaniennes aux XIX et XIX siècles*. Paris: INED.

Shineberg, Dorothy (1967) *They Came for Sandalwood*. Melbourne: Melbourne University Press.

Totman, Conrad (1989) *The Green Archipelago*. Berkeley: University of California Press.

—— (1993) *Early Modern Japan*. Berkeley: University of California Press.

Weeramantry, Christopher (1992) *Nauru: Environmental Damage Under International Trusteeship*. Melbourne: Oxford University Press.

Wester, Lyndon (1991) "Invasions and Extinctions on Másatierra (Juan Fernández Islands): A Review of Early Historical Evidence," *Journal of Historical Geography* 17: 18–34.

4

MARITIME TRADE AND THE AGRO-ECOLOGY OF SOUTH CHINA, 1685–1850

Robert B. Marks

Introduction

This chapter focuses on trade patterns in the South China Sea, what the Chinese called the Nanyang, from 1685 to 1850, and the impact that that commerce had upon agricultural land-use patterns in Guangdong province. I look first at the Chinese resurrection of the Nanyang trade after 1685, and then the creation of a domestic trade circuit of sugar and raw cotton that arose because of the Nanyang trade, before turning to a consideration of the nature and extent of European trade with China from about 1700 to 1850. What I argue is that long before European trade with China became significant for either Europeans or China, the Chinese already had established a thriving trade in the Nanyang; the size of Europe's trade with China, I estimate, only by the end of the eighteenth century reached the level of China's *c.* 1700 Nanyang trade, and the European trade reached that level only by tapping into the circuits of trade that satisfied China's domestic market demand. We already know that China in the eighteenth century was as commercialized as the most advanced parts of Europe (Marks 1991); what this chapter suggests is that, in addition, our views of the incorporation of China into the world economy need revision as well. Moreover, both the Nanyang and the European trade precipitated important changes in land use and cropping patterns, contributing to the linked processes of the commercialization of agriculture and ecological change in South China.

Background

The first 40 years of Manchu (Qing dynasty, 1644–1911) rule over South China, from the initial assertion of sovereignty in 1644 to the end of 1683, were difficult ones. The ravages of war, epidemic disease, and depopulation in the early years were followed first in the 1660s by the forcible relocation of the coastal population in an attempt to deprive the Ming loyalist Koxinga of his supply sources, and by what one historian (Kishimoto-Nakayama 1984) calls the "Kangxi depression," a reference to the depressed economic conditions attending the early years of the Kangxi emperor's reign (1661–1722). Only the defeat of Koxinga's successors in 1683 and the taking of their bases on Taiwan prompted the Kangxi emperor to consider reopening the China coast for trade.

The restoration of peaceful conditions in Guangdong provided one condition for the revival of the economy. And while peace itself may have removed obstacles to economic recovery, it did not itself stimulate growth. Yet, we know that by the eighteenth century, the economy of South China not only had revived, but that most of China too was about to experience one of the best economic climates ever. Moreover, the economic recovery was not gradual, but explosive. The cause, the evidence suggests, was a sudden, substantial increase in foreign and domestic seaborne trade beginning in 1684 and continuing, albeit with some important changes, right through to the middle of the nineteenth century, driving economic growth and the commercialization of agriculture. In brief, Chinese overseas and foreign trade after 1684 stimulated demand for raw cotton and silk, thereby prompting some peasant farmers to change their cropping patterns, growing non-food commercial crops instead of rice, which in turn led to the further commercialization of rice. By the end of the eighteenth century, the agricultural economy of South China had become thoroughly commercialized, with even peasant farmers in westernmost Guangxi province affected by market demand centered on Guangzhou and the Pearl River delta (see Marks 1998: Ch. 8).

Chinese overseas trade

When we think about China's foreign trade in the eighteenth and nineteenth centuries, the image that mostly comes to mind is that of European and American clippers arriving in China's ports and then loading up with tea, silk, sugar, and porcelains bound for their home markets. While it is true that European and American trade became the largest part of China's foreign trade by the end of the eighteenth century, the largest number of merchants to take to the seas when the Kangxi emperor reopened the coast to trade in 1684–5 were Chinese, plying both the domestic coastal routes and conducting overseas trade with the many states of what the Chinese called the Nanyang, or the Southern Ocean.[1]

The Nanyang

Chinese merchants and other residents of Guangdong's coastal regions thought of the ocean to the south as being comprised of two parts: the Nan Hai, or South Sea, which was contiguous to the coast and blended with the inland waterways of the Pearl River delta; and the Nanyang, or Southern Ocean, which encompassed both mainland and insular Southeast Asia. The coastline of Guangdong province stretches for some 2,000 miles, and, because of the gradual subsidence of the land, is irregular and dotted with good harbors. Not all of the harbors are deep or sheltered, but there were sufficient places either on the coast or up the coastal rivers for the Kangxi emperor to authorize the establishment of 70 customs houses on the coast of Guangdong when he reopened the coast for trade and shipping.

Many of those customs houses were situated at what the Chinese called "portals onto the sea" (*hai men*), and, as Qu Dajun claimed around 1700, "the portals onto the Nan Hai are the most numerous [of any in China]." The central and largest portal, the Tiger's Mouth, or Bocca Tigris, as Europeans called it, straddled the Pearl River delta and controlled access to Guangzhou. Qu lists scores of other portals for the "eastern route," that is, up the coast from Xin'an (Hong Kong) to Denghai, and for the "western route," stretching from the Pearl River down the coast, including the Leizhou peninsula and Qinzhou (on the northern shores of the Gulf of Tonkin) (Qu 1974: 33).

Beyond the coastal waters of the Nan Hai lay the Southern Ocean, or Nanyang. As described by Cushman, the Nanyang

"should be conceived of as a circle encompassing the mainland Southeast Asian countries bordering the South China Sea [the Nan Hai] and the Gulf of Siam, i.e. Vietnam, Cambodia and Siam, southern Burma, the

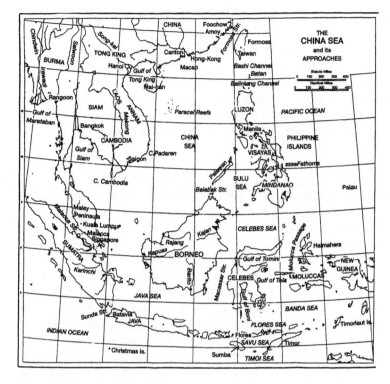

Figure 4.1 The South China Sea
Source: Morse 1966: 24–5

Malay peninsula, Sumatra, western Java, and the north-east coast of Borneo"

(Cushman 1993: 4–5)[2]

The map provided by H.B. Morse in his chronicle of the East India Company (1966, see Figure 4.1) labels the Nanyang the "China Sea," clearly showing both its extent and unity. Stretching from the Tropic of Cancer (which runs just to the north of Guangzhou) to just south of the equator, the Nanyang is longer than it is wide, and it lies more or less on a southwest to northeast axis, a shape made to order for the monsoons. As soon as the tell-tale signs of the northeasterly winds of the winter monsoon appeared in December or January, junks set sail from one of the numerous "portals on the sea" – the busiest being Guangzhou, Chaozhou, and Haikou (on Hainan Island) (Qu 1974: 33) – for

88

ports to the south, taking on cargoes in Siam or Malacca and waiting for the winds to change with the summer monsoon. Then in April, gently at first but then with more strength in May, the southerly and southeasterly monsoon winds provided the Chinese junks with the wind power to return home. Ocean currents too facilitated the return voyage, especially for those merchants who plied the Southeast Asian coast up to Tonkin. Easterly currents south of Hainan Island pushed water against the coast of Vietnam, trending then northerly into the Gulf of Tonkin before circling westward and through the Hainan Straight separating the island from the Leizhou Peninsula. Chinese junks could thus easily ride the winds and the currents from the Straights of Malacca or the Gulf of Siam right back to ports on Hainan Island, Guangzhou, or Chaozhou.[3]

With both a natural shape and wind and ocean currents conducive to an annual round of trade, Chinese merchants had long maintained trading relations with the countries of the Nanyang, going back at least to Han times (Chen 1985; Wang 1988), but especially from the eleventh and twelfth centuries when Chinese traders supplanted Arabs as the primary carriers of goods throughout the Nanyang (Cushman 1993: 1). But the transition from the Ming to the Qing dynasties, and especially the closure of the coast from 1662 through 1683, had severed the trade links between Guangdong and the Nanyang (Marks 1998: 151–7). To be sure, both tribute missions from Siam (Viraphol 1972: 28), and smuggling kept some goods moving along the old routes (Ng 1983: 52–3; Viraphol 1972: 23–4), but the legal trade had been virtually extinguished (Fan 1992: 239).

Reopening of the coast for trade

With the capture of Taiwan in 1683 by Qing forces, though, the last serious challenge to Qing rule was crushed, and the Kangxi emperor then moved quickly to reopen the coast to shipping and to foreign trade. And as soon as the emperor did so, Chinese merchants set sail up and down the China coast as well as overseas for ports to the south in the Nanyang as well as to the north in Japan. The numbers must have been impressive, for the provincial governor Li Shizheng commented that "in any given year, a thousand ships come and go [from Guangdong]" (Huang 1987: 6). Whether Governor Li had statistics on the numbers of ships passing through the various ports, or was merely estimating, he does convey the sense of a fairly large fleet of Chinese-owned and -manned junks plying the Nanyang in the years after the coast was opened. Moreover, Governor Li's impression of "thousands" of junks is confirmed by the English Captain Hamilton, who, on a trading mission to Guangzhou in 1703, observed that "there is no Day in the Year but shews 5,000 Sail of Jonks, besides small Boats for other Services, lying before the City" (Morse 1966, vol. 1: 104).

The number of junks "lying before the City" in 1703 was impressive not merely because of its magnitude, but also because most of that fleet had been built anew only after 1684. By all accounts, the Chinese commercial fleet had been virtually destroyed during the disastrous relocation of the coastal population in 1662. "All ocean-going junks," the order closing the coast had read, "are to be burned; not an inch of wood is allowed to be in the water" (Ye 1989: 140). Qing troops apparently carried out the order almost to the letter: according to local gazetteers, in Haiyang county "not a junk was left at the docks," and in Xin'an county "not more than one in a hundred junks remained" (quoted in Ye 1989: 140). And yet by 1685, thousands of junks once again sailed the seas. To be sure, not all had been destroyed in the 1660s; some smugglers and pirates had managed to avoid capture, keeping up a small but lucrative trade from new bases in Tonkin or Siam. By and large, though, it seems certain that most of the junks plying the Nanyang had to have been constructed quickly in the years after 1684. "Rich households compete to build ships," one observer wrote at the time (quoted in Huang 1987: 6). And build they did.

Of the thousands of junks lying before Guangzhou, most were smaller one- or two-masted junks plying the coastal trade; the largest, though, with three to five masts, had been built to sail the Nanyang, principally to Siam but also to the Philippines, Malacca, and Batavia. How many ocean-going junks called at ports in Guangdong in any given year is difficult to say, but a variety of sources allow us to get some perspective on the issue. In 1685, the English pirate, adventurer, and author, Captain William Dampier, arrived in the Philippine Islands intent upon seizing one of the Spanish galleons laden with Mexican silver. At Manila, Dampier observed, "the Harbour is so large, that some Hundreds of Ships may ride here; and is never without many, both of [the Spaniards'] own and Strangers. . . . [T]hey do allow the Portuguese to trade here, but the Chinese are the chiefest Merchants, and they drive the greatest Trade; for they have commonly twenty, thirty, or forty Jonks in the Harbour at a time, and a great many Merchants constantly residing in the City, besides Shopkeepers and Handy-crafts-men in abundance" (Dampier 1968: 263). Japanese sources too confirm a large and growing number of Chinese junks at Nagasaki after the China coast was reopened: from 24 junks in 1684 to 73 in 1685, 84 in 1686, 111 in 1687, and 117 in 1688 (Viraphol 1972: 59). From 1684 to 1757, a total of 3,017 junks visited Japan; not all of these were from Guangdong, but we can assume that a substantial number were (Huang 1987: 7–8). The South China Sea, in short, was a Chinese-dominated lake.

But how many ocean-going junks were there, and how large and how important to the economy of Guangdong was the trade that they carried? We can make some estimates by examining data from later periods. Early nineteenth-century sources put the number of Chinese junks from all ports engaged in the trade with Siam at 150–200 (Cushman 1993: 86), while *The Chinese Repository* estimated in 1833 that "the whole number of Chinese vessels, annually visiting foreign ports south of Canton, is not probably, less than one hundred; of these one third belong to Canton; six or eight go to Tungking; eighteen or twenty to Cochinchina, Camboja, and Siam; four or five visit the ports of Singapore, Java, Sumatra, and Penang; and as many more find their way to the Celebes, Borneo and the Philippine islands. These vessels never make but one voyage in the year, and always move with the monsoon" (Anon 1833: 294). Certainly there were fewer ocean-going junks in 1700 than in 1800; Fan I-chun cites early-to mid-Qianlong era sources (*c.* 1750) stating that up to 40 Guangdong junks had received licenses to trade in the Nanyang (Fan 1992: 248). Thus I think that in the years around 1700, when Fujian-licensed junks (which also stopped in Guangzhou) are added, perhaps 50–100 ocean-going junks traded goods to and from Guangzhou. This amounts to one-third to one-half the number of junks engaged in the Nanyang trade in the early nineteenth century.

At first glance those numbers may not seem like much, but they were – at least when placed into comparative perspective with the size of the European trade. In the early 1820s, for instance, the amount of goods exported from Siam to China totaled 35,083 tons (and the two-way trade presumably about double that amount) (Cushman 1993: 83), an amount equivalent to the combined exports from Guangzhou in 1790 carried by British East India Company and American ships (Morse 1966, vol. 2: 180). Those comparisons mean that in 1700, Chinese junks were carrying perhaps as much as 20,000 tons of goods back to Guangdong. By comparison, the volume of European exports from Guangzhou totaled just 500 tons in 1700, 6,071 tons in 1737, and probably did not reach 20,000 tons until the 1770s.[4] In short, Chinese trade with the Nanyang in 1700 was already at a level not reached by the European trade until the 1770s.

To place these trade figures into global perspective, some comparisons with Europe might help. According to Jan deVries, for the decade of 1731–40, annual Dutch trade in colonial goods to the Baltic passing through the Danish Sound totaled 16,000 tons, and the maximum yearly tonnage of all European ships trading in Asian waters was about 19,000 tons (deVries 1976: 120, 131). And according to Fernand Braudel's estimates, the two-way trade between England and Russia during the eighteenth century (which included considerable quantities of grain) may have amounted to as much as 120,000 tons annually (Braudel 1984: 207).[5] Thus the amount of Chinese trade with the Nanyang was between the amounts of the Dutch- and English-circuits trade in Europe.

That comparison, though, excludes China's domestic grain trade, which was every bit as large as that between Eastern and Western Europe.[6] I estimate that during the eighteenth century, around 240,000 tons of grain flowed into Guangzhou on both the riverine traffic from Guangxi province, and on coastal junks, rendering the total amount of trade in Guangdong somewhat larger than most measures of trade between various points in Europe. The grain trade along the Yangtze River was even larger, perhaps three times that pouring into Guangzhou.[7] The total amount of grain entering long-distance trade in China thus clearly outpaced that in Europe, and should be taken into consideration in comparing the amount of goods entering the market in China, which happened to be a single political entity, with those traded between various European countries.

In addition to excluding the grain trade, Chinese customs statistics did not distinguish among the Chinese inter-port (i.e. domestic) trade, trade with the Nanyang, and the European–American trade. Nonetheless, it is possible to gain some perspective on the value of the combined Chinese domestic and Nanyang trade by examining some data from the early century. In 1735, the

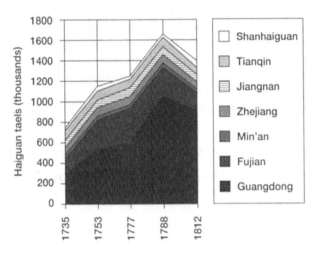

Figure 4.2 Chinese maritime customs revenue, 1735–1812
Source: Adapted from Fan 1992: 241

total amount of duty collected by all of China's customs houses totaled 729,000 taels; of that, 37 percent (272,000 taels) was collected in Guangdong alone (see Figure 4.2). The Guangdong total includes customs duty collected from Chinese merchants trading only on the coast, from Chinese merchants trading with the Nanyang, and from European ships as well. The latter, however, coming from fewer than 10 ships paying perhaps 3,000 taels each, was as yet relatively a small amount. It therefore seems reasonable to conclude that, for Chinese coastal and Nanyang trade, the Guangdong customs house reported duty on the order of 250,000 taels. Assuming that to be a low estimate,[8] and that the duty averaged 5 percent *ad valorem*,[9] then the value of annual Chinese coastal and Nanyang trade approached five million taels; that seems to have been a fairly consistent level of trade throughout the eighteenth century (Fan 1992: 242–3). When the grain trade is included, the value of the annual trade through Guangdong ports swells by another three million taels to a total of eight million.

The trade flows between China and the Nanyang were characterized by Chinese exports of manufactured or processed goods, and imports of raw materials and food, in particular rice. According to Cushman, junks from China carried chinaware, earthenware, silk and cotton textiles, brass- and copperware made into utensils or dishes, paper, as well as dried and salted vegetables and fruits and a variety of smaller manufactured items; Viraphol adds iron works of all kinds – pans, axes, cast iron, metal tubes, and wire – to the list (Viraphol 1972: 51). Imports from Siam included rice, wood for building and for extracting dyes used in the textile industry, raw materials for drugs, hides for farm equipment, various spices, and, importantly, raw cotton (Cushman 1993: 82–3, 87).

The Nanyang trade and changes in cropping patterns

The raw cotton originated in India, and was brought to Siam either by Indian, Muslim, or Portuguese traders where it was in turn purchased by Chinese merchants. The raw cotton is interesting because it points to aspects of China's coastal trade and to cropping and land-use patterns in Guangdong that became increasingly important during the eighteenth and nineteenth centuries. Clearly, the raw cotton was imported in order to be spun and woven into cloth of varying grades, some of which was in turn exported back to Siam as finished goods, but most of which was sold within Guangdong. According to Qu Dajun (writing about 1700), "The cotton cultivated in Guangdong is not sufficient to satisfy the needs of the ten prefectures" (Qu 1974: 426).[10] The importation of the raw cotton meant that local sources could not satisfy the demand, and so producers looked elsewhere for their supplies. But did this demand then spur the planting of cotton in Guangdong and thereby change land use patterns?

To be sure, some peasant farmers did plant cotton in and around the Pearl River delta. According to seventeenth-century gazetteers cited by Sucheta Mazumdar (a scholar who has studied extensively the commercialization of agriculture in the Pearl River delta), cotton was planted in rotation with sugar cane in Panyu county. Of all the delta counties, Panyu had higher and drier land than lower-lying Pearl River delta counties like Nanhai or Xiangshan, rendering it more suitable to either cotton or sugar cane. Nonetheless, according to Mazumdar, "cotton was not grown extensively in the Delta" (Mazumdar 1984: 292), and its rotation with sugar cane disappeared some time during the eighteenth century. It is possible that peasant farmers had begun to experiment with cotton after coastal trade resumed, responding to the demand of the textile industry in and around the city of Foshan (located about 20 kilometers west of Guangzhou). But the little evidence that we have indicates that cotton cultivation died out. For whatever reasons – perhaps because of quality, perhaps because of price, perhaps because of unexpected ecological problems with the cultivation of cotton – the Foshan textile industry turned instead to importing raw cotton not just from India, but also from central and northern China.

Indeed, the importation of raw cotton from the Yangtze River delta constituted one half of an important coastal trade circuit during the eighteenth century, where merchants brought sugar from Guangdong to the markets of the Yangtze River delta to exchange for raw cotton grown in Jiangsu and Hubei:

> In the Second and Third month, people from Min (Fujian) and Yue (Guangdong) come carrying crystallized sugar to sell. In the autumn they don't buy cloth, but only buy ginned cotton and return. Hundreds and thousands of ships all load up pile upon pile of bags because there [in Guangdong], among themselves, they can spin and weave it.
>
> (Mazumdar 1984: 350)

Mazumdar rightly calls this an "interlinked structure of the sugar–cotton trade," and devotes considerable attention to analyzing how it worked (Mazumdar 1984: ch. IV). What is important to note here, though, is that the growth of the cotton textile industry in Foshan did not stimulate the expansion of cotton cultivation in the Pearl River delta, but instead, because of the trade circuits, of sugar cane. In other words, to obtain raw cotton for the spinners and weavers in Guangdong, merchants established a triangular trade: sugar produced in Guangdong was sold (or traded) in Jiangnan for raw cotton; the raw cotton then was sold in Guangzhou, the proceeds of which became either profit or capital to finance another round of trade.

In the crop-rotation system of many Guangdong peasant farmers, then, sugar cane therefore replaced rice, and as the amount of land allotted to sugar cane increased, the amount devoted to rice shrank, more or less on a one-for-one basis. By the middle of the eighteenth century, substantial portions of the land in several counties had become devoted to sugar cane: "In Panyu, Dongguan, and Zengcheng [counties], four out of ten [peasant farmers] produce sugar; in Yangchun, six out of ten do. The cane fields almost equal the rice fields" (Li 1915: *juan* 14). By the nineteenth century, entire villages specialized in only sugar cane (Anon 1849:

237). In 1819, for instance, the shipwrecked English Captain J. Ross observed "continued fields of sugar-cane" and "plantations of sugar-cane" on the Leizhou peninsula and to the north in Gaozhou prefecture (ibid.).

The process by which peasant farmers replaced rice fields with sugar cane in order for merchants to purchase raw cotton, of course, we now label the commercialization of agriculture. But what is important to note here about sugar cane is its place in Guangdong's coastal and overseas trade circuits, in particular the linkage with raw cotton. For the demand which spurred the production of sugar cane came not directly for sugar, but for raw cotton which could be spun and woven into thread and cloth that was then sold within Guangdong or exported to the Nanyang. The expansion of trade with the Nanyang following the opening of the coast after 1684 increased demand for cotton cloth and raw cotton. But rather than the cotton being grown in Guangdong, it was imported both from India (see the next section for figures on the increase in raw cotton imports carried by British ships) and from central and northern China, the latter in exchange for locally produced sugar. As domestic and foreign demand for cotton goods produced in Guangdong increased, then, the amount of land devoted to rice decreased. The resumption of Chinese overseas and coastal trade in the late-seventeenth and early eighteenth centuries thus provided the impetus not just to economic expansion following the mid-seventeenth century crisis, but also to the commercialization and specialization of agriculture in Guangdong.

In summary, several aspects of the Chinese overseas and coastal junk trade are noteworthy. First, by all indications both the volume and the value of the trade, beginning immediately with the lifting of the ban on coastal shipping in 1684–5, were very large, providing the stimulus needed for the economy to begin growing again from the end of the seventeenth century onwards. Second, the Nanyang demand was mostly for Chinese manufactured goods produced either in or around Guangzhou, or gathered in that great emporium from other parts of the empire. The impact of the increased export trade upon Guangdong's agricultural economy was indirect, mediated by the need to import raw cotton: rather than growing cotton, peasant farmers grew sugar cane which, after being refined and processed, was exchanged for cotton from central and northern China. The increased demand for cotton textiles, whether domestic or from the Nanyang, thus drove the substitution of sugar cane for rice, and although the expansion of cane fields did not result in the clearance of more land to grow sugar cane for sale in the market, it did decrease the amount of rice produced in and around the Pearl River delta, and thus increased the market demand for rice.

A similar conversion of paddy fields to a non-food, commercial crop occurred when the demand for silk increased. And like the demand for cotton textiles which was satisfied by expanding the acreage devoted to sugar cane, the demand for silk had an indirect impact on cropping patterns, increasing the acreage devoted to the "fish pond–mulberry tree" combination which had first developed in the early Ming dynasty (1368–1644). The driving force behind the demand for silk, though, was not the Chinese coastal or Nanyang trade, but rather the European trade.

European trade

The story of European and American trade with China – from the re-opening of the ports to Europeans in 1685 to the Opium War in 1839–42, the multiport trading system from 1685 to 1760, the rise to dominance of the English, and the use of opium to balance the accounts of the British East India Company (B.E.I.C.) – is better known than China's native coastal or Nanyang trade, and I will not repeat it here.[11] What I do want to do is to examine those aspects of the trade that are relevant both to understanding the development of the economy of South China in the eighteenth and nineteenth centuries, and to changes in cropping patterns.

European trade was layered on top of the base established by the Chinese coastal and Nanyang trade, beginning with just a few ships in the early 1700s, rising only to 20 or so by the middle of the century, and increasing dramatically in the 1780s when the British discovered the Chinese demand for raw cotton. Even the restriction, after 1757, of English trade to the single port of Guangzhou did not result in an immediate increase in the amount of trade at Guangzhou. If 250,000 taels of customs revenue represents the amount of Chinese overseas trade, then foreign (i.e. European) trade did not attain that level until the 1770s. By the end of the eighteenth century, though, European trade had eclipsed the Chinese coastal and Nanyang trade, easily reaching four times the Chinese trade. Figure 4.3 shows both the total duty collected by the Guangdong customs houses, and the number of European and American ships trading at Guangzhou. Clearly,

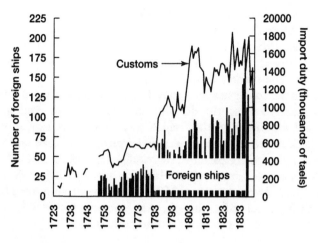

Figure 4.3 Foreign trade at Guangzhou, 1723–39
Source: Huang 1934: 166–70, 180–4

both the increase in the customs collected and its annual fluctuations are a function of the number of foreign ships arriving in Guangzhou.[12]

The nature of the eighteenth and nineteenth century trade between China and Western countries is well known, but a brief summary is warranted. Europeans purchased porcelain, lacquered ware, silk, cotton cloth ("Nankeens"), refined and raw sugar, and, increasingly, tea. Europeans could not trade for these commodities with any of their products or commodities (although they tried), and for the most part paid in silver bullion. As the English demand for tea increased throughout the eighteenth century, and the B.E.I.C. came to dominate the China trade, the B.E.I.C. also successfully imported raw cotton from India to pay in part for the tea.

We have already seen the place that the cotton textile industry played in the commercialization of the rural economy through its connection with sugar cane. By all indications, the demand for cotton textiles increased so much during the eighteenth century that increasingly large quantities of raw cotton were imported from India via the B.E.I.C. As the B.E.I.C.'s purchases of Chinese products increased, especially to satisfy the growing British thirst for tea, the company searched for products it could bring in trade to minimize the need to pay in silver. At first it looked like Indian raw cotton would fit the bill (see Figure 4.4). By the late eighteenth

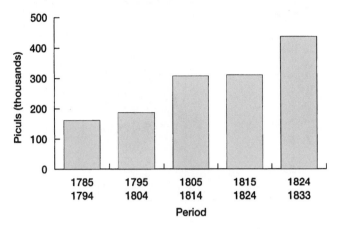

Figure 4.4 Indian raw cotton imports, 1785–1833 (10-year averages)
Source: Complied from Morse 1966, vols 1–4

century, Indian raw cotton accounted for one-third of B.E.I.C. funds, and on the eve of the Opium War totalled one-half of the value of opium imports (Fairbanks 1964: 60, 288).

As can be seen from Figure 4.4, raw cotton imports doubled from the late eighteenth century through the first quarter of the nineteenth century, and increased by another 50 percent by the 1830s. About one-quarter of the imported cotton was woven in urban workshops in Foshan, and the rest was distributed to rural households for spinning and weaving, satisfying about two-thirds of the domestic demand from Guangdong and Guangxi provinces.[13] The rest of the domestic demand was met by raw cotton imports from the lower Yangtze in exchange for sugar. Thus, while consumer demand in South China drove the rapid increase in the imports of Indian raw cotton carried by B.E.I.C. ships, it was insufficient to cover B.E.I.C. purchases of tea and silk in Guangzhou.

The balance of trade thus remained strongly in China's favor (see Figure 4.5). For a while, as John McNeill has recently pointed out, a triangular trade with the Pacific islands helped the Europeans: "European, American, and Australian merchantmen organized the exchange, in which Pacific island products were acquired for Western manufactured goods, then exchanged for Chinese silk and tea" (McNeill 1994: 319). But European demand for, and Chinese exports of, silk and tea increased dramatically in the 1780s, accompanied by a smaller increase in imports – the

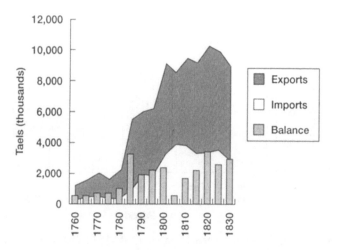

Figure 4.5 China's foreign trade balances, 1760–1833 (5-year averages)
Source: Adapted from So 1986: 57

balance of some 2 million taels annually was in silver bullion imports into Guangzhou, leading to substantial positive balances of trade for China.

If the silver imports lubricated the Guangdong economy, to the Europeans their reliance on silver bullion to balance their trade deficits was a problem in search of a solution. To stem the flow of silver to China, the B.E.I.C. had been searching for a commodity that the Chinese would purchase in sufficient quantities to pay for their purchases; raw cotton supplied part of the answer, but it was insufficient, and so silver continued to flow into China. According to data compiled by Yan Zhongping, on balance millions of taels of silver poured into China in the first decades of the nineteenth century. As is well known, the British increasingly used opium to balance their trade,[14] not merely stemming the flow of silver into China, but reversing the flow by 1827 (see Figure 4.6).[15]

Until the British found opium to cure their trade imbalance ills, the B.E.I.C. had tried, with some success, using Indian raw cotton and South Pacific island products, both of which met a substantial demand in the Chinese domestic market. In effect, until the early nineteenth century, China was *the* industrialized country in the world – it had the textile manufacturing prowess in centers like Guangzhou and Shanghai – manufacturing raw cotton into finished goods that satisfied not merely domestic demand but provided for the export market too. This provides a new context

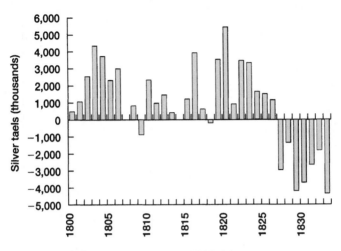

Figure 4.6 Silver flows at Guangzhou, 1800–33
Source: Yan 1953: 31, 32

for understanding the British opium trade. As the story usually gets told, the B.E.I.C. turned to opium because Europe's demand for Chinese products, in particular porcelain, tea, and silk, could not be balanced with imports of any other kind. That is only partially true, for there was a Chinese demand for Indian raw cotton. The Chinese domestic textile market, and its circuits of trade, including the sugar-raw cotton one linking Guangdong to the lower Yangtze, thus also are important elements in the story. But as it was, the Chinese market for Indian raw cotton did not expand fast enough to sate European appetites for tea and silk. With opium pouring into China in the nineteenth century, exports of silk (and tea[16]) increased substantially, precipitating changes in agricultural land-use patterns in Guangdong's Pearl River delta.

Silk

Where we can only guess at the amounts of sugar entering the export trade, figures for silk are available (So 1986: 80–1), and, for the most part, parallel the general pattern for trade between Europe and China. From about 25,000 piculs in 1723, exports of Guangdong silk increased steadily for the next century, reaching about 1.1 million piculs in 1828 (see Figure 4.7). The trend was virtually linear, with the silk exports increasing by 10,000 piculs

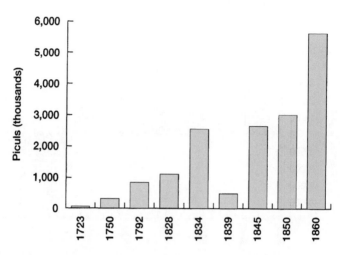

Figure 4.7 Exports of Pearl River delta silk, 1723–1860
Source: So 1986: 80–1

each year. From 1828 to 1834 the silk exports doubled, largely because the vast increase in the amount of smuggled opium gave the B.E.I.C. greater resources to buy silk (as well as tea). The Opium War (1839–42) disrupted trade, but afterwards silk exports quickly rebounded to the 1834 level before doubling again from 1850 to 1860. The story of silk exports thus can be characterized by steady if not unspectacular growth during the century followed by exponential growth in the 1830s and the 1850s.

To meet this demand, the increased silk production in the eighteenth and nineteenth centuries came not from any technological advances, but from expansion of the tried and true "mulberry tree–fish pond" method pioneered centuries earlier. In the Pearl River delta, the silk industry developed on a base that had been created by a particular combination of fish ponds with fruit trees. From Song times on, fish ponds had been scooped from the swamplands of the upper Pearl River delta (So 1986: 200–01). The mud and the muck raked up into embankments above the flood plain protected the ponds from flooding, while the high water table filled the hole with water, and the pond was stocked with various kinds of carp fry netted from local waters.[17] On the embankments, peasant farmers by the early Ming period planted mostly fruit trees (long-yan, litchee, etc.), giving rise to the "fruit tree and fish pond" (*guo ji yu tang*) combination. The carp fed on organic matter that either dropped or was thrown into the pond, while the muck scooped up from the pond fertilized the fruit trees and the rice fields, and added height to the embankments and more protection for the fish ponds. As the demand for silk increased, peasant farmers replaced the fruit trees with mulberry trees, giving rise to the "mulberry tree–fish pond" (*cang ji yu tang*) system, and then began digging up even more paddy fields to expand the "mulberry tree–fish pond" system.

According to Alvin So's calculations, to increase silk exports from 25,000 to 1.1 million piculs required expanding the acreage devoted to mulberry trees from 500 to 22,000 *mu*, nearly all of which occurred in the Pearl River delta counties of Nanhai, Shunde, and Xiangshan. However, because of the "mulberry tree–fish pond" combination, the amount of land converted to the system as a whole was substantially greater. Indeed, So states that the rule of thumb was that "the land in about four-tenths of any given area was dug out and large ponds were formed. The excavated soil was thrown on the other six-tenths of the land, thereby raising the level" (So 1986: 84–5). Thus the amount of land converted to the "mulberry tree–fish pond" combination by 1828 was more than 35,000 *mu* (about 6,000 acres).

Like the expansion of acreage devoted to sugar cane, the increase in the "mulberry tree–fish pond system" came at the expense of paddy fields. Nanhai and Shunde county gazetteer entries are quite explicit on this point: "Rice fields were turned into mulberry embankments and fish ponds; mulberry bushes were planted on the newly constructed embankments; . . . lower part with fishing, upper part with mulberry" (So 1986: 85). By the twentieth century, according to the geographer Trewartha, virtually all the land in Nanhai and Shunde counties had become devoted to sericulture:

> From one of the low hills in the delta's specialized mulberry area as far as the eye can reach in any direction, there are closely spaced fields of dark green mulberry shrubs inter-sected by narrow canals and dotted with ponds of water scattered irregularly between the fields.
>
> (quoted in So 1986: 85)

Demand for silk thus prompted a series of changes in land use patterns in Guangdong, with peasant farmers in the Pearl River delta converting rice paddies to the "mulberry tree–fish pond" system.

Conclusion

Stimulating and then driving the commercialization of agriculture in Guangdong was the explosive growth of Chinese coastal and foreign trade immediately following the lifting in 1684 of the ban on coastal shipping. Just as domestic demand for cotton cloth stimulated the conversion of paddy fields to sugar cane fields, so did the foreign demand for silk result in the transformation of paddy fields into fish ponds and mulberry tree embankments. When the peasant farmers in the Pearl River delta turned to these cash crops, they then looked to the market to supply food. The demand for rice stimulated peasant farmers along the river systems draining Guangdong and Guangxi provinces to sell their rice downstream, while they substituted New World foods, in particular sweet potatoes, for rice in their diets. The markets for silk, sugar cane, and cotton then turned rice, the basic food staple of most people in South China, into a commodity.

These markets existed within the context of six trade circuits, ranging from local through regional, national, and global, all interconnected and linked through activities centered on Guangzhou:

1 To get the entire cycle started, merchants contracted with peasant families growing sugar cane in the counties near Guangzhou (or within easy water access, such as Zengcheng or Yangjiang) for raw sugar, exchanging raw cotton for the sugar.

2 These merchants then exported raw and refined sugar to Jiangnan, bringing back raw cotton that was spun and woven in Guangdong.

3 The cotton cloth and yarn was sold throughout the Guangzhou hinterland to peasant families, who in turn sold rice for export to Foshan and Guangzhou.

4 From Foshan, some rice then was sold in markets in the Pearl River delta, where peasants produced raw silk that was shipped to Foshan for finishing there in the silk filatures.

5 From the Nanyang to Foshan and Guangzhou came raw cotton, rice, and dyes, while silk, cotton cloth, and refined sugar all produced or warehoused in Foshan were sold to the Nanyang.

6 Europeans purchased silk, cotton goods, and tea in Guangzhou, and brought raw cotton, silver, and opium in return.

Thus, a highly articulated set of six trade circuits integrated the regional economy of Guangdong and linked it not just with an emerging national market in Jiangnan, but also to the Chinese-dominated overseas trade in the Nanyang, and to the growing European world economy.

Trade through these circuits both stimulated commercialization of Guangdong's agrarian economy, and changed patterns of land use throughout the region. The growing domestic and foreign demand for cotton goods propelled the conversion of rice paddies into sugar cane fields, while the exports of silk prompted peasant farmers to convert paddy fields to the "mulberry tree–fish pond" combination. To meet the food needs of these increasingly commercialized farmers, peasants further inland, especially in Guangxi province, began producing rice for export down river to Guangzhou and the Pearl River delta.[18]

All of this commercialization, it must now be remembered, started with Chinese trade in the Nanyang, not with European trade. Indeed, the European trade tapped into Chinese trade circuits designed to meet domestic Chinese demand, rather than creating new ones to serve the needs of Europeans. Chinese demand for Indian raw cotton allowed Europeans to expand their purchases of tea and silk, thereby both stoking further European demand for those commodities, and transforming south China's agro-ecology. To be sure, Europeans introduced opium into the equation, but basically the linking of China to the European world economy was less a new phenomenon than a continuation of existing patterns set deep within the functioning of the Chinese economy. And since that is the case, we might want to revise the usual view of the place of China in the emerging world economy, from the passive object of European stimulation to an active force in the shaping of the modern world economy.

Notes

1 Jennifer Cushman surely was correct to note that

"modern Western scholarship has generally neglected to analyze the role of the overseas junk trade in China's economic development. The primary concern of twentieth-century historians has been with the expansion of Western commercial activities in China, which is legitimate given the greater volume and monetary value of that trade."

For her attempt to correct that oversight, see Cushman 1993: 6. Two other works of note are Viraphol 1972 and Ng 1983. I have relied heavily on these works for this section.

2 The Philippines, Taiwan, and Japan, although not considered part of the Nanyang, but the "Eastern Ocean" (*dong hai*), were also part of China's junk-trade circuits. Anthony Reid calls attention to "water and forest [as] the dominant elements in the environment of Southeast Asia," with "ubiquitous sealanes," "moderate and predictable" winds, and warm water combining to make the Nanyang "more hospitable and inviting a meeting place than that deeper and stormier Mediterranean in the West." A vast supply of wood at the water's edge made the Nanyang "a region uniquely favourable to maritime activity," (Reid 1988: 2). An interesting comparison might be made of the Nanyang with the Mediterranean, but such a comparison is beyond the scope of this book.

3 Captain William Dampier, perhaps ignorant of the strength of the summer monsoon, found out the hard way how inexorable the winter and summer winds were in determining where one could sail in the South China Sea. Wintering in the Gulf of Siam, Dampier planned on returning to Manila "by the latter End of May [1687], and wait [to pirate] the Acapulco Ship that comes about that time" (Dampier 1968: 264). Setting sail on June 4, Dampier encountered such strong southeasterlies that he was driven, three weeks later and contrary to his plans to raid ships in Manila, to the south China coast near the mouth of the Pearl River.

4 Morse 1966 does not provide total European tonnage figures from 1737 to 1790.

5 Braudel estimated that the trade was conducted on about 400 ships of 300 tons each.

6 For the imperial court's discussion about whether or not to tax the grain trade, see Liang (*c*. 1840) juan 8: 8a-9b.

7 For an estimate of the total amount of grain and cotton cloth entering the market in China *c*.1840, see Xu and Wu 1985: 282–9, 318–29.

8 Smuggling, corruption and embezzlement lowered the amount of duty reported from that which could have been collected and reported. For a discussion of the nature of the customs statistics, see Fan 1992: Appendix A.

9 This is a gross estimate only; since duty was levied on each commodity based on volume or weight, not value, reconstructing *ad valore,* duty is difficult if not impossible.

10 Also quoted in Mazumdar (1984: 350), but translated slightly differently.

11 The best and most accessible standard accounts include Wakeman 1975: ch. 7; Spence 1990: chs 6–7; and Hsü 1983: chs 7–8.

12 The correlation coefficient is 0.9, and a linear regression of customs duty in the number of foreign ships has an R^2 value of 0.8.

13 The Foshan textile industry employed "about 50,000 [people]; when there is pressing demand for work the number of laborers is considerably increased; they occupy about 2,500 shops, averaging usually twenty in each shop" (Anon 1833: 305–06). My estimate

is based on calculations from per capita consumption figures in Xu and Wu (1985: 322) and production figures in Huang (1990: 84).

14 Ironically, the English discovery of opium as the means to balance their trade imbalance with China spelled a reprieve for Pacific island wildlife. According to McNeill,

> "By 1850 Chinese tea could be had without hunting down the last seals or sandalwood. Opium provided the key that unlocked Chinese trade. As the British East India Company converted tracts of Bengal to opium production, China's commercial horizons shifted, and the Pacific trade lapsed into insignificance"
>
> (McNeill 1994: 325)

15 This whole sordid story has been told elsewhere, and will not be repeated here. See Chang 1970; Fay 1975; and Waley 1958.
16 Although virtually all tea was exported from Guangzhou (because of the restrictions on trading), mostly it came from the hills of Fujian and Jiangxi (see Gardella 1994). The increased European demand for tea thus had little impact on land-use patterns in Guangdong.
17 In the 20th century, five kinds of fish were reared in the ponds, all from fry secured from local rivers (Hoffman 1929: 167–8).
18 For a full exploration, see Marks 1998.

References

Anon (1833) "Description of the City of Canton," *The Chinese Repository*, vol. 11 no. 7.

Anon (1849) "Journey of a Trip Overland from Hainan to Canton in 1819" The Chinese Repository XVIII (5).

Braudel, F. (1984) *The Wheels of Commerce*, vol. 2 of *Civilization and Capitalism 15th–18th Century*, translated by Sian Reynolds. New York: Harper and Row.

Chang, H-p. (1970) *Commissioner Lin and the Opium War*. New York: W.W. Norton and Co.

Chen Guanghui (1985) *Zhongguo gudai dui wai maoyi shi* (A history of foreign trade in ancient China). Guangzhou: Guangdong Renmin Chubanshe.

Cushman, J. (1993) *Fields from the Sea: Chinese Junk Trade with Siam during the Late Eighteenth and Early Nineteenth Centuries*. Ithaca NY: Cornell University Press.

Dampier, W. (1968) *A New Voyage Round the World*. New York: Dover Publications.

deVries, J. (1976) *The Economy of Europe in an Age of Crisis, 1600–1750*. New York: Cambridge University Press.

Fairbanks, John K. (1964) *Trade and Diplomacy on the China Coast: The*

Opening of the Treaty Ports, 1842–54. Cambridge, MA.: Harvard University Press.

Fan, I-c. (1992) "Long Distance Trade and Market Integration in the Ming-Ch'ing Period 1400–1850," Stanford University unpublished PhD thesis.

Fay, P. (1975) *The Opium War 1840–1842*. Chapel Hill: University of North Carolina Press.

Gardella, R. (1994) *Harvesting Mountains: Fujian and the China Tea Trade, 1757–1937*. Berkeley and Los Angeles: University of California Press.

Hoffman, W. (1929) "Preliminary Notes on the Fresh-Water Fish Industry of South China, Especially Kwangtung Province,' *Lingnan Science Journal* vol. 8.

Hsü, I. (1983) *The Rise of Modern China*, 3rd edn., New York: Oxford University Press.

Huang Juzhen (1987) "Qingdai qianqi Guangdong de dui wai maoyi" (A history of Guangdong's foreign trade during the early Qing), paper presented at the 4th International Conference on Chinese Social and Economic History.

Huang, Philip C.C. (1990) *The Peasant Family and Rural Development in the Yangzi Delta, 1350–1988*. Stanford: Stanford University Press.

Huang, Shansheng (1934). "Qing dai Guangdong maoyi ji qi zai Zhongguo jingji shi shang zhi yiyi–yapian zhi yu zhi qian" (The Qing-era foreign trade of Guangdong prior to the Opium War and its significance in China's economic history), *Lingnan xuebao* 3 (4).

Kishimoto-Nakayama, Mio (1984) "The Kangxi Depression and Early Qing Local Markets." *Late Imperial China* 10 (2).

Li Diaoyuan (1915) *Yuedong biji* (Sketches of Guangdong), Shanghai: Huiwentang.

Liang Tingnan (*c*.1840) *Yue hai guan zhi* (Guangdong maritime customs gazetteer). Taibei: Wenhai chubanshe, 1975.

Marks, R. (1991) "Rice Prices, Food Supply, and Market Structure in Eighteenth-Century South China," *Late Imperial China* 12 (2).

Marks, R. (1998) *Tigers, Rice, Silk, and Silt: Environment and Economy in Late Imperial South China*. New York and London: Cambridge University Press.

Mazumdar, S. (1984) "A History of the Sugar Industry in China: The Political Economy of a Cash Crop in Guangdong, 1644–1834," University of California, Los Angeles, unpublished PhD dissertation.

McNeill, J. (1994) "Of Rats and Men: A Synoptic Environmental History of the Island Pacific," *Journal of World History* 5 (2).

Morse, H. (1966) *The Chronicles of the East India Company Trading to China, 1635–1834*. Taibei: Chengwen Reprint.

Ng C-k. (1983) *Trade and Society: The Amoy Network on the China Coast, 1683–1735*. Singapore: Singapore University Press.

Qu Dajun (1974) *Guangdong xinyu* (New sayings about Guangdong). Hong Kong: Zhonghua Shuju.

Reid, A. (1988) *Southeast Asia in the Age of Commerce 1450–1680*, vol. 1 *The Lands below the Winds*. New Haven: Yale University Press.

So, A. (1986) *The South China Silk District: Local Transformation and World-System Theory*. Albany: State University of New York Press.

Spence, J. (1990) *The Search for Modern China*. New York: W.W. Norton.

Viraphol, S. (1972) *Tribute and Profit: Sino-Siamese Trade 1652–1853*. Cambridge MA: Harvard University Press.

Wakeman, F. (1975) *The Fall of Imperial China*. Boston: The Free Press.

Waley, A. (1958) *The Opium War Through Chinese Eyes*. Stanford: Stanford University Press.

Wang, Gungwu (1988) *Nanhai maoyi yu nanyang huaren* (Trade in the South China Sea and Chinese in the South China Sea). Hong Kong: Zhonghua Shuju.

Xu, Dixin and Wu, Chengming (1985) *Zhongguo zibenzhuyi de mengya* (The sprouts of capitalism in China). Beijing: Renmin chuban she.

Yan Zhongping (ed.) (1953) *Zhongguo jindai jingji tongji ziliao xuanji* (Selected statistical material concerning China's modern economy). Beijing: Kexue chubanshe.

Ye Xian'en (ed.) (1989) *Guangdong hang yun shi gu dai bu fen)* (A history of shipping in Guangdong in ancient times). Beijing: Renmin jiaotong chuban she.

5

RICE IS A LUXURY, NOT A NECESSITY

The sources of Asian growth

A.J.H. Latham

After 1800 an international market in rice became established. Burma, Siam and French Indo-China exported rice and Ceylon, Malaya, the Dutch East Indies, the Philippines and China imported it (Latham and Neal 1983: 260–80). There is no puzzle about the flow of rice to most of these countries, where there were immigrant workers in mines and plantations. But why was rice imported to China in such quantities? Hamashita discusses these imports of rice to Southern China, and argues that local production was never sufficient to supply the provinces of Kwangtung and Fukien, and that large imports were always necessary to supplement the deficiency. Rice came from the Lower Yangtze area through the ports of Wuhu and Chinkiang, and this rice was preferred, but rice also came from Siam and French Indo-China (Hamashita 1989: 142–53). Rice imports to China are shown in Figure 5.1. The implication is that there was an inherent production problem. So was this an economy in crisis which could not feed itself? Or is there a more favourable interpretation?

Rice and other grains

Rice came late to many parts of Asia, particularly Japan, the Malay Penisula and Java. The earliest remains of cultivated long-grain *Indica* rices were found in northern India and eastern China dating back about 7,000 years. The oldest round-grain *Japonica-sinica* rices found in China are dated to about 5,300 years ago (Swaminathan 1984: 63–8). From linguistic and ethnographic

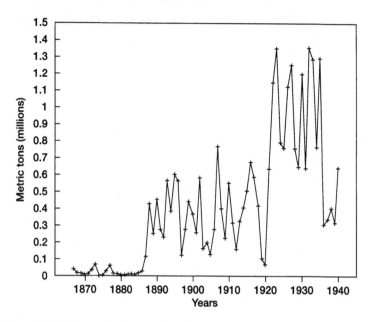

Figure 5.1 Chinese rice imports, 1867–1940

evidence it appears that the earliest staple foods grown in monsoon Asia were millets and tubers, which were then augmented and gradually replaced by rice.

Rice seems to have come to Japan as late as 300–400 BC having been introduced from China. It spread northward from Kyushu, only reaching northern Honshu about AD 250. The Japanese were dependent on other staples until this time. Millets remained important in the Malay peninsula until at least AD 800 and irrigated rice was brought to Java only in medieval times, perhaps as late as *c.*AD 1200. Rice, then, is a comparatively recent introduction in much of Asia, but once people had started eating rice, they were unwilling to go back to their previous staples (Bray 1986: 8–11). The terracing of fields in hilly parts of Asia which is often thought to be characteristic of rice production was probably practised before the introduction of rice. Even today these terraces are used for dry crops after the rice has been harvested (Bray 1986: 33). To emphasize the late arrival of rice, it has recently been indicated that although rice has been grown in Korea for the last 2,000 years, it was not a very important crop. Koreans actually depended upon other grains and foods. As late as the 1920s only 36 percent of cultivated fields were producing rice, and the economy was based on dry rice and dry field crops like millet, barley and soybeans which were less vulnerable to drought than wet rice. It was only as a result of Japanese colonial government programmes that rice production increased sufficiently to become the staple Korean food, and this was not until the mid 1930s (Lee 1990: 21). An early FAO report confirms that in this period rice was grown in Korea largely for export to Japan, and the growers themselves consumed a good deal of millet and other cheap grains, some of which were imported (FAO 1955: 5).

So what were these other staple crops which rice came to supercede? Of the grains, the most important were the millets. The main millets were finger millet (*Eleusine coracana*), foxtail millet (*Setaria italica*), Japanese barnyard millet (*Echinochloa crusgalli*), bulrush or pearl millet (*Pennisetum glaucum*) and broomcorn millet (*Panicum miliaceum*), the latter being the staple millet of ancient Rome, where it was called *milium*. These millets were generally consumed as porridges and unleavened bread, and they could be used for brewing beer. They were of very ancient origin and cultivated across Asia. In India they were known collectively as *bajra*. In addition there was sorghum (*Sorghum vulgare*), which is often confused with millet, which it superficially resembles. This too was used for porridges and breads. The Indian variant is known as *jowar* or *shallu*, and the Chinese variant as *kaoliang* (Brouk 1975: 24–9: Doggett 1988: 1).

Finger millet, called *ragi* in India, is grown widely there and in Malaya and China. In India the principal growing area is Mysore, and one of the great advantages of the crop is that it can be stored for up to 10 years without suffering weevil or other damage, making it an ideal emergency reserve against famine. The grains can also be germinated and dried (i.e. malted) for brewing (Simmonds 1976: 29). Foxtail millet is known to have been cultivated in China as early as 2700 BC. Japanese barnyard millet or *sanwa* millet, is grown extensively in Japan and Korea where it is consumed mainly as porridge. Bulrush millet is grown in India where even in recent times it has been the fourth most important grain after rice, sorghum and wheat. Grown in very dry rainfed areas unsuitable for finger millet it is ground into flour for bread and porridge (Pursglove 1972 205–6: Simmons 1976: 90). Broomcorn millet is grown in India, China and Japan and as previously noted, sorghum is also important in India and China (Brouk 1975: 24–9).

The other ancient grain which was extensively cultivated was barley (*Hordeum vulgare* or *sativum*). It originated in South West Asia and Tibet, and was known to the ancient Egyptians, Greeks and Romans. Cultivated in ancient China, it had been brought to Japan by 100 BC. But besides true cereals, there were also psuedo-cereals, crops which could be made into flour and used in exactly the same way. If the acorn is the classic European example, in Asia there was buckwheat, and also the water chestnut. Buckwheat (*Fagopyrum sagittatum*) is cultivated much like wheat, then ground into flour and used for porridge and pancakes. The plant originated in Central Asia, and is still to be found there in the wild, but it has been grown in China for many centuries. As for the water chestnut (*Trapa natans*), this was once consumed extensively in Europe, and is still grown widely in China, Korea and Japan, where it is made into flour. Even in the 1930s it was one of the five most important food crops in China. It is not to be confused with the Chinese water chestnut (*Eleocharis tuberosus*), a native plant of East Asia whose corms are eaten raw, boiled or roasted, and often diced to add to soups and other dishes (Brouk 1975: 19–20, 34–8, 142).

There were also two principal tuberous plants which were eaten. There was the yam (*Dioscorea alata*), a climbing plant native to Southeast Asia. The tubers can grow to huge sizes, and some weighing 15 kg have been recorded. They are peeled, then boiled or roasted like potatoes. The yam is not to be confused with the sweet potato (*Ipomoea batatas*) which is of American origin, and often called yam there. The other tuber is taro, also known as eddo and cocoyam (*Colocasia antiquorum*), which again is native to Southeast Asia. From there it was carried to Polynesia where it is a staple. The corm is peeled, and boiled or baked, often being eaten mashed. The commonest dish made from taro in Polynesia is *poi*, a thick paste. Taro is propagated by planting the tops of the corms, where the buds are situated (Brouk 1975: 140–4, 130–1).

Rice: a preferred grain

So it appears that rice was just one of an array of grains and other food items available in Asia. But it seems to have been a preferred grain, seen in the mind of consumers as a superior food to the others. Even after the arrival of the American crops, maize, cassava, potatoes and sweet potatoes, rice seems to have maintained this preferred status.

Hayami has shown how in Tokugawa Japan there was a developed market economy, within which individual peasant farmers farmed for their own gain (Hayami 1990: 3). Tsubouchi adds that as much of the farmers' rice went to pay tax demands, they did not eat much rice themselves, but subsisted on inferior grains and foods. In Java, rice was produced from irrigated fields in the lowlands, but there was also dry rice from slash-and-burn agriculture in the uplands, which also produced millets and maize. Later cassava was introduced as an inferior food. A similar situation existed in Northern Thailand, China, the Deccan in India, Eastern Indonesia and the Philippines, with irrigated wet rice co-existing with dry rice, millets, maize and other inferior foods (Tsubouchi 1990: 9–14). The FAO adds that in Indonesia even in the 1950s maize, cassava, yams and sweet potatoes were regarded as "poor man's food" but farmers tended to sell their rice and eat the cheap foods when their incomes were low (FAO 1955: 5).

Mizoguchi writes that in Japan in the mid-Tokugawa period 40 percent of the arable area was available for dry rice and other crops after the area under wet rice had been taken into account. Dry rice came both from field and slash-and-burn cultivation, all three systems sometimes existing side-by-side, some slash-and-burn continuing even up until 1945. Farmers in dry-rice areas also grew tobacco, fruit and vegetables to sell to wet-rice areas, using the money to buy wet rice. Even in the wet-rice areas people ate millet, wheat and potatoes because they had to sell paddy to meet tax payments (Mizoguchi 1989: 21–40).

Kito confirms that in the Tokugawa period rice was the most important food, but it was substantially augmented by millets, barley, rye, buckwheat, maize, soybeans, red beans and sweet potatoes. Rice was the preferred grain, but was not eaten in great quantities as part of the everyday diet. Poor people could afford to eat very little, and consumption of rice only rose with income. Many poor peasants who grew rice had to sell it for cash, and to pay their taxes. For the poorest, rice was a treat only to be enjoyed on feast days. Yet for many peasants, about 50 percent of their food was rice, which is nearly as much as was consumed by many people of Southeast Asia in the 1970s. Because rice was in such demand as the preferred grain it was the leading item of commerce in the country, and regions which did not produce rice bought it in exchange for the products of their own areas. Eating three meals a day, and consuming white rice spread amongst the common people after 1400, and was firmly established by the

1730s. The sweet potato was introduced to south-western Japan after 1650 and from about the 1720s became increasingly wide-spread, adding a fresh source of vitamin C to a diet generally deficient in it (Kito 1989: 41–54).

The late conversion of Korea to a rice-based diet has already been referred to, but Yi (1989) indicates that there were developments in Korean agriculture between 1400 and 1600, involving both the introduction of crop rotation, and local markets. Slash-and-burn areas were reduced as fields were established, and with crop rotation came fertilizers, and irrigation schemes for wet rice. There was a complementary relationship between the development of markets and the specialisation required by irrigated wet rice, because it was only through the markets that rice producers could sell their paddy and obtain the money to buy fertilizer and other grains, fruit, and vegetables. So specialist irrigated rice producers depended on markets and the establishment of a market economy! To facilitate exchange, commodity monies were introduced, of which the two most important were rice itself, and cloth (Yi 1989: 72–90).

As for Southern China, Liu indicates that rice culture goes back 7,000 years, and by AD 1600 was providing 70 percent of grain production. As New World crops like maize and potatoes were introduced, they were added to rice production so that the proportion of rice in total basic food production fell, and by the 1930s was down to 36 percent. Wheat was also important. From 1660 fertilizers were used and crop rotations introduced, in which dry rice and yellow beans were used as a second crop to wet rice. Other second crops were wheat, barley, beans and rape seed. In the lower Yangtze region there was competition for land as early as AD 1100 between rice and mulberry trees for silk worms, with mulberry trees gradually displacing rice as returns from sericulture were better. From about 1700 came the rise of cotton handicraft textile production with cotton often being grown in rotation with rice, the rice year breaking the pest cycle in the cotton crop. So the three major crops of the lower Yangtze area became rice, cotton, and mulberry leaves according to natural conditions, with other crops like wheat, rapeseed and beans as second crops. In the Pearl River delta fields were converted into fish ponds after 1700 and fruit trees and mulberry trees planted on the surrounding dykes. Mulberry leaves were used to feed the silkworms, and their excreta was fed to the fish. Sugar cane and tobacco were supplementary crops, but wherever these cash crops replaced rice, the farmers had to buy rice through the market instead. This was true of Kwangtung, Fukien and the Yangtze delta. So the market system was reinforced, because if rice had not been available, the farmers would have had to continue with food production rather than turning to cash crops. Pig and sheep rearing was also taking place (Liu 1990: 50–68). That the region was increasingly turning to cash crops like cotton, silk, tobacco and sugar, and expensive food items such as fish, meat and fruit indicates rising living standards.

The intimate relation between silk production and rice production is also emphasised by Furuta (1989), who indicates that the silk trade to Western markets increased enormously during the nineteenth century. Opportunities were created for export merchants and the network of middlemen, down to the peasants who produced mulberry leaves and cocoons. Some areas became specialist silk producers, but they could only do so because they had market links with other areas which were specialist rice producers, and could supply them with food. But in many areas rice and silk were produced together, with silk as an ancillary to rice, mulberry trees growing along the edge of the paddy fields, and on the banks of creeks. The major silk-producing areas saw increasing imports of rice because they were no longer growing sufficient rice for themselves, and because their silk sales gave them higher incomes with which they could purchase this preferred grain (Furuta 1989: 91–118).

Shi (1989) also examines China, showing how from 1750 the northeast became an important grain producing area, and a three-crop two year rotation system spread into the North China plain using barley or winter wheat in turn with beans, maize or millet. In the south, double or treble cropping spread widely from the lower reaches of the Yangtze, bringing wheat and other dry crops into rotation with wet rice. In Fukien and Kwangtung a rotation of two crops of wet rice and one of wheat became common. Inter-cropping and inter-planting became more various with other crops being introduced in additon to wheat. These were barley, soya-beans, broad beans, peas, and cash crops like cotton and mulberry leaves. Maize and sweet potatoes were also introduced, both being able to produce high yields from poor dry lands, maize producing a marginally higher yield than millet or *kaoliang*. Southern crops like wet rice tended to move northwards, and northern crops like wheat southwards, and were increasingly grown in rotation. The southwards movement of northern crops enabled uncultivated dry land to be brought into production and, by the 1930s, half the land in cultivation in the Yangtze valley was dry, and more than that in Yunnan and the southwest. This caused a big rise in agricultural production, with crops like *kaoliang*, broomcorn and other millets, maize and sweet potatoes being encouraged (Shi 1989: 154–91). The FAO noted in 1955 that although wheat was the grain of northern China, and rice the grain of southern China, there was an overlap between the two crops in the region between the Yangtze valley to the south and the Yellow River in the north, with consumers switching from one grain to the other. Millets were a competing cheaper cereal (FAO 1955: 5).

A model of rice consumption

Rice, then, was one in an array of other grains and foods in Asia, but it was regarded as superior to the others, and preferred to them all. It gradually took over from the other grains, just as white wheat bread replaced brown bread, barley, and rye in Europe (Drummond and Wilbraham 1957 41–3, 74, 105-6, 178, 186–90, 209–10, 295–9, 329). This process is still continuing in Asia. Grist records that *ragi* (finger millet) is the main diet in certain parts of India, but once a *ragi*-eater becomes accustomed to rice, it is with the greatest reluctance that he will return to eating *ragi* (Grist 1986: 487). Even in 1991 the FAO could report that in India among the lower income groups there was a proportionately heavy reliance on inferior crops like sorghum and millet (FAO 1991: 76). This report studies patterns of rice consumption in Bangladesh, China, India, Indonesia and the Philippines who together account for 70 percent of world rice production and consumption. It concludes that income plays a major role in most countries in increasing per capita consumption of rice. In the first four countries' income, elasticity of demand for rice was positive, consumption of rice increasing as income rose. But the Philippines was an exception, for there, at least in the urban areas, increases in income brought about a decline in rice consumption (FAO 1991: 2). The reason for this appears quite clear. The Philippines enjoyed higher per capita income levels than the others. At the time of the report, per capita income there stood at $700 1984–5 (FAO 1991: 114). This compares very favorably with Bangladesh $150 1987 (FAO 1991: 26). Indonesia, a middle-income developing country had a per capita income of $550 1988 (FAO 1991: 90). In other words, the urban areas of the Philippines had reached the level of income at which rice consumption begins to fall as vegetables, fruits, fish and meats enter the diet in quantity. In Bangladesh, the poorest country, the proportion of income spent on food was very high, over 50 percent, with 35 percent on rice. Many Bangladeshis cannot even cover their basic calorie requirements (FAO 1991: 26). In India, in rural areas, 52 percent of family expenditure was on cereals, and of the cereals 73 percent was spent on rice. In urban areas 40 percent of total expenditure was on cereals, rice taking 85 percent of the total spent on cereals. In other words, in the higher-income urban areas, an increased proportion of grain consumption was in rice (FAO 1991: 70). As for Indonesia, Timmer and Alderman indicated (1979: 984) that income elasticity of demand was extremely high for low-income groups, and that rice was almost a luxury good for the bottom 30–40 percent of the Indonesian population. Even for high-income groups rice intake increased with higher income, especially in rural areas. This continues to be the case (FAO 1991: 98). In the Philippines, the wealthiest of the five countries in per capita income terms, negative elasticity of demand for rice is observed in urban areas, and urban dwellers consume only 85 percent of the quantity of cereals consumed by rural dwellers (FAO 1991: 124).

This general pattern of consumption was first observed in an obscure paper prepared for the FAO in 1970:

When rice is the preferred cereal, past trends suggest that its per caput consumption increases as soon as incomes improve often at the expense of coarse grains such as millets and barley, or starch roots and beans. Moreover, in rice consuming countries, rice remains at all income levels the principal base around which meals are planned, so that it does not become supplementary in the way bread or potatoes tend to be in other high income countries.

(FAO 1970: 8)

A footnote adds:

Sooner or later, however, as a dietary maximum intake is reached, the quantity of rice consumed tends to be stabilised, but expenditure continues to increase because rice of a better quality is substituted. *At still higher levels of income, as in Japan now, rice itself may begin to be displaced by meat and other non-cereal foods* (my italics). However, an actual decline in absolute per caput consumption levels of rice seems to be very far for most developing countries.

(FAO 1970: 8)

These observations lead one to recognize a simple model of rice consumption and its relationship to income, in which at lower levels consumption of rice rises as incomes rise, the preferred grain rice displacing inferior cereals and foods. But at somewhere about the $700 per capita income level, rice consumption begins to fall as vegetables, fruit, fish and meat take over. However, at a certain point, rice consumption stabilizes and continues at that level regardless of further increases in income. To illustrate this point dramatically this relationship may be plotted, with income on the vertical axis, and expenditure on rice on the horizontal axis, a "b" or belly-shaped curve is observed. This is shown in Figure 5.2. What is being observed is a line showing positive income-elasticity of demand for rice up to $700, and negative income elasticity of demand for rice above this level. This is shown more conventionally with income on the horizontal axis and rice consumption on the vertical axis in Figure 5.3. It is interesting to note that if this principle is correct, then rice is not a Giffen good, contrary to what might be expected.

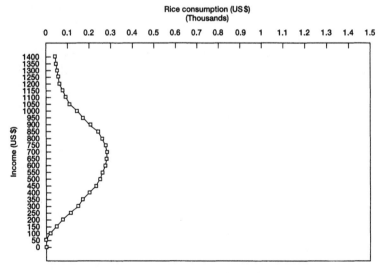

Figure 5.2 Income and rice consumption (belly-shaped curves)

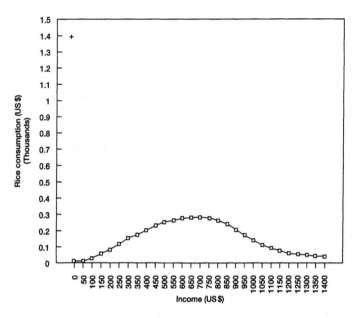

Figure 5.3 Income and rice consumption (hypothesis)

Conclusion

The issue for this chapter is what these findings imply about rice imports to China in the nineteenth century and, indeed, up to the Pacific War. We know that in the late nineteeth century considerable commercialization was taking place in Chinese agriculture, with both cotton and silk becoming important cash crops, as were tobacco and sugar. Farmers increasingly specialized in these crops to secure a gain in income. As farmers specialized in cash crops they had to move out of rice and food grain production. They were able to do this because they were linked through an expanding market economy to those who were choosing to specialize in rice production. As rice was the preferred grain, they chose to purchase more of it as their incomes rose. Rawski has described the situation in China in the early decades of the twentieth century. He confirms that between 1914–18 and 1931–36 total output as measured by gross domestic product rose by two-fifths which, when corrected for inflation, suggests an increase in output per head of 20–25 percent. But as a rising share of output went to investment and government spending, average private consumption per capita only increased by about 10 percent. However he indicates that the most dynamic part of the

Table 5.1 Chinese rice imports, 1867–1940 (metric tons)

Year	Tons	Year	Tons
1867	43,121	1904	203,027
1868	21,107	1905	134,747
1869	20,986	1906	283,404
1870	8,527	1907	772,014
1871	14,998	1908	407,446
1872	39,855	1909	229,699
1873	69,913	1910	557,676
1874	362	1911	320,720
1875	5,140	1912	163,293
1876	34,835	1913	327,493
1877	63,563	1914	412,103
1878	18,022	1915	512,619
1879	15,059	1916	682,444
1880	1,814	1917	594,931
1881	11,974	1918	422,385
1882	14,091	1919	109,466
1883	15,301	1920	69,671
1884	9,192	1921	642,831
1885	19,171	1922	1,158,535
1886	32,658	1923	1,356,846
1887	117,571	1924	798,201
1888	431,336	1925	764,152
1889	258,305	1926	1,131,017
1890	458,067	1927	1,275,622
1891	283,344	1928	765,422
1892	238,771	1929	654,564
1893	573,038	1930	1,202,987
1894	389,545	1931	649,604
1895	610,595	1932	1,359,991
1896	569,409	1933	1,295,399
1897	127,247	1934	771,046
1898	280,924	1935	1,296,427
1899	445,427	1936	310,378
1900	375,393	1937	345,697
1901	266,833	1938	406,116
1902	588,521	1939	320,236
1903	169,462	1940	649,544

Source: Hsiao, Liang-lin (1974) *China's Foreign Trade Statistics, 1864–1949*: 32–3, 297. Cambridge: Harvard University Press.

Chinese economy was the Lower Yangtze area and the northeastern provinces (Rawski 1989: 344–5). Loren Brandt has looked at the situation in the southern provinces of China, to which the majority of rice imports came. He confirms the importance of rice imports to the region, but adds that Shanghai was also a major importer, rice prices there moving in accordance with international levels. The Lower Yangtze was traditionally a rice-deficit area attracting rice from the Middle and Upper Yangtze provinces. This rice competed with rice from overseas, and he argues that the rice markets in Shanghai and South China were highly integrated. So the prices there were set by those prevailing in Monsoon Asia and the international rice market (Brandt 1989: 18–37). However, Brandt is mainly concerned with the situation in Central and Eastern China, and whilst confirming the importance of rice imports to southern China he does not explicitly deal with the forces drawing in the imports, although he is certainly aware of rice's importance as a superior grain (Brandt 1989: 54).

So we may return to the suggestion that the movement of rice in trade is not a response to adversity, but to prosperity. Rising incomes in southern China drew in rice from other parts of China, and from abroad. By this interpretation then, the flow of rice imports to China was not a reaction of an economy finding it difficult to provide for itself, but the response of an economy which was prospering and seeking to indulge itself with the luxury of rice. Incomes were increasing in an economy which was expanding under favourable market conditions. The source of the dynamism was increased productivity in agriculture and rising incomes due to advancing specialization. To this Brandt would surely agree (Brandt 1989: 78–9). Rice is a luxury not a necessity and China was on the move.

References

Brandt, L. (1989) *Commercialisation and Agricultural Development: Central and Eastern China 1870–1937*. Cambridge: Cambridge University Press.

Bray, F. (1986) *The Rice Economies: Technology and Development in Asian Societies*. Oxford: Blackwell.

Brouk, B. (1975) *Plants Consumed by Man*. London: Academic Press.

Doggett, H. (1988) Sorghum, 2nd edn. Harlow: Longman Group UK Ltd.

Drummond, Sir J.C. and Wilbraham, A. (1957) *The Englishman's Food: A History of Five Centuries of English Diet*, 2nd edn. London: Jonathan Cape.

FAO (1955) *The Stabilization of the International Trade in Rice: A Report on Possible Measures*. Rome: FAO.

FAO (1970) *Committee on Commodity Problems. Study Group on Rice.*

Fourteenth Session. Recent Trends and Patterns in Rice Trade and Possible Lines of Action. Rome: FAO. CCP: RI 70/6 6 April.

FAO (1991) *Demand Prospects for Rice and other Foodgrains in Selected Asian Countries*. Rome: FAO.

Furuta, K. (1989) "Peasant, Market Town and Handicraft Technology: Nineteeth Century Huzhou," in A. Hayami and Y. Tsubouchi (eds) *Economic and Demographic Development in Rice Producing Societies: Some Aspects of East Asian Economic History, 1500–1900*. Tokyo Workshop, September 11–15. Private limited edition, Tokyo: Keio University.

Grist, D.H. (1986) Rice, 6th edn. London: Longman.

Hamashita, T. (1989) "The Importation and Cultivation of Rice in Southern China," in Hayami and Tsubouchi.

Hayami, A. (1990) "Preface," in A. Hayami and Y. Tsubouchi *Economic and Demographic Development in Rice Producing Societies: Some Aspects of East Asian Economic History (1500–1900)*, Session B–3, Proceedings, Tenth International Economic History Congress, Leuven: Leuven University Press.

Kito, H. (1989) "History and Structure of Staplefoods in Japan,' in A. Hayami and Y. Tsubouchi *Economic and Demographic Development in Rice Producing Societies: Some Aspects of East Asian Economic History, 1500–1900*. Tokyo Workshop, September 11–15. Private limited edition, Tokyo: Keio University.

Latham, A.J.H. and Neal, L. (1983) "The International Market in Rice and Wheat, 1868–1914," *Economic History Review*, 34: 260–80.

Lee, H. (1990) "Rice Culture and Demographic Development in Korea C 1429–1918" in A. Hayami and Y. Tsubouchi *Economic and Demographic Development in Rice Producing Societies: Some Aspects of East Asian Economic History (1500–1900)*, Session B–3, Proceedings, Tenth International Economic History Congress, Leuven: Leuven University Press.

Liu, T-j. (1990) "Rice Culture in South China, 1500–1900: Adjustment and Limitation in Historical Perspective,' in A. Hayami and Y. Tsubouchi *Economic and Demographic Development in Rice Producing Societies: Some Aspects of East Asian Economic History (1500–1900)*, Session B–3, Proceedings, Tenth International Economic History Congress, Leuven: Leuven University Press.

Mizoguchi, T. (1989) "Economic Development of Non-rice Producing Villages in Pre-modern Japan," in A. Hayami and Y. Tsubouchi *Economic and Demographic Development in Rice Producing Societies: Some Aspects of East Asian Economic History, 1500–1900*. Tokyo Workshop, September 11–15. Private limited edition, Tokyo: Keio University.

Pursglove, J.W. (1972) *Tropical Crops. Monocotyledons*. 1, London: Longman.

Rawski, T.G. (1989) *Economic Growth in Pre-War China*. Berkeley: University of California Press.

Shi, Z. (1989) "The Development and Underdevelopment of Agriculture during the Early Quing Period (1644–1840)," in A. Hayami and Y. Tsubouchi *Economic and Demographic Development in Rice Producing Societies: Some Aspects of East Asian Economic History, 1500–1900*. Tokyo Workshop, September 11–15. Private limited edition, Tokyo: Keio University.

Simmonds, N.W. (1976) *Evolution of Crop Plants*. London: Longman.

Swaminathan, M.S. (1984) "Rice," *Scientific American*, 250: 62–71.

Timmer, C.P., and Alderman, H. (1979) "Estimating Consumption Parameters for Food Policy Analysis", *Amer. J. Agr. Econ.*, 18: 982–87.

Tsubouchi, Y. (1990) "Types of Rice Cultivation and Types of Society in Asia," in A. Hayami and Y. Tsubouchi, *Economic and Demographic Development in Rice Producing Societies: Some aspects of East Asian Economic the History (1500–1900)*, Session B–3, Proceedings, Tenth International Economic History Congress, Leuven: Leuven University Press.

Yi, T. (1989) "New Tendencies in the Korean Socio-Economy of the fifteenth and sixteenth Centuries: Population Increase and Cultivation in the Lowlands," in A. Hayami and Y. Tsubouchi *Economic and Demographic Development in Rice Producing Societies: Some Aspects of East Asian Economic History (1500–1900)*. Tokyo Workshop, September 11–15. Private Limited edition, Tokyo: Keio University.

6

GOLD RUSHES AND THE TRANS-PACIFIC WHEAT TRADE

California and Australia, 1848–57

James Gerber

Introduction

Gold was discovered in California on January 24, 1848. The region was technically a part of Mexico at the time, but 18 months earlier U.S. naval forces had seized the regional capital of Monterey from an overextended Mexican empire. Nine days after the discovery, the U.S. and Mexico signed the Treaty of Guadalupe Hidalgo, ceding California and much of the Far West to the United States. The discovery was both confirmed and publicized on December 5, 1848, by President Polk. The ensuing rush to the gold fields turned the territory of California into an American state and the town of San Francisco into one of the busiest commercial centers in the United States.

The contours of this resource boom are well known; what is less well appreciated, at least in the U.S., is that a similar discovery occurred three years later in the British colonies of New South Wales and Victoria. Equal in magnitude, the discovery in the British colonies was the result of efforts by Australian prospectors who returned home empty handed after failing to find riches in the California gold fields, only to strike it rich in their homeland.

This was not the only connection between the two mining booms, neither was it necessarily the most important. California's boom resulted in significant growth and development of the regional agricultural economy; so much so, that the state became one of the most important grain-producing regions in the U.S.

during the second half of the 19th century. Given the difficulties facing farmers in the form of distances to markets, unfamiliar soils and climates, and labor scarcity generated by the gold-mining boom, the growth of export agriculture into a major supplier of world grain markets was remarkable. The discovery in 1851 of gold in the British colonies of Victoria and New South Wales turned out to be critical to California's agricultural development. From 1854 to 1860, the important initial years of expansion of grain exports, the high level of demand created by the Australian mining boom provided a relatively protected outlet for California's surplus production.

Gold discoveries on the Australian continent turned that region from self sufficiency to a net importer of grain. The high prices offered as a result of the mining boom enabled California's wheat producers to sell their output at a profit, while learning how to reduce costs. It is at least possible that California grain farmers would not have survived long enough to accumulate the experience they needed in order to bring down costs and overcome the transportation problems which made it possible to penetrate the much larger European market. By the 1860s, however, California grain began to enter England and throughout the remainder of the nineteenth century after the U.S. Civil War, California shipments made up about half of total U.S. wheat exports to England.[1]

In the next section, the size of the gold discoveries and their impact on population growth in California and Australia are compared. The following section digresses from the main narrative in order to provide a brief review of the economic theory of the economy-wide effects of the discovery of large mineral deposits. A brief excursion into economic theory is useful for conveying a sense of the anomaly of California's agricultural development, and the critical role played by New South Wales and Victoria. Section 4 examines the effects of the mining booms on wages and prices. Evidence in both regions points to the occurrence of a classic resource boom of the sort that has been well described in economics literature, although the magnitude of the effect on prices and wages in California was attenuated by the high starting level. In Section 5, the impact on agriculture in both regions is examined in detail. California's experience is seen as somewhat anomalous, or contrary to the general expectation of economic theory, and Section 6 ties this development to the Australian gold boom. Section 7 concludes by placing this first American decade of California history in the larger context of the growth of commercial centers and trade networks in the Pacific Basin.

A comparison of the California and Australian gold booms

The discovery in California

The discovery of California's gold occurred during the construction of a millrace for a sawmill owned by John Sutter. Sutter was a Swiss emigrant who became one of the first settlers of European ancestry to locate in the interior of California. He took Mexican citizenship, acquired land from the Mexican government, and used Native American labor to build a tenuous foothold in the California interior. Sutter was anxious to keep the discovery a secret, not necessarily to monopolize it, but because of his more immediate concern to protect his agricultural enterprise. He instinctively understood that his operation would be overrun by gold seekers, and that he would be unable to keep a labor force if the word got out.

Nevertheless, the news soon reached San Francisco, some 75 miles away, and the town began to empty. By late spring, the leading newspaper, The *Californian*, ran the following announcement in its last edition:

> The majority of our subscribers and many of our advertising patrons have closed their doors and places of business and left town . . . We have also received information that very many of our subscribers in various parts of the country have left their usual places of abode, and gone to the gold region, showing that this fever (to which the Cholera is a mere bungler in the way of depopulating towns) is not confined to San Francisco alone . . . The whole country from San Francisco to Los Angeles and from the sea shore to the base of the Sierra Nevada resounds with the sordid cry of "gold! GOLD!! GOLD!!!" while the field is left half planted, the house half built, and everything neglected but the manufacture of shovels and pickaxes . . .
>
> (*Californian* May 29: 1848)

Once word was out, normal commerce became impossible, as the newspaper announcement makes clear. Gold seekers from Mexico,

Hawaii, and Oregon began to trickle in through the summer of 1848, to be joined by South Americans in the fall. Word of the gold strike was not confirmed on the East Coast, however, until December, so that the big rush did not begin until a full year after the discovery.

The discovery in Australia

Gold was discovered several times in Australia before the news got out in 1851. As early as 1839, a man named Hartley found gold in the Blue Mountains of New South Wales, but kept the find a secret for fear of its effects on the colony's convict labor. Two years later, in 1841, gold was again found near Bathurst but not widely reported. In 1851, partly out of fear of a continual loss of labor to California, the government of New South Wales paid the highly qualified English geologist, Sutchbury, to come and look for gold. He reported that Australia was devoid of the metal.

In the meantime, however, Edward Hargreaves found his way home from California, and using the experience he had gained there, showed the geologist how to prospect. On February 12, 1851, Hargreaves found a few specks in Lewis Pond Creek, New South Wales. More discoveries in New South Wales followed quickly. Not to be outdone, and in fear of losing population, the southern district of Port Phillips in New South Wales (which was to divide into the separate colony of Victoria on July 1, 1851) held a town meeting in the Hall of the Mechanics Institution in Melbourne to offer a reward of £200 for a similar discovery in Victoria. Discoveries were soon made and after publication in The *Geelong Advertiser* on July 22, the rush began.

The immediate effects were similar to those in San Francisco three years earlier. Charles Joseph La Trobe, Lieutenant-Governor of Victoria, described the rush as follows:

> Not only have the idlers and day labourers, shopmen, artisans, and mechanics of every description thrown up their employments . . . but responsible tradesmen, clerks of every grade, farmers, and not a few of the superior classes have followed . . . some unable to withstand the mania, but others because they were, as employers of labour, left in the lurch and had no other alternative. Cottages are deserted, houses to let, business is at a standstill, and even schools are closed.
>
> (Quoted in Coghlan 1918: 565–6)

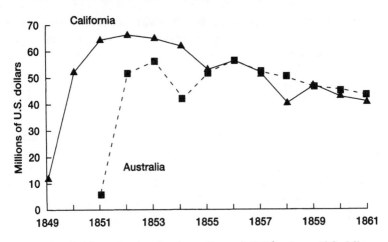

Figure 6.1 Gold production in Australia and California at U.S. Mint prices

Note: Berry's estimates are "best estimates" of California gold at U.S. mint prices ($20.67 per fine troy ounce). The Australian estimate is converted from tons (1 troy pound is equivalent to 0.82286 lbs avoirdupois) and valued at U.S. Mint prices for the sake of comparability

Source: Berry 1976: Table 1, series B; *AHS* 1987: series M6.

Estimates of the quantity of gold produced

Figure 6.1 compares the best estimates of gold output in the two regions (see Table A in the Appendix, for the actual values). The pattern is similar: a year of learning, exploring, and positioning resources, followed by several years of much higher production. A production peak is reached within four to six years, from which a gradual decline begins.

The gold rushes of Australia and California shared another similarity: for several years, individuals and small groups of miners could successfully work the fields with very little capital. After 1851 in California, wage labor in the mines becomes more common, and increasingly there was a need for capital to build quartz mills, acquire hydraulic equipment, and construct flumes (Paul 1947: Ch. 9 and 10). Coghlan (1918: 732) describes similar changes in the technique of Australian mining by 1854, also three years after its initiation.

The effects on population

As news of the discoveries spread, both regions experienced spectacular population growth. Gold catapulted California from a tiny colony on the far edge of a collapsing Mexican empire, to a major Pacific Basin commercial center and a U.S. state. Estimates put the population of California (exclusive of Native Americans) at about 15,000 in 1848 (Wright 1940). By 1852, a special state census counted 255,122 non-Native Americans in the state (DeBow 1853).

Population growth in San Francisco was equally spectacular. In 1847, one year before the gold discovery, San Francisco contained 459 persons, not counting several hundred troops that were part of the American occupation. By 1852, the state census counted 36,154 in the city (*California Star* 1847; DeBow 1853). The commercial implications of this growth were enormous and, by 1851, the port of San Francisco was raising more than $2 million in customs duties, a figure that was exceeded only by the ports of New York, Boston, Philadelphia, and New Orleans (*Alta California* September 25, 1852).

Australia's population growth was similar to California's but with the difference that it began from a larger base of existing towns and commercial centers. The Census of 1851 counted 197,186 persons in New South Wales, the colony of the first gold discovery, and another 97,489 in Victoria, the colony where gold soon proved to be the most abundant. By 1861, the population figures had swollen to 350,086 and 541,800 in New South Wales and Victoria, respectively (Coghlan 1918: 520).

The relative population increases were even greater for Sydney and Melbourne, the leading cities of, respectively, New South Wales and Victoria. Sydney's population increased between the censuses of 1851 and 1861 from 53,924 to 95,789 (78 percent) while that of Melbourne went from 23,143 to 139,916 (505 percent) (Coghlan 1918: 521).

A comparison of population figures is necessary to draw out one of the most important contrasts between the two gold rushes. In the case of Australia, the discovery took place in a well-established colonial economy. The commercial centers of Sydney and Melbourne, along with several other smaller towns and ports, were functioning as urban markets for manufacturers, service providers, and a growing agricultural sector in the hinterland. In addition, warehousing and other port facilities provided services for an important import and export trade. Furthermore, as components of the British Empire, the Australian colonies were subject to a rule of law which included well defined property rights.

By contrast, the gold boom in California occurred in an undeveloped region of a collapsing Mexican empire. Outside the tiny capital of Monterey, there were no cities in Northern California at the time of the gold discovery. The onslaught of people and goods that were to make their way to the port of San Francisco in 1849 would find that there were no port facilities, lighterage, longshoremen, warehouses, or hauling and carting services. Furthermore, as a Mexican colony which had recently come under U.S. military occupation, property rights and the rules of law were less well defined.

The differences in the effects of the resource discoveries in the two regions can largely be ascribed to this factor. In the case of Australia, the discovery occurred in established British colonies which had significant urban and agricultural development. In the California case, there were no cities, little agriculture, and only a handful of people accustomed to the commercial life of Western civilization.

At the beginning of the boom, virtually all goods consumed in the gold fields and the newly created cities of San Francisco, San Jose, Sacramento, Placerville, and so forth, were imported. Ships sailed into San Francisco Bay from around the world; when they arrived they discovered that the warehousing facilities were non-existent, that longshoremen's wages were outrageously high, and that the market was subject to scarcities and gluts which could as easily ruin a merchant as make his fortune. When the market was oversupplied, prices fell below costs; when it rained, goods left out were ruined; and to top it off, ship's crews regularly jumped ship to head for the gold fields. In July of 1850 "500 abandoned vessels lay rocking in front of the city, some with cargoes undisturbed, for it did not pay to unload with costly labor upon a glutted market" (Bancroft 1890: 125).

General effects of resource booms

Before proceeding to a more detailed, sectoral comparison of the two gold rushes, it is helpful to consider what economic theory tells us about such episodes. One of the best models for analyzing the economy-wide effects of a mining boom is the so-called "Dutch disease" model (Corden 1984; Corden and Neary 1982). The model takes its name from the fact that it was first used to explain the de-industrializing effects on the Dutch economy of the discovery of natural gas in the North Sea. As the Dutch shifted resources into natural gas production, it bid up the price of inputs used by that sector and caused a decline in the manufacturing sector which competed for the same factors. These models have been used to analyze a wide variety of positive supply side shocks, including the Australian gold boom (Maddock and McLean 1984).

The model divides the economy into three sectors: a booming sector which produces the newly discovered mineral, a lagging sector which produces tradable goods, and a service sector which produces non-tradable goods and services. The lagging sector is usually thought of as the manufacturing sector since the model was developed to analyze the decline in national manufacturing output (de-industrialization) which usually occurs simultaneously with the boom. There is no *a priori* reason why manufacturing should be considered synonymous with the lagging sector, however, and for the purposes of this chapter, agriculture is considered an important part of the lagging sector, along with manufacturing.

There are two general forces pushing against each of the three economic sectors. These are conveniently labeled the *resource effect* and the *spending effect*. The resource effect stems from the sudden rise in the productiveness of labor, capital, and land in the booming sector. This draws inputs to the booming sector from other sectors (depending on the extent of factor mobility). Overall, the resource effect pushes up the costs of land, labor and capital, to the extent that they can be productively employed in the booming sector. This effect spills over onto the lagging and service sectors as a rise in their input costs and a decline in their output.

The spending effect stems from the rise in real incomes resulting from exploitation of the new resource. Miners flush with gold dust spend it on services and lagging sector goods, either imported or domestically produced. As spending on services (non-tradables) occurs, it bids up the price of services and allows service producers the revenue they need to pay for their more expensive inputs. Spending on services will partially or, perhaps, fully offset the decline in service sector output which resulted from the resource effect (see Table 6.1). The fact that the lagging sector produces tradable goods causes it to stagnate and decline. Lagging sector prices are constrained by import prices. Local producers of grain and other imported goods, face a degree of competition which is absent from the service sector. Given the inability of producers in the lagging sector to raise prices to cover their higher input costs, stagnation and decline is inescapable.

Table 6.1 The spending and resource effects of a resource boom

The resource effect	The spending effect
1 Productivities and compensation of mobile inputs rise	1 Higher real incomes leads to increased spending
2 Inputs are drawn into the booming sector	2 The price of services rises relative to the price of traded goods
3 Inputs leave the lagging sector and the service sector	3 Inputs are drawn into the service sector from the booming sector and the lagging sector

Several testable hypotheses result from this analysis. Given that labor is mobile between sectors, we should observe a rise in wages. Prices for imported goods should rise less (or not at all if arbitrage is effective) than the prices of services. Both the resource producing sector and the service sector should expand, while the remaining sectors (manufacturing and agriculture) should contract.

Wages and prices in Northern California and Melbourne

The evidence of wages and prices in both regions of gold discovery strongly supports the economic predictions of the effects of resource booms. An important difference, however, between Northern California and Melbourne stemmed from the scarcity of (non-Native American) population and the lack of market centers in the former region. As a consequence, the Californian boom occurred within the context of an economy that already had high wages and prices. The subsequent run-up in prices and wages, while dramatic and highly variable month-to-month, does not appear to have been as great as in Melbourne on a year-to-year basis.

Wages

Figures 6.2 and 6.3 show a sample of wages for Northern California (San Francisco mainly) and Melbourne. Wage data for the Melbourne labor market was regularly reported in the *Argus*; San Francisco data are less regular prior to 1854 when the *Prices Current and Shipping List* (hereafter, simply *Prices Current*) began to report wage data. Wages prior to the gold discovery are particularly

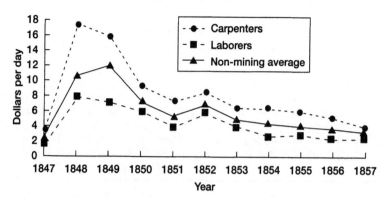

Figure 6.2 Money wages, Northern California, 1849–57
Sources: See Appendix 2

problematic given the small population and the relatively personal nature of economic relations.

Wages in San Francisco and Northern California

Prior to 1850 there are no systematic, comprehensive, reports of wages. The first systematic account can be found in the decennial manuscript census of 1850 which reported wages for a handful of

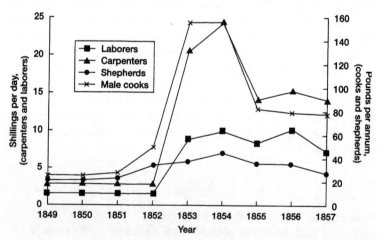

Figure 6.3 Money wages, Melbourne, 1849–57
Note: In some cases the reports are signed by John Whiteoak or G. Whiteoak and Co., Australian Labour Market, 92 Bourke-street east
Source: *The Argus*, various edns 1849–57

occupations; its usefulness is marred, however, by the loss of the returns for several key counties, including San Francisco. Beginning in 1851, scattered accounts in newspapers begin to make note of wages for a variety of occupations. Prior to then, there are the observations of travelers, government officials, settlers, and the inevitable booster.

The *Californian*, a pre-gold San Francisco paper, cites $1 to $3 as the daily money wage prior to the discovery of gold (July 15, 1848, quoted in Cross 1935), which is the range also cited by Bancroft in his *History of California* (1890, p. 110). The earliest history of San Francisco puts the pre-gold wage of laborers in the $1 to $2 per day range (Soule *et al.* 1855: 202). Whether accurate or not, the $1 to $3 seems to have been accepted as a reasonable approximation.[2]

This level of wages probably persisted into the late spring of 1848, by which time Californians were beginning to realize that the rumors of a gold strike were true. On June 1, 1848, Thomas Larkin, the U.S. Consul in San Francisco, wrote that mechanics and teamsters were earning $5 to $8 per day, while cooks were offered $25 to $30 per month. This was early in the first stage of the Gold Rush, and Larkin noted that these wages "will not be an inducement a month longer" (Larkin 1951–68, vol. 7, letter dated June 1, 1848). Moerenhout, a French observer, put the wage of the cook at Sutter's Fort at $150 a month when he visited near the end of July, 1848, and in August, the leader of the U.S. military forces in California listed the wages of blacksmiths and wagon-makers at $10 per day, and carpenters and other mechanics at $15 to $20 per day (Moerenhout 1935, see letters dated July 30, 1848, and Feb. 15 and October 28, 1849; Mason 1848).

By 1849, immigrants from the East Coast were arriving in great number, along with Europeans, Mexicans (who began arriving from Northern Mexico in 1848), Chileans, Australians, and Hawaiians. Two competing forces began to push against the level of wages. On the one hand, wages were pushed up by the real or imagined level of compensation in the placer mines. This effect was re-enforced as the sudden increase in demand for locally produced services and perishable (non-tradable) agricultural commodities such as fresh fruits and vegetables, increased both wages and the demand for labor. On the other hand, immigration increased the supply of labor enormously. The mines, however, were the deciding factor (Figure 6.2).

Through much of 1849, it was assumed that the average take in the placer mines was around an ounce per day per person. Given that gold could be sold for approximately $16 per ounce in San Francisco, this set the level of wages for skilled workers. By 1850, more systematic accounts of wages became available, first in the form of the U.S. Census, and second in a more frequent reporting of wages in the local press. The manuscript census for six counties in the gold region and around San Francisco have average wages for day labor at $6 and for carpenters at $9.42. Clearly, wages were beginning to fall by 1850.[3] Except for the brief rise in 1852, the downward trend continued until approximately 1857 when money wages seem to have stabilized at a level slightly above that of the pre-gold period.

Wages in Melbourne

Data sources for wages in the Australian colonies are more regular and, perhaps, more reliable. In any event, wages were regularly reported in the *Argus* both for the Melbourne and surrounding labor markets. The values in Figure 6.3 for Melbourne show that the most significant increases occurred between 1852 and 1853. Wages peaked in early 1854, and by late in that year were falling. They continued to trend downward for the rest of the decade.

Two interesting features of the wages reported in Figure 6.3 should be noted. First, there is a significant increase in the skill premium for carpenters and cooks. Less skilled workers, such as shepherds and laborers, saw much smaller increases in their money wages than did skilled workers. Shepherds, however, were also given rations so that as retail prices of foodstuffs rose, the real value of their compensation rose independently of any increase in the money wage.[4] A second feature of wages during this period is that there was a shortening of the contractual period for hiring labor from a per week or per annum basis to a per day basis. The shift in the contracting period is simultaneous with the greatest increase in wages – from late 1852 to early 1853.

The relationship between wages and the expected returns to gold mining were very close, as in the California case. For example, Coghlan (1918: 730) notes that there were various estimates of miner's returns, but at the peak of the boom it was about £430 per year. Carpenters in the same period earned £400 per year, while laborers earned half as much.

Prices in San Francisco, New South Wales, and Victoria

Money wages are not informative about the standard of living of the persons receiving them unless there is some accounting for the costs those people face. Prices, it is safe to say, increased dramatically in all three regions. Again, however, the lack of a well developed market economy in San Francisco prior to the gold rush makes the pre- and post-gold comparisons questionable. It is certain that most things were expensive in San Francisco prior to the discovery. The market was small, it was a long way from anywhere, and before the Gold Rush it did not pay merchants to supply the area with large quantities of commodities.

Prices in San Francisco

Price quotations for San Francisco, unlike the Australian case, are wholesale rather than retail. While this limits their usefulness for determining real wages, the general trend in wholesale and retail prices tends to be the same over the medium to long run.

The key difference between San Francisco and Melbourne is, once again, the small market and high level of wholesale prices in the former before the discovery of gold. Figure 6.4 shows several items of interest to consumers in the San Francisco market. It should be noted that there was significant month-to-month fluctuation around the plotted annual averages of monthly prices. The outstanding feature of the data in Figure 6.4 is the lack of a dramatic price increase. This is perhaps surprising to anyone who is casually familiar with anecdotal history of California's Gold Rush.

The picture of San Francisco wholesale prices shown in Figure 6.4 does not contradict the notion that prices were high during the Gold Rush. Rather, it supports the idea that the increase in prices was not as great as might have been assumed given the high levels that were reported for several years from 1849 onwards. Prices were high before the Gold Rush, and one effect of the discovery of gold was that it put San Francisco on the map as a destination for goods of every sort. In other words, the market creation effect of the resource boom partially counteracted the price increases in the short run, and in the medium run of three to five years, it completely counteracted the boom.

Given that wages seem to have risen somewhere between three and five times, the evidence of wholesale prices indicates that there

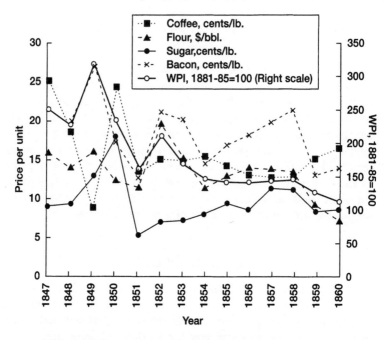

Figure 6.4 Wholesale prices, San Francisco, 1847–60

Note: Annual average of monthly prices. The price coverge for 1847 is limited to March; for 1848, the four months from March through June; and for 1849, for the six months of July through December. The lack of prices quotes between July 1848 and June 1849 (inclusive) may cause 1848 and 1849 to be underestimated. The wholesale price index (WPI) covers 76 commodities, of which 62 commodities and 74 percent of the weight are farm products and food

Source: Berry 1984: 230–43

was a very real and very significant increase in the standard of living for Northern Californians.

Prices in New South Wales and Victoria

Two price indices for basic commodities are plotted in Figure 6.5, one for New South Wales and one for Victoria. The commodities included in each price index are 7 food items, plus soap and candles weighted "as appropriate for an artisans family" (*AHS* 1987: series PC 1 and 2). Figure 6.5 amply illustrates the greater effect of the gold boom on the colony of Victoria. By 1855, the year of peak prices in Victoria, that colony had produced approximately 86.4 percent of the gold output, hence the greater effect (*AHS* 1987: series ME 2 and 6).

138

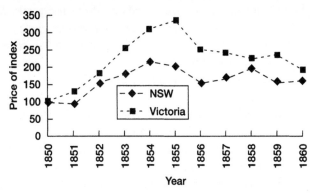

Figure 6.5 Prices of basic commodities, New South Wales and Victoria, 1850–60
Source: AHS 1987: series PC 1 and 2

A comparison of Figures 6.4 and 6.5 is useful. Whereas San Francisco's prices began high and then rose 41 percent from their low point in 1848 to their peak in 1849, in both Victoria and New South Wales, prices rose for three to four years before peaking at levels of 236 percent and 117 percent above those of the pre-gold period.[5] Nearly a decade after the first discovery (1860) prices in both colonies remain significantly higher than their pre-gold levels. San Francisco prices, on the other hand, trend down throughout the decade after peaking in the second year of the gold discovery.

A comparison of lagging sectors: agriculture

In the Dutch Disease economic model, every branch of the economy that produces a traded good which is not part of the mineral discovery is lumped together under the label "Lagging Sector." In effect, this includes manufactured items and non-perishable agricultural commodities. These sectors are expected to shrink due to the increase in their input costs (driven up by the resource boom) and the essentially constant level of output prices (due to the availability of imports at existing world prices).

Agricultural expansion in California

The traditional story of Californian agriculture is that it took off as a direct result of the mining boom. For example, Bancroft's

encyclopedic history of the state explains that immigrant farmers
became discouraged in the gold fields and turned their hand to
what they knew best. "As surface mining became less remunerative, diggers began to swell the agricultural ranks, first as raisers
of potatoes, and other vegetables . . . cereals followed, first barley.
. . . (Bancroft 1890: 2)."

Perishables such as fruit and vegetables were highly remunerative to miner–farmers. The spending effect of the gold boom
meant that miners had exceptional purchasing power with little
opportunity to satisfy it on imports of fresh fruit and vegetables
that would perish in transport. Consequently, prices for the output
of truck gardens were high enough to provide stimulus to the
investment of labor and capital. Grains, however, were another
matter. Why would a miner–farmer turn his hand to wheat or

Table 6.2 The expansion of grain production during the gold rush

Region	1850	1852	1855
San Francisco Bay Area[1]			
Wheat (bu.)	15,000[4]	205,385	620,696
Barley (bu.)	101,790[4]	1,020,133	910,352[5]
Central Valley[2]			
Wheat (bu.)	7,700	41,622	1,129,441[6]
Barley (bu.)	3,500	930,194	1,845,001[6]
South/Central Coast[3]			
Wheat (bu.)	8,528	38,892	50,833[7]
Barley (bu.)	4,872	37,115	18,000[8]

Sources: For 1850 and 1852: DeBow 1853a, b. For 1855: Thomas 1859.

Notes:
1 Alameda, Contra Costa, Napa, San Francisco, Santa Clara, and Sonoma
counties
2 Butte, Colusa, Sacramento, San Joaquin, Solano, Sutter, Yolo, and Yuba
counties
3 Los Angeles, Monterey, Santa Barbara, San Diego, and San Luis Obispo
counties
4 The 1850 manuscript census returns for San Francisco, Contra Costa (which
included Alameda county in 1850), and Santa Clara counties were destroyed
in a fire. Santa Clara was an important agricultural county; the total includes
estimates for 1851 that come from Werth (1851: 71–4)
5 Production reports for Contra Costa and San Francisco counties are missing
6 Production reports for Solano county are missing
7 Wheat production reports for Santa Barbara are missing
8 Barley production reports for Los Angeles, Monterey, and Santa Barbara are
missing

barley when they were readily available as imports from Oregon, Chile, and the East Coast?

While the nearly simultaneous boom in agriculture and mining is beyond dispute, it is curious that no one has explored the mechanisms that made grain agriculture possible given that its development seems to contradict standard economic theory. While this would be far from the first instance of economic theory breaking down in the real world, the contradiction between theory and fact points to an interesting and unique set of occurrences which are worthy of further exploration.

Table 6.2 underscores the development of grain farming in California. While the estimates for 1850 are marred by the absence of reliable estimates for the San Francisco Bay Area, there can be no mistaking the tremendous growth in output between 1850 and 1852, the year in which gold production peaked. Particularly noticeable is the huge increase in production in the vast Central Valley region of the state where, other than Sutter's operation, there had been almost no farming as of 1850.

One indicator of the growth of wheat farming in California by 1852 was that San Francisco newspapers began to carry intelligence about wheat prices in their current prices section. Another indicator was the repeated attention given by the business press to the lack of milling facilities in the state and the bottleneck to further growth. Throughout 1852, The *San Francisco Prices Current and Shipping List* (PC) called for investment in milling operations, either by local capital or by Eastern manufacturing interests ("Review of the Market," PC June 1, July 14, October 15, 1852).[6]

Plantings of Californian wheat, barley, and oats during the 1852 season seemed to foretell a not too distant time when the state would be self sufficient. In its May 1 and June 15 editions, the *Prices Current* gave warnings to Chilean and Oregonian suppliers that:

> " . . . shippers cannot rely on a sale here for their produce in the future. Already heavy contracts have been entered into between consumers and domestic growers, for the delivery of growing crops at rates that would not clear cost and charges to foreign consignors."

While the turning point in grain production probably came in 1852, by 1854 the state was, in the words of its leading historian, "practically self supporting" in grains (Bancroft 1890: 2). Nevertheless, self sufficiency and an export surplus did not come without a significant amount of last minute uncertainty. Throughout the spring of 1854, information reached San Francisco predicting a more than adequate planting to satisfy demand in the California market (*PC* February 22, April 14, and May 15, 1854). There remained questions about the quality of California flour. Through the summer, the San Francisco press worried about smut, grains mixed with seeds from native plants, uncleanliness and the extreme dryness of the flour (*PC* August 24, and September 9, 1854). In addition, low prices for wheat and flour in the local markets raised questions about the profitability of harvesting the local product (*PC* May 15, June 6, 1854). And the attempt by Chilean millers to corner the San Francisco market with the intention of stifling the development of California production, while too late to be effective, put market watchers on edge (*PC* May 9, 1854).

Combined wheat and flour exports for 1854 totaled $538,000, a sum that was far behind the value of gold exports, but not far from California's second most important export of the 1850s, quicksilver ($649,000 in 1854). The value of grain exports was also far ahead of cow hides ($108,000 in 1854), the traditional leading export before the discovery of gold (*PC* January 4, 1859). While the numbers for each individual product jump around in the subsequent years, it is clear that by 1854, wheat and flour exports were real and that their long-run trend was positive.[7]

Agricultural contraction in New South Wales and Victoria

The response of Australian agriculture to the sudden development of gold mining stands in contrast to California. In the latter locale, farmers immediately abandoned their crops during the 1848 season (and those who did not had a hard time finding labor for the harvest), but by 1849 and 1850, grain, vegetables, and livestock were entering a period of rapid growth. By contrast, in New South Wales and Victoria, wheat acreage continued to expand for at least a year after the gold discovery, beef and dairy cattle herds continued a permanent expansion, albeit at a slower pace through 1855, and sheep flocks grew until 1854. After this somewhat more delayed response, a downturn in production occurred which lasted until 1856 for wheat while sheep flocks

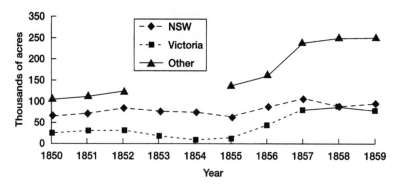

Figure 6.6 Australian wheat acreage, 1850–9
Note: Other includes South Australia, Tasmania and Western Australia. The
Nothern Territories is included in South Australia, but had no wheat
production. Queensland had less than 1,000 acres of wheat until 1863
Source: AHS 1987: series AG 37–45

in New South Wales and Victoria continued to shrink until at
least 1858 (*AHS* 1987: series AG 37–72).

Figure 6.6 shows a plot of wheat acreage in New South Wales,
Victoria, and all the other Australian colonies.[8] The importance of
the drop in production implied by the acreage reductions was
magnified by the sudden influx of fortune seekers, many of whom
came from California in 1851 and 1852. The inevitable result of
the simultaneous fall in supply and increase in demand was that
Australia became an importer of grains.

California's good fortune in the Australian boom

The surplus of wheat realized by California farmers in 1854
presented them with the problem of finding a market. In the
weekly "Market Review" column, the editors of the *Prices Current*
expressed constant anxiety over the lack of a "foreign outlet" for
the grain coming to market (*PCS* April 14, April 29, June 6,
1854). At the end of 1854, the paper proclaimed that " . . . the
only thing required to make us exporters instead of importers is
the absence of any convenient foreign market for our surplus
production" (*PCS*, December 30, 1854).

Several possibilities existed. As early as June 15, 1853, the
paper had noted an increase in exports to numerous destinations
around the Pacific, including Hawaii, Australia, Hong Kong,
Russian North America, Central America, Mexico, and Chile.
California's location on the Pacific Rim gave it a natural advantage

over other major producers and distributors, as did the fact that many of these markets were too small to attract major attention. Throughout 1854, occasional shipments of surplus wheat, flour, barley, and oats were made to these ports, as well as to Vancouver, Manila, Shanghai, New York, and Liverpool.

Table 6.3 shows the distribution of wheat and flour exports by destination from the harvest season of 1854 through the harvest of 1859. Led by its grain and quicksilver[9] exports, California established itself as a major commercial center in the Pacific Basin during the second half of the 1850s. Table 6.3 shows that in general, the markets of the Pacific, and specifically Australia and New Zealand, were far more important during this early phase of agricultural growth than either European or U.S. markets. In effect, California's trade relations were those of a separate nation rather than those of a U.S. region. Australia and New Zealand took more than 52 percent of California's combined wheat and flour exports during the first six years of export trade.[10] Further-

Table 6.3 Exports of Californian wheat and flour, 1854–60

Destination	Wheat (centals)[1]	Flour (barrels)[2]
China, Japan, East Indies[3]	9,237	37,506
Pacific Islands[4]	12,796	15,846
Central America and Mexico	40	13,522
British Columbia, Alaska, and Siberia	6,564	47,195
South America	29,163	24,354
Australia and New Zealand[5]	319,099	138,214
New York, Boston, and Philadelphia	106,472	2,257
Europe[6]	11,231	25,733
Total	494,602	304,627
Australia and New Zealand as a percent of the total	64.5	45.4

Source: Author's calculations based on data from Davis 1894.

Notes:
1 A cental equals 100 lbs
2 Barrels are 196 lbs of flour
3 Primarily China
4 Primarily the Hawaiian Islands and the Society Islands
5 Primarily Australia
6 Primarily England

more, as shown below, the trade led to premium prices for California producers who were struggling to become competitive on world markets.

By the 1860 harvest season the pattern was to change and European markets, specifically Liverpool, would begin to take the lion's share of California wheat. Before then, however, production costs and uncertainties about markets and shipping methods kept the grain markets of England out of reach.[11]

The timing of the Australian boom could not have been better for California. The sudden drop in Australian grain production and the price increases which followed were an important stimulus to California's transition from mining to an export-oriented agricultural economy. Nowhere is this importance better perceived than in a comparison of wheat prices in Australia, California, and New York. Figure 6.7 illustrates the wholesale price of wheat in the three cities of Melbourne, San Francisco, and New York. High labor costs in San Francisco were an obstacle to exports to nearly any destination – particularly the large grain markets of New York and Philadelphia which were well supplied by the Mid-Atlantic and the Midwestern states.

By 1854, however, the surplus in California was bringing prices down to a level familiar to Eastern U.S. markets. Simultaneously, the Australian market presented an opportunity for Californians,

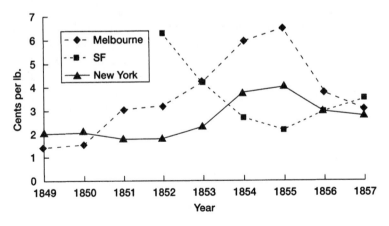

Figure 6.7 Wholesale wheat prices in three cities, 1849–57
Notes: Prices are the annual average of monthly prices. Melbourne prices were converted to cents at the exchange rate of $4.848 per pound sterling
Sources: San Francisco prices are from Berry 1984; New York prices are from Cole 1938; Melbourne prices are from *The Argues*, 1849 through 1857

both in its ability to absorb a significant part of the excess supply, and in the premium prices it offered. The Australian market was also closer than the East Coast of the United States and therefore required lower transportation costs. Who could have designed a more fortunate set of occurrences?[12]

Conclusion

The parallels between the discovery of gold in California and Australia are striking: the size of the discoveries were similar, they occurred within three years of each other, and they stamped independent identities on each region. In the California case, the gold discovery created an important regional economy and quickly gave the U.S. a significant political presence on the West Coast of North America from which it could deal more effectively with its English, Russian, and Mexican competitors. In the Australian case, the discovery led to the rapid growth of the colonies and, in the words of Coghlan, created a public identity separate from that of England (Coghlan 1918: 524).

The differences are striking as well, not the least of which was the fact that the Australian colonies were well established with commercial centers and a developed regional economy. The presence of a recognized and accepted civil authority in Australia led to significantly more regulation of mining claims and a more secure rule of law and order in the Australian mining camps.

Perhaps no greater difference between the two regional experiences with gold was the rapid development of agriculture in California which followed close on the heels of the discovery. Particularly in the case of grains, this development was anomalous when viewed through the lens of economic theory, but yet it led to the development of California as a major U.S. grain producer. Since grains no longer figure prominently in California agriculture, it is worth stressing how significant they once were. Relative to other states, California became the single largest producer of barley by 1860, and it continued to climb among the ranks of wheat-producing states, until it finally reached the number two position in 1890 at a level of output equal to nearly nine percent of the entire U.S. production.

The economics of the development of California's grain sector in the midst of a gold boom has not yet been fully explained. Somehow, California farmers were able to overcome their extraordinarily high labor costs to produce a competitively priced product which, by 1860, was a major source of supply to the world's grain markets.[13] One part of this story must be the gold discovery in Australia, and the opportunities it presented to Californian farmers at a critically early stage in their learning.

On a broader note, it is also worth pointing out that the history of these linkages across the Pacific offers another cautionary tale to those who see today's rise of a global economy as something entirely new. In the 1850s, California and Australia were well integrated into a regional Pacific economy in which the international forces of supply and demand were shaping the opportunities and activities of local producers.

Appendix 1

Table 6.4 Gold production in California and Australia, in millions of U.S. dollars

Year	California	Australia
1849	12.48	
1850	53.02	
1851	64.68	6.00
1852	66.64	52.12
1853	65.72	56.88
1854	62.83	42.59
1855	53.49	52.67
1856	56.75	56.97
1857	52.37	52.95
1858	40.89	50.72
1859	47.46	47.05
1860	43.64	45.79
1861	41.60	43.93

Source: See Figure 6.1.

Appendix 2: Sources for Figure 6.2

- Pre-Gold Rush wages are from: Bancroft 1890: vol 7: 110; Hastings 1846: 131–2. Wages for 1848 are from: Lotchin 1974: 86; Mason, letter dated August 17, 1848. Average wages include weighted observations of laborers, cooks, blacksmiths, and carpenters.

- Wages for 1849 are from: Bancroft 1890: vol 7: 110; Hittel 1863: 305; Larkin 1951–68; Moerenhout, letters dated February 15, 1849 and October 28, 1849; and Mason 1848. Average wages include (weighted) observations of wages for laborers, cooks, blacksmiths, carpenters, and teamsters.
- Wages for 1850 are from the Census of the United States, manuscript version, 1850. Occupations for the index include laborers, carpenters, tinsmiths, blacksmiths, coopers, mill workers, lumbermen and sawyers, bakers, and masons.
- Wages for 1851 are from: *Alta California*, October 12, 1851; and Hittel 1863: 305. Occupations for the index are carpenters, smiths, laborers, and engineers.
- Wages for 1852 are from: *Alta California*, January 1, February 15, 1852; Bancroft 1890: 639; and *Sacramento Daily Union*, October 30, 1852. Occupations are the same as 1851.
- Wages for 1853 are from: *Alta California*, March 3 and May 2, 1853. Occupations are blacksmiths, carpenters, coopers, cooks, engineers, jewelers, laborers, masons and plasterers, millers, painters and glaziers, printers, sawyers, tailors, teamsters, and tinsmiths.
- Wages for 1854–7 are from: *Prices Current and Shipping List*; and *Mercantile Gazette and Shipping Register*, various editions of each. For 1854, occupations are the same as 1853, plus barbers, butchers, gunsmiths, hatters, lumbermen, porters, upholsterers, watchmakers, and wheelwrights, and omitting sawyers. For 1855, occupations are the same as 1854, plus bakers. For 1856, occupations are the same as 1855, plus sawyers. For 1857, occupations are the same as 1856, minus gunsmiths and tailors.

Notes

1 See Rothstein (1975).
2 By comparison, wages for laborers on the Erie Canal were $0.88 per day from 1847 to 1851. Farm labor in 1850 averaged 10.85 per month (with board) in the United States, but $68.00 in the Far West. The Far West figure includes areas less affected by the Gold Rush and therefore underestimates the wage in Northern California (*Historical Statistics of the United States*, 1975, series D 705 and D 718).
3 The destruction of the manuscript census returns for San Francisco and two other important counties in the San Francisco Bay Area (Contra Costa and Santa Clara), along with the severe undercount of miners in the gold regions, led to the implementation of a second census for California in 1852. However, the lack of data for San Francisco in 1850 may cause the decline to be overstated.

4 Basic commodities (7 food items plus soap and candles) in Victoria rose 163 percent from 1851 to their peak in 1855 (*AHS* 1987).

5 While it is true that the Californian and Australian price indices are not identical in coverage, and that the California index suffers from missing data for the months between July 1848 and June 1849, the general point of this paragraph remains: Californian prices rose less and peaked sooner than prices in Australia. Note also that this repeats the comparative pattern of wages.

6 The *San Francisco Prices Current and Shipping List* became simply the *Prices Current and Shipping List* in November of 1852.

7 There are several sources of data on export quantities and export values. The figures reported here come from the most commonly cited source, the San Francisco business press (*San Francisco Prices Current and Shipping Register*). The British Consul's report of January 19, 1858, has grain export figures that seem to be drawn from the same source (*BPP* 1971: v 19: 166). Horace Davis, an observer and participant in the grain trade, provided export data for wheat and flour separately by quantity rather than value, and by harvest year rather than calendar year. Given San Francisco prices for wheat and flour, his estimates for the 1854–5 season exports are approximately $569,743 (Davis, 1894). The lone dissenter is the table in Langley (1859: 116) which has total exports of wheat and flour of $82,273 in 1854. Langley's 1855 figure is considerably higher – $908,646. Regardless of the actual number, all observers agree that 1854 and 1855 were the years in which California grain exports took off.

8 South Australia was a significant wheat producer and underwent substantial expansion in acreage after about 1856; Tasmania was another important producer. The "other" category in Figure 6.6 includes these two colonies, plus a small amount produced in Western Australia.

9 See St. Clair (1994–5) for an interesting description of the development of California's quicksilver production.

10 300 lbs of wheat is approximately equivalent to one barrel (196 lbs) of flour.

11 In order to sell grain in England, California shippers had to make a 14,000 mile journey, cross the equator twice, and were limited to sailing vessels due to the high costs of coal for such a long voyage. In addition, the wheat had to be shipped in sacks rather than in bulk due to the length and roughness of the trip (Paul 1958).

12 It is also interesting to note that the outbreak of the Crimean War closed the Black Sea, a major grain supply route to England's wholesalers and distributors. The resulting shortage of grain supply to English markets certainly did not hurt California's ability to exploit the Australian market for several years relatively free from English competition. The Crimean War also cut short the development of a regular steamship communication with England. The initial arrival of steam vessels in 1852 did not lead to regular service until 1856 (Coghlan 1918: 549).

13 Gerber (1993) briefly explores the economic contradictions in more detail and offers an interpretation based on the exploitation of Native

American labor. Paul (1958, 1973) stresses the effects of mechanization, but these came very late in the 1850s.

References

Alta California (1849–1853) Various editions. San Francisco: E. Gilbert and Co.

Argus, The (1849–1857) Various editions. Melbourne: Edward Wilson.

AHS (Australian Historical Statistics) (1987) New South Wales: Fairfax, Syme, and Weldon Associates.

Bancroft, H.H. (1884) *History of California. Vol. I.* San Francisco: The History Company.

—— (1890) *History of California. Vol VII.* San Francisco: The History Company.

Berry, Thomas (1976) "Gold! But How Much?" *California Historical Quarterly* 55(5): 246–55.

—— (1984) *California Prices and California Gold.* Richmond, Virginia: Bostwick Press.

BPP (British Parliamentary Papers 1854–1865) (1971) Irish University Press Area Studies Series: United States of America. Embassy and Consular Commercial Reports. Shannon, Ireland: Irish University Press.

Californian, The (1848) May 29. San Francisco: J.D. Hoppe and Co.

California Star, The (1847) August 28. San Francisco: Samuel Brannan.

Coghlan, T.A. (1918 [1969]). *Labour and Industry in Australia: From the First Settlement in 1788 to the Establishment of the Commonwealth in 1901.* Melbourne: Macmillan of Australia.

Cole, Arthur Harrison (1938) *Wholesale Commodity Prices in the United States, 1700–1861.* Cambridge, MA: Harvard University Press.

Corden, W.M. (1984) "Booming Sector and Dutch Disease Economics: Survey and Consolidation," *Oxford Economic Papers* 36: 359–80.

Corden, W.M. and J. Peter Neary (1982) "Booming Sector and De-Industrialization in a Small Open Economy," *The Economic Journal* 92: 825–48.

Cross, Ira B. (1935) *A History of the Labor Movement in California.* Berkeley: University of California Press.

Davis, Horace (1894) "California Breadstuffs," *Journal of Political Economy* 2: 517–612.

DeBow, J.D.B. (1853a) "California," *The Seventh Census of the United States: 1850.* Washington, DC: Robert Armstrong Printers.

—— (1853b) "Population and Industry of California by the State Census for the Year 1852," *The Seventh Census of the United States: 1850.* Washington, DC: Robert Armstrong Printers.

Gerber, J. (1993) "The Origin of California's Export Surplus in Cereals," *Agricultural History* 67(4): 40–57.

Hastings, Lansford (1846) *The Emigrant Guide to Oregon and California.* Cincinnati: G. Conclin.

Historical Statistics of the United States (1975) Washington: U.S. Government Printing Office.

Hittel, J.S. (1863) *The Resources of California*. San Francisco: A. Roman and Co.

Langley, Henry G., and Morison Samuel (1859) *State Register and Yearbook of Facts: for the Year 1859*. San Francisco: H.G. Langley.

Larkin, Thomas O. (1951–1968) *The Larkin Papers, Volume 7* edited by George P. Hammond Berkeley, CA: University of California Press.

Lotchin, R.W. (1974) *San Francisco, 1846–1850: From Hamlet to City*. New York: Oxford Press.

Mason, R.B. (1848) "Letter to R. Jones," House Exec. Doc. No. 17. 31st Congress, 1st Session: 528–36.

Maddock, Rodney and McLean, Ian (1984) "Supply-side Shocks: The Case of Australian Gold," *Journal of Economic History* 44(4): 1047–67.

Mercantile Gazette and Shipping Register (1856–57) Various editions. San Francisco: T.M. Bosworth.

Moerenhout, Jacques Antione (1935) *The Inside Story of the Gold Rush*, translated by A.P. Nasatir. San Francisco: California Historical Society.

Paul, Rodman (1947) *California Gold*. Lincoln: University of Nebraska Press.

—— (1958) "The Wheat Trade between California and the United Kingdom," *The Mississippi Valley Historical Review* 45(3): 391–412.

—— (1973) "The Beginnings of Agriculture in California: Innovation *vs*. Continuity," *California Historical Quarterly* 52(1): 16–27.

PC (Prices Current and Shipping List) (1852–7) Various editions. San Francisco: S.O. Johnson & Co.

Rothstein, Morton (1975) "West Coast Farmers and the Tyranny of Distance: Agriculture on the Fringes of the World Market," *Agricultural History* 49(1): 272–80.

Sacramento Daily Union, The (1852) October 30. James Anthony and Co: Sacramento.

San Francisco Prices Current and Shipping List (1852) Various editions. Merchants' Exchange: San Francisco.

Soule, Frank, Gihan, John, and Nisbet, James (1855) *The Annals of San Francisco*. New York: D. Appleton and Co.

St. Clair, David J, (1994–5) "New Almaden and California Quicksilver in the Pacific Rim Economy," *California History* Winter: 279–95.

Thomas, D. (1859) "On Agricultural Statistics of the State," *Transactions of the State Agricultural Society 1859* in Appendix to the *Assembly Journal*, 11th Session: 323–48.

Werth, John J. (1851) *A Dissertation on the Resources and Policy of California: Mineral, Agricultural, and Commercial, including a plan for the disposal of the mineral lands*. Benicia, CA: St. Clair and Pinkham.

Wright, Doris Marion (1940) "The Making of Cosmopolitan California: An Analysis of Immigration 1848–1870," *California Historical Society Quarterly* 19(4): 12–40.

7

AMERICAN TRADE DOLLARS IN NINETEENTH-CENTURY CHINA

David J. St. Clair

Introduction

The Coinage Act of 1873 ended the minting of regular silver dollars in the United States and led to the de-monetization of silver the following year. It also created a new silver coin, the trade dollar, to replace the discontinued silver dollar. The trade dollar was a larger coin, containing more silver than the regular silver dollar, and was never intended for circulation in the United States. Produced solely for export, the American trade dollar was to be a commercial or trade coin that would circulate abroad, primarily in China.

From 1873 through 1878, trade dollars were minted in quantity for export. After 1879, only proof coins were struck through 1885. A total of 35,965,939 trade dollars were minted, including 8,773 proof coins struck for collectors.[1] Prior to 1873, the United States Mint had only minted 8,045,838 regular silver dollars. In just four years, more than four times as many trade dollars were coined. Trade-dollar production was equivalent to 25 percent of all American silver coinage minted before 1873 (i.e., all silver dollars and subsidiary silver coins).[2] Regular silver dollar coinage was restored under the Bland–Allison Act in 1878 and later increased under the Sherman Silver Purchase Act of 1890. Regular silver dollars minted under these two acts quickly dwarfed trade-dollar production, but at the time, the trade dollar marked a dramatic increase in silver coinage in the United States. Between 1873 and 1878, trade-dollar coinage consumed about 23 percent of the silver mined at the Comstock Lode.

The trade dollars were intended for export and indeed more than 81 percent of them were shipped abroad.[3] Of those exported, a little less than 85 percent left through San Francisco, destined for China. It is estimated that another five percent were sent home by Chinese laborers working in the United States.

The Coinage Act of 1873 gave the trade dollar the legal tender status of a subsidiary coin. Since 1853, subsidiary coins – coins in fraction of a dollar denominations – were only legal tender for payments under five dollars. The limited legal tender status of the trade dollar was repealed amidst controversy in 1876 as the price of silver fell and some trade dollars began circulating in the United States. The trade dollar was soon embroiled in the bitter debate over a domestic bimetallic monetary standard. Volume production of trade dollars ended in 1879 when silver was re-monetized and the regular silver dollar restored. The Bland–Allison Act called for the U.S. Mint to coin two to four million silver dollars per month, dramatically increasing silver coinage for domestic circulation. However, the restoration of domestic silver dollars only added to the confusion over the status of the trade dollar. After 1879, the trade dollar languished in limbo, its fate hotly debated until the coin was finally recalled in 1887.

The trade dollar was quickly dubbed a failure. President Arthur called the coin a "disturbing element" and "an embarrassment to our currency."[4] Merchants came to hate the coin because its legal tender status was unclear. Gold standard partisans saw in the trade dollar a perfect example of the dangers inherent in a bimetallic monetary standard. On the other hand, most pro-silver advocates had come to view the trade dollar as a threat and an annoyance. By 1879, silver lobbyists had moved on to the bigger pie of expanded silver coinage under the Bland–Allison Act, and the trade dollar had become a potential threat to silver purchases under that act.[5] The trade dollar become a despised orphan.

Most historians and numismatists have also deemed the trade dollar a failure. John Willem dubbed the trade dollar "America's only unwanted, unhonored coin" (Willem 1965: xiii–xiv). Charles Little claimed that the trade dollar was recalled because it was "unpopular at home and unwanted abroad" (Little 1941: 130).[6] Coin historian David Watson characterized the trade dollar's "creation a misfortune, its existence a failure, and its retirement a necessity" (Willem 1965: xiv).

The trade dollar lived its short life in the midst of controversy that ultimately resulted in its repudiation and recall. Aside from a few enthusiastic partisans, it was never really understood in its day. Today, it remains an oddity, a numismatic enigma. It remains the only American coin to ever be recalled. While the coin was only intended for export, it was dragged into domestic political wrangling over the silver question and bimetallism. Prior to its recall, the larger trade dollar, with more silver than the regular silver dollar, was only worth a fraction of its smaller replacement in the market.

This chapter attempts to unravel the enigma of the American trade dollar. It argues that, if its purpose is understood, the trade dollar was not a mistake or failure or embarrassment. It was instead quite a success.

But beyond salvaging the reputation of a long-forgotten coin, there is a larger, more important issue here. The American trade dollar can shed some light on an important aspect of American and European trade with China in the nineteenth century. I argue that the trade dollar can only be appreciated if one understands the nature of Chinese demand for foreign silver. Low opinions of the trade dollar stem from a failure to understand this demand.

Before discussing the American trade dollar, a discussion of the nature of trade or commercial coins is in order. This will be followed by a brief discussion of some earlier attempts at introducing trade coins into China.

Characteristics of trade coins

Many coins throughout the world have been created as trade or commercial coins. Other coins were never created to serve as trade coins, but acquired this status de facto. A "pure" trade coin is a coin made by one country expressly for circulation outside of that country.[7] A pure trade coin is not legal tender and does not circulate in its country of origin. It circulates abroad based on its bullion value and on the integrity of the issuing mint. Pure trade coins have been issued by many countries, including Great Britain, Italy, France, Holland, Japan, and Austria. European pure trade coins began to circulate in Asia in the eighteenth century and were still in use in the twentieth century.

The world's most durable pure trade coin must have been the Maria Theresa thaler. This was a silver coin that was first minted in Austria in the eighteenth century. It was still being minted in the 1970s (McDonald 1975: 14). The thaler (the term from whence we derive the word "dollar") was never legal tender in

Austria. It circulated primarily in East Africa and the Middle East where its value fluctuated with the price of silver. Its appeal rested on its near universal acceptance in these markets.

De facto trade coins are regular issue coins that have legal tender status in their country of origin, but which acquire a circulation far beyond their national borders. Historically, the most important coins of this type were the Spanish and Mexican silver dollars minted from the sixteenth to the nineteenth century. These coins, variously known as dollars, pesos, peso duros, eight reales, piastres, or pieces-of-eight, depending on time and place, were always legal tender in their country of issue. However, they circulated freely and extensively abroad and figured prominently in world trade.

The Spanish dollar, first minted in 1497, was extensively minted in Mexico from 1535 and soon became the most popular medium of exchange in China (Kann 1927: 128). These coins were an important part of the silver flow to China that began in the sixteenth century. Early on, Spain adopted a policy of coining its New World silver as soon as possible. Coins were easier to handle and control than bullion. At the same time, Chinese merchants, for reasons discussed below, also preferred coinage to bullion. An official of the British East India Company noted in 1736 that "Silver in the lump seldom answers in China so well as Dollars" (Willem 1965: 70).

The Chinese demanded silver to meet their commercial needs.[8] Silver was the preferred commercial medium of exchange in China from the fifteenth century, but China produced little silver and did not mint its own silver coins until 1889.[9] In addition, silver commanded a higher value in China than in Europe and America. Consequently, foreign silver coins flowed into China in response to its higher price and to fill the coinage void. Foreign silver coins became the medium of exchange in Chinese domestic as well as international trade.

After the Mexican revolution, Mexican dollars were usually minted in quantities that greatly exceeded domestic requirements. They were routinely exported and circulated abroad. Like their Spanish predecessors, they played an important role in European trade with East Asia. Silver dollars coined by the Mexican Republic, with the same weight and fineness of the earlier Spanish dollars, were coined after 1824. The Mexican silver dollar became the primary circulating medium in North America, South America, the West Indies, the Pacific Islands, Japan, and the greater part of Asia (Kann 1927: 145). By the 1850s, the Mexican dollar was the *de facto* coin of commerce in China. The American trade dollar was later created to compete with the Mexican dollar in China.

The essential requirement of any successful trade coin – pure or *de facto* – was acceptance. Acceptance in turn depended on recognition, familiarity, and trust. It must be remembered that these coins were issued by foreign governments and circulated on their reputation, not on legal mandate.

The Maria Theresa thaler illustrates this very well. It featured the likeness of the Empress Maria Theresa and was dated 1780. Because the likeness and the 1780 date became recognized and trusted symbols, they were never changed. For almost two centuries, the Empress's likeness and the 1780 date were featured on the coin. Even the copies of the Maria Theresa thaler produced by Great Britain, Belgium, France, and Italy, featured the same likeness and 1780 date. Recognition and familiarity were more valuable than dynastic or chronological accuracy.

Recognition and acceptance were sometimes problems for Spanish and Mexican silver coins in China. These coins were periodically changed as conditions in Spain and Mexico changed. New coin designs often met with suspicion and discounting. The Mexican 8-reales dollar was first coined in 1824 to replace the Spanish dollar previously coined at Mexican mints. With a new design, the Mexican dollar initially encountered some resistance. However, it was widely understood in China that the Spanish dollar had in fact been coined in Mexico and the Mexican silver dollar was soon accepted as the heir to the Spanish dollar (Willem 1965: 39–40).

A more difficult problem arose with the introduction of a new Mexican silver dollar – the balance scale peso – in 1869. This coin was minted from 1869–73 and proved difficult to keep in circulation in China. The problem was not only its unfamiliar design, but also its new designation as a "peso." Even more problematic was its smaller size. The balance scale peso had a diameter two millimeters smaller than the previous dollar. The balance scale peso actually had the same silver content as the earlier Mexican silver dollars, but this fact was not widely known or appreciated in China. Buttrey and Hubbard noted that the unfamiliar design and smaller size of the balance scale peso "counted against it in the China trade" and made its withdrawal "imperative" (Buttrey and Hubbard 1986: 8). In 1873, the old familiar design was reinstated and "8R" replaced peso to "satisfy foreigners, not Mexicans" (ibid.)

Early trade coins in China

Great Britain made its first trade coin for use in China in the late-eighteenth century. In 1778, an official of the British East India Company suggested that his government coin silver money to facilitate its trade with China (Willem 1965: 33–4). A 1778 Spanish Carolus Pillar silver dollar was sent to London as a pattern piece. Dies were made in London and dispatched to Canton where the Spanish coin was minted under British control. The date of "1778" was maintained.

The Canton dollar ended in failure and left a sour legacy for all future trade coins in China to follow. The coin failed because it was quickly debased at the mint. Its initial silver content of 92 percent was debased to as low as 60 percent. In addition, corrupt local Chinese officials encouraged local craftsmen to turn out cruder versions of the coin containing even less silver.

The Canton dollar fiasco cast a pall over all foreign money and led Chinese merchants to develop their own means of self-protection. They began a practice called "chopping" coins. Chopping should not be confused with either the "clipping" or "sweating" of coins, both of which deliberately short-weight coins.[10] A coin was "chopped" when a merchant's mark was stamped on the face of the coin. A chop mark indicated that the merchant who was paying with the coin guaranteed its purity and weight and would stand by it later if it was shown to be short-weighted or adulterated.

Chopping was a practical, private solution to the problem of fraud and debasement. It was also symptomatic of the weakness of China's central government. Chinese authorities could not guarantee the integrity of the money supply, foreign or domestic, so the private sector developed its own solution through chopping. Chopping was an established practice in China when the American trade dollar was introduced and most trade dollars sent to China were chopped.

The Canton dollar was quickly abandoned and Britain did not try again to create a trade coin for more than eight decades. In 1863–4, Britain minted silver dollars in Hong Kong in an attempt to meet the increased demand for silver coins following the opening of new treaty ports in 1858 and 1860. Over 2.1 million Hong Kong dollars were coined, but British officials were disappointed with their initial reception and discontinued minting after only two years. Chinese merchants were skeptical of the new coin and were also confused about whether it was legal to chop it.

A new design featuring a dragon and the inscription "One Tael Shanghai, Hong Kong 1867" was introduced, but it was rejected by Chinese merchants.

The Hong Kong dollar was discontinued because Chinese merchants only accepted them at a discount to their silver value. This initial discounting stopped after a few years, but the Hong Kong Mint had already been closed in 1868. British officials seemed not to have understood that any new coin or change in design would invariably meet with initial suspicion and discounting.

The Hong Kong minting equipment was sold to the Japanese who later used it to mint their own trade coins patterned after the American trade dollar. The Japanese persisted through the initial discounting and produced trade coins for their China trade through 1914. The British returned to the trade coin arena for a third time in 1895 and successfully coined more than 274 million trade dollars through 1935.[11] These trade dollars were minted in Bombay.

The American trade dollar

The American trade dollar grew out of two needs. First, American merchants in the China trade needed silver to trade for Chinese products, mostly tea. Second, the trade dollar sought to provide a market for silver from American mines.

The first need was a long-standing, chronic problem that had plagued American trade with China from its inception. The second problem was quite new, a need created by the rapid outpouring of silver from the Comstock Lode after 1859. Each of these will be discussed in turn.

Silver figured prominently in American trade with China throughout the nineteenth century. The first American ship entered a Chinese port in 1784, laden with silver, sandalwood, ginseng, and other items. However, export products for China proved hard to come by and silver dominated the trade (Hoa 1986). Between 1784 and 1833, more than $88.6 million in silver was sent to China, compared to $50.3 million in non-silver American goods (Willem 1965: 30). During the period 1805–14, specie comprised 70 percent of American exports to China. From 1816 through 1844, specie comprised 65 percent of American exports to China (Hoa 1986: 22–3).

Although silver was the most important American export to China, silver production in the United States was virtually nonexistent before 1859. American silver production averaged only $19,000 per year between 1835 and 1844, and $39,000 per year for the period 1845 to 1858 (U.S. Bureau of the Census 1976: 606). This did not come close to meeting the coining needs of the U.S. Mint, let alone export demand. Between 1831 and 1860, $147 million worth of silver was imported into the United States, while domestic production amounted to only one percent of this sum (Willem 1965: 46). Generally, silver flowed into the United States from Mexico, was coined, and then flowed out to Europe and Asia. American silver coins minted during these years were seldom seen in domestic commerce. China drained off much of this silver. For example, between 1856 and 1860, only $400,000 in silver was mined in the United States and silver imports exceeded exports by $9 million (Schran 1986: 255). Silver exports to China during these years totaled $10 million.

After 1827, Americans acquired another means of financing trade with China – bills of exchange drawn on London. These were increasingly relied upon by American merchants to alleviate the silver shortage. For example, in 1827, Americans financed its trade with China by exporting $2.0 million in goods, sending $1.8 million in specie, primarily silver, and utilizing $400,000 in London bills of exchange (Willem 1965: 30). By 1833, exported goods totaled $2.9 million while specie exports fell to $682,500 and bills exceeded $4.7 million.

But bills drawn on London added to the cost of doing business in China and were often perceived as putting American merchants at an unfair and costly disadvantage. The American Consul in Hong Kong reportedly characterized the commissions charged on London bills as a three to four percent tax on American commerce with China.[12]

To acquire silver for the China trade, American merchants often paid a premium for silver coins. Regular American silver dollars and subsidiary silver coins (half-dollars, quarter-dollars, and dimes) were collected and exported. However, the supply of American silver coins was seldom sufficient. American merchants usually had to seek out foreign coins, mostly Mexican dollars.

Mexican dollars were crucial to filling the silver shortfall, but they were expensive. Premiums paid by American merchants for Mexican dollars were usually higher than the premiums that they paid for American coins. Enjoying greater acceptance in China, Mexican dollars often sold at premiums ranging from two to 22

Table 7.1 Pure silver in various coins

Coin	Silver content (troy grains)
Mexican dollar	377.25
Japanese yen	374.10
American dollar	371.25
Trade dollar	378.00

percent above their bullion value.[13] These premiums were a constant source of complaint from American merchants.

Part of the reason why Mexican dollars commanded such high premiums was due to the smaller size of the American silver dollars (see Table 7.1). It was difficult doing business in China with a coin that was smaller than the standard, that is, the Mexican dollar. Size was important, but it was not the main problem. As Willem points out, regular American silver dollars were an unknown *brand* silver in China (Willem 1965: 47). There had never been sufficient quantities circulating in China to give the Chinese the opportunity to become as familiar with the American silver dollar as they were with the Mexican dollar. The Chinese simply did not like the smaller, unfamiliar U.S. coin whose supply had been so limited.

In 1861, the Director of the Mint reported that the regular American silver dollar:

> was supposed to be needed for our China and East Indies trade. But our consular advices [sic] are to the effect that our silver dollars are very reluctantly taken at the (treaty) ports, and not at all in the Interior of China. They are believed by the Chinese to be of less value than they are.[14]

Edgar Adams writes that Mexican silver dollars were in such short supply in San Francisco that they were actually produced in the city in the early 1850s (Adams 1913: xxvi–xxvii). Willem describes a second, unsuccessful attempt to mint Mexican dollars in San Francisco in 1861 (Willem 1965: 19–20). A contract was signed with the Mexican government, but the plan fell apart over a last-minute contract dispute.

It is interesting to note that Californian gold did not enter the China trade to any significant extent. *Merchants Magazine* reported in 1859 that every ship leaving San Francisco for China carried large amounts of Mexican dollars.[15] Edgar Adams writes that silver was:

> required for purchases in China; under no conditions would the Orientals accept gold for their merchandise, and thus the San Francisco buyers were compelled to pay a premium in gold for silver coins . . . a remarkable example of the important part played by that now despised metal in the greatest of the days of gold.
>
> (Adams 1913: vii)

Although gold was being exported out of California, sometimes at a rate that left little in the state, it was not destined for China.[16]

In 1856, *Merchants Magazine* printed an article from an American correspondent in Shanghai suggesting that the Americans ought to pressure the Chinese to make gold legal tender for commerce in China.[17] In China, an American $5 gold piece was worth only a little more than four dollars in trade. He also argued that a heavier silver dollar was needed to better compete with the Mexican dollar.

Dennis Flynn and Arturo Giráldez have noted the same phenomenon in European trade with China during the sixteenth through the eighteenth centuries, i.e., that gold did not join the silver flow to China.[18] In fact, they point to gold flows in the opposite direction up to at least 1640, suggesting that the Chinese wanted silver, not merely a trade-balancing bullion flow. They see the flow of European silver to China as the primary catalyst for the development of world trade.

The experience of California suggests a similar pattern in the nineteenth century. The Chinese were silver customers, not passive recipients of silver money. If this had not been the case, California gold would have entered the China trade. It did not.

The United States became a significant silver producer after 1859, but Comstock silver did not automatically flow into the China trade. Even as large quantities of Comstock silver became available, American merchants were still seeking Mexican dollars. Premiums paid for Mexican dollars appear to have been as high, if not higher, in the 1860s than in the 1850s. It should be noted that the failed scheme to produce Mexican dollars in San Francisco occurred in 1861, when American silver output was more than 38 times higher than the pre-Comstock level of 1858. In addition, American merchants had to contend with a 12 percent excise tax imposed by the Mexican government on the export of Mexican dollars in 1867 (Willem 1965: 50).

Comstock silver seems to have had such a limited impact on the China trade because it was originally channeled into regular American silver dollars. In 1859, 636,500 silver dollars were minted, the bulk exported to China (Willem 1965: 46–7). The following year, another 733,930 silver dollars were minted. Again, most were exported. The silver dollars produced in these two years amounted to 11 percent of the entire minting of silver dollars in the United States between 1793 and 1873. Yet Mexican and Spanish dollars still commanded premiums of four to 15 percent in Shanghai. Between 1870 and 1873, another surge of silver dollar coinage occurred. Regular silver dollars, amounting to 30 percent of the total number of silver dollars produced from 1793 and 1873, were minted and largely exported.[19] But like the earlier exports in 1859 and 1860, these exports "in no way improved the competitive position of the American coin in China, nor its acceptance by the Chinese" (Willem 1965: 51).

Getting Comstock silver into the China trade was a difficult problem. Dr Henry Linderman, Director of the Mint and enthusiastic proponent of the trade dollar, saw a solution to this problem in the American trade dollar. He argued that "the true policy of this country . . . is to seek a market in China for its silver bullion, and to do this, it must be put in form to meet a favorable reception in that empire."[20]

But to accomplish this, Comstock silver had to be packaged and name-branded in order to make it appealing to Chinese customers. To do this, a new coin was created to compete with the Mexican dollar – the American trade dollar.

Table 7.1 shows the trade dollar compared to the Mexican dollar, the regular American dollar, and the Japanese silver yen, a trade coin. The American trade dollar offered superior weight, fineness, and quality control. It was, in essence, a superior brand of silver. Willem writes that:

> the major point here is that Nevada silver had to be refined to the Chinese standard, and that there was a cost factor involved which had to be reckoned with in the competition with the Mexican dollar, which for all practical purposes, was the Chinese standard.
>
> (Willem 1965: 67)

Chinese customers wanted a coin, not bullion. They wanted a reliable coin of dependable weight and purity. They wanted a coin that was comparable to, or superior to, the Mexican dollar. The American trade dollar provided such a coin.

Success or failure?

The trade dollar was abandoned after only four years despite clear evidence that it was doing the job for which it was intended. Consular reports from China cite favorable acceptance in South China, with more moderate success in Northern China (Willem 1965: 95–102). Given the skepticism that invariably accompanied all new coins or revisions of established coins, these consular reports are remarkably positive.

The reception accorded the trade dollar was apparently good enough to prompt plans for striking other denominations of trade coins – $5, $10, $20, and 50-cent pieces. The success of the American trade dollar also prompted the Japanese to initiate their own trade coin. Interestingly, the original Japanese trade coin carried, in English, the name "Trade Dollar" and the same inscription of weight and purity as found on the American trade dollar.

Congressional testimony in 1877 claimed that the American trade dollar was enjoying a two percent premium over the Mexican dollar in the China trade (Laughlin 1888: 103). This clearly indicates acceptance since it reversed the long-standing tendency for American coins to exchange at a discount in China.

Porter Garnett wrote about how the trade dollar succeeded in its goal of getting American silver into the China trade. In 1878, when the trade dollar figured prominently in the China trade, domestic specie accounted for 82 percent of American silver exports, with foreign silver making up the remaining 18 percent. After the suspension of trade-dollar coinage, the relative shares were reversed (Garnett 1917: 97).

Mint statistics for the period 1873–8 also confirm a marked decline in silver imports into the United States relative to silver exports (US Bureau of the Mint 1897: 284). This is also consistent with the trade dollar successfully channeling American silver into the China trade. Table 7.2 also shows how the trade dollar quickly came to dominate American silver flows to China.

Virtually all of the evidence suggests that the trade dollar was a

Table 7.2 Shipments of silver from San Francisco, 1873–5

Fiscal year ending	Bullion	Trade dollars
June 30, 1873	$1,730,398	–
June 30, 1874	2,004,944	$1,905,122
June 30, 1875	87,007	4,405,420

Source: Willem 1965: 93.

huge success. How, then, does one explain the widespread opinion to the contrary? Misunderstanding and confusion about what the trade dollar was – and about what it was supposed to do – was a significant factor. For example, it was quite common for contemporary writers to explain Asian demand for silver with racist stereotypes. J. Laurence Laughlin, a well-known monetary economist at Harvard University, attributed Asian demand for silver to "their barbaric taste for ornaments and their want of civilized methods of exchange" (Laughlin 1888: 122). With such an attitude, it would be difficult to appreciate how the trade dollar effectively satisfied Asian customers.

Ignorance can also be seen in the wild estimates of how many "non-mutilated" trade dollars might be presented for redemption in 1887. The ignorance involved the practice of chopping. Not understanding circumstances in China, many in the United States equated chopping with clipping or wanton mutilation. Estimates of the number of eligible trade dollars that might be redeemed were as high as 20 million, or 70 percent of those exported. The redemption regulations therefore stipulated that to be eligible for redemption, a coin could not have been mutilated.

But virtually all trade dollars that circulated in China had been chopped, not because they were mutilated, but because they had been accepted. Chopping was a sign of success, not vandalism or mutilation. Partisan motives aside, the failure to understand chopping reflects a basic ignorance about how trade dollars satisfied the Chinese demand for a reliable silver coin. In fact, the number of trade dollars actually redeemed was 7,689,036. Records show that only 114,935 trade dollars were ever returned directly from China, through San Francisco (Willem 1965: 121, 131). Of the trade dollars that had come back to the United States, 80 percent were re-exported, not redeemed.

The legal tender controversy

If the trade coin was, in fact, so successful in doing what it was intended to do, then why the controversy? How did a coin made solely for export become so mired in domestic disputes?

The answer to these questions lies in the legal tender dispute. The relevant question here is how did a coin that was never meant to circulate in the United States, a coin that was meant to be nothing more than a branded silver disk for export, ever acquire legal tender as a domestic subsidiary coin?

It should be pointed out that this issue would never have arisen if it were not for the dramatic fall in the price of silver after 1876. The trade dollar originally had a bullion value that exceeded its monetary value. Consequently, it would not have circulated domestically regardless of its legal tender status. But as silver prices fell, this was reversed – the trade dollar's monetary value exceeded its value as a silver disk. While there is little evidence that trade dollars ever really circulated to any significant extent in this country, the threat of domestic circulation dragged the trade dollar into the silver question.

Most supporters of the trade dollar argued that the coin was given limited legal tender status in error. Garnett called the decision a "palpable oversight" (Garnett 1917: 96). He points out, quite correctly, that the supporters of the coin did not even want to call it a dollar, preferring instead "Silver Union" or "Silver Arbiter."

Laughlin concluded that the decision to grant the trade dollar limited legal tender was the product of "inadvertence, and without any intent" (Laughlin 1888: 104). Henry Linderman thought bestowing legal tender had been "inadvertent".[21]

Most writers have tended to accept this "mistake" explanation, but there have been some exceptions. Neil Carothers claims that the decision was a deliberate attempt by silver interests to give the new coin a better standing.[22] A. Barton Hepburn also points out that when many of the politicians who voted in favor of the Coinage Act of 1873 were confronted about their vote to effectively de-monetize silver, they pleaded ignorance of that feature of the bill! (Hepburn 1903: 272–3). Ignorance of the trade dollar's inclusion as a subsidiary coin smacks of the same duplicity.

Willem offers a more plausible explanation. He points out that the processing of Nevada silver to the standard of the Mexican dollar incurred an extra cost (Willem 1965: 66–7). Coining always entails minting costs, but these were not the problem. Silver brought to the mint was exchanged for minted trade dollars with the bullion owners paying minting costs and seigniorage. The problem came from the additional cost incurred in preparing Comstock bullion for coining. Nevada silver tended to have a higher gold content than Mexican ore. While a higher gold content was beneficial in Europe, it was a liability in Asia. Gold would have to be separated from Comstock bullion prior to coining and the cost of separation added to the cost of the trade dollar.

Private refiners, with limited capacity, were charging from two to six percent to separate the metals. This would have increased the cost of coining trade dollars and reduced their attractiveness vis-à-vis the Mexican dollar. In addition, it was not clear if private refiners could have even handled the refining task created by the trade dollar. The U.S. Mint did have the capacity and, by law, was required to keep processing fees at cost. Consequently, the Mint only charged one and a half percent for separation. But to qualify for Mint processing, the trade dollar had to be a legal *coin*. Consequently, the trade dollar was given the status of a subsidiary coin with limited legal tender to cap separation charges at the Mint.

Seen in this light, the legal tender controversy appears to have been a classic example of rent-seeking gone awry. What was intended as a means to shift processing costs to the government ended up creating a controversy that eventually killed the program.

Willem is correct about the cost advantages derived from Mint processing, but he is on less firm ground when he argues that the trade dollar had to be a legal tender coin *somewhere* in order to survive (Willem 1965: 76). There were indeed added costs incurred in holding "non-money" trade dollars in the United States. If trade dollars were not money that circulated, then holding them would require a commitment of funds. A Congressional Commission estimated these holding costs at nine percent per year (ibid.).

But Willem's assertion is contradicted by the success of pure trade coins like the Maria Theresa thaler. It should also be pointed out that holding cost would only be incurred prior to export. There would be no holding costs once the coin circulated abroad, regardless of its legal status at home. This would dramatically mitigate these costs and exclude any necessity for legal tender status.

Conclusions

The trade dollar was created to increase American silver exports and to facilitate American trade with China. By this criterion, it succeeded.

To accomplish this, American silver had to be packaged, or name-branded, in order to make it appealing to Chinese customers. Selling silver to the Chinese was no different from selling any product to anyone else. The Chinese customer wanted a coin with a weight and purity similar or superior to the Mexican dollar. The trade dollar provided such a product.

This dimension of Chinese American trade is difficult to appreciate if silver flows to China are merely treated as a trade-balancing monetary flow. In this regard, the American trade dollar episode supports the view that silver flows to China were primarily the result of Chinese demand for silver as a circulating medium.

Notes

1 Statistics on trade dollar coinage are from (U.S. Bureau of the Mint 1887), and (Willem 1965: 163–7). The figures cited in this chapter exceed the figures from these sources by a total of 15 coins, all proof coins struck for collectors, that were coined in 1884 and 1885. These proof coins were not reported in Mint records until 1908. Willem and the Mint report cited here did not count these coins in their coinage tally or in their dating of trade dollar coinage.
2 Calculated from Mint figures (U.S. Bureau of the Mint 1900: 223).
3 This and the following export figures were calculated from (Willem 1965: 169).
4 Address of President Chester Arthur to Congress, 3 December 1883. Reprinted in (Willem 1965: 126).
5 The Bland–Allison Act required the Mint to coin between two and four million silver dollars per month. After the passage of the Bland–Allison Act, silver advocates considered the trade dollar a threat because the controversy over the coin jeopardized domestic silver coinage. In addition, opponents argued that trade dollar redemptions should be counted against the monthly silver purchases mandated by the act.
6 Little claimed that the poor reception of the trade dollar abroad resulted from its lower silver content compared to the Mexican silver dollar. This is simply not true (see Table 7.1). Little's erroneous assertion illustrates the confusion surrounding the trade dollar and ignorance about its apparent failure (Little 1941: 130).
7 I am coining (no pun intended) the terms "pure trade coin" and "*de facto* trade coin" here. If there is another name for these types of coins, or a more apt term, I am unaware of it.
8 On the nature of Chinese demand for silver from the sixteenth century

through eighteenth centuries, see: Flynn and Giráldez 1994; 1995; 1996a; and 1996b. On Chinese money and monetary policy, see: Von Glahn 1996a; and 1996b.

9 Lien-sheng Yang describes the changing nature of Chinese coinage and currency, including China's two thousand years of copper coinage at Chinese mints. In addition, the Chinese coined gold and silver coins during earlier times as well as pioneering paper money in the eleventh century. However, the inflationary debasement of paper money led to its replacement by silver after 1400. The central government's inability to assure the quality of silver and gold coinage led to a virtual cessation of minting these coins until 1889 (Yang 1952).

10 In theory, chopping and clipping are separate, distinct practices carried out for very different purposes. However, in the hands of a skilled craftsmen, chopping could serve as a disguise for clipping. Although this certainly occurred at times, it does not negate the primary intent and purpose of chopping, that is, as a means to insure against fraud.

11 Calculated from figures presented in (Willem 1965: 176).

12 Cable from the Washington correspondent of The *Daily Alta California*, February 10, 1873. Quoted in (Willem 1965: 72–3).

13 Reported premiums varied. The figures cited here are from Garnett 1917: 91–2; Laughlin 1888: 103; Willem 1965: 68; and Adams 1913: 26.

14 Cited in (Willem 1965: 19).

15 Cited in (Willem 1965: 19).

16 California's experience also illustrates the point about coin being preferred to bullion. The state was rich in bullion, yet suffered from a severe coin shortage. A mint was not opened in San Francisco until 1855, and custom duties and port fees had to be paid in legal tender, i.e., U.S. coin or foreign coins that enjoyed legal tender status in the U.S. Gold dust was not accepted, or only accepted at extreme discounts of up to 50 percent. California suffered from a silver-coin shortage and foreign silver coins poured in, attracted by huge premiums paid for these coins. California merchants often found themselves competing with merchants in the China trade for silver coin, thus raising premiums even higher.

17 *Merchants Magazine*, October, 1856. Quoted in (Willem 1965: 46).

18 See the citations to the work of Flynn and Giráldez in note 8 above.

19 This figure was calculated from United States Bureau of the Mint 1900: 238–45 and Willem 1965: 46, 51.

20 *Banker's Magazine*, March, 1873: 710–16 (quoted in Willem 1965: 70).

21 Henry R. Linderman quote is from Willem 1965: 77.

22 Neil Carothers quote is from Willem 1965: 77.

References

Adams, E. (1913) *Private Gold Coinage of California, 1849–55: its History and its Issues*. Brooklyn: Edgar H. Adams.

Buttrey, T. and Hubbard, C. (1986) *A Guide Book of Mexican Coins: 1822 to Date*. Iola, WI: Krause.

Flynn, D. and Giráldez, A. (1994) "China and the Manila Galleons," in A. J. H. Latham and H. Kawakatsu (eds) *Japanese Industrialization and the Asian Economy*. London: Routledge.

——— ——— (1995) "Born with a 'Silver Spoon': The Origins of World Trade in 1571," *Journal of World History* 6 (2): 201–21.

——— ——— (1996a) " Introduction: Monetary Substances in Global Perspective," in D. Flynn and A. Giráldez (eds) *Metals and Monies in an Emerging Global Economy* Aldershot: Variorum.

——— ——— (1996b) "China and the Spanish Empire," *Revista de Historia Economica* 14 (2): 309–38.

Garnett, P. (1917) "The History of the Trade Dollar," *American Economic Review*, VII: 91–97.

Hepburn, A. (1903) *History of Coinage and Currency in the United States and the Perennial Contest for Sound Money*. New York: Greenwood (1968 reprint).

Hoa, Y. (1986) "Chinese Teas to America – A Synopsis," in J. Fairbank and E. May (eds) *America's China Trade in Historical Perspective: The Chinese and American Performance*. Cambridge: Harvard University Press.

Kann, E. (1927) *The Currencies of China*. Shanghai: Kelly and Walsh.

Laughlin, J.L. (1888) *The History of Bimetallism*. New York: Appleton.

Little, C. (1941) "The Trade Dollar," in American Numismatic Association, *Selections from The Numismatist – United States Coins*. Racine, WI: Whitman.

McDonald, D. (1975) "The History of Silver," in A. Butts, (ed.) *Silver: Economics, Metallurgy, and Use*. New York: Kreiger.

Schran, P. (1986) "The Minor Significance of Commercial Relations between the United States and China, 1850–1931," in J. Fairbank and E. May (eds), *American's China Trade in Historical Perspective: The Chinese and American Performance*. Cambridge: Harvard University Press.

United States Bureau of the Census (1976) *Historical Statistics of the United States: Colonial Times to 1970, Part One*. Washington DC: Government Printing Office.

United States Bureau of the Mint (1887) *Annual Report of the Director of the Mint*. Washington DC: Government Printing Office.

——— (1897) *Annual Report of the Director of the Mint*. Washington DC: Government Printing Office.

——— (1900) *Annual Report of the Director of the Mint*. Washington DC: Government Printing Office.

Von Glahn, R. (1996a) "Myth and Reality of China's Seventeenth-Century Monetary Crisis," *The Journal of Economic History*. 56: 2.

Von Glahn, R. (1996b) *Fountain of Fortune: Money and Monetary Policy in China, 1000–1700*. Berkeley: University of California Press.

Willem, J. (1965) *The United States Trade Dollar: America's Only Unwanted, Unhonored Coin.* Racine, WI: Whitman.

Yang, L. (1952) *Money and Credit in China.* Cambridge: Harvard University Press.

8

ALFRED CROSBY'S *ECOLOGICAL IMPERIALISM* RECONSIDERED

A case study of European settlement and environmental change on the Pacific Rim

Warwick Frost

Introduction

In *Ecological Imperialism: The Biological Expansion of Europe, 900–1900* (1986), Alfred Crosby posed the question – "why were Europeans so successful in settling the temperate parts of the Americas, Australia and New Zealand?" Not only had they successfully established themselves, but in many instances European migrants, culture and landscape had almost completely replaced their indigenous counterparts (Crosby 1986: 2–5).

Crosby's explanation for this success was that, apart from superior weaponry and military organization, the Europeans brought with them a superior biota of germs, plants and animals. Smallpox, influenza and other contagious diseases devastated the indigenous populations. Cattle, sheep, pigs, European trees, grasses and weeds all flourished. Why was the European biota superior? Crosby argued that thousands of years of trade and migration between the "Old World" of Europe, Asia and Africa had exposed Europeans and their plants and animals to many competing organisms. Europeans had developed a high level of relative immunity to many germs. European plants and animals were tough, hardy and especially opportunistic. In contrast the biota of the isolated "New World," especially the Pacific Rim, had not been previously exposed to new competitors and was therefore relatively weak and unable to cope (Crosby 1986: 270–308).

While Crosby's work has been greatly influential on comparative historians of European settlement on the Pacific Rim, he has had less impact on country-specific writers. In particular Crosby has had relatively little effect on Australian environmental historiography.[1] This is probably due to three reasons. First, the impact of exotic introductions on the Australian environment had previously been explored by Australian writers, though not to the same analytical detail as Crosby. In particular Eric Rolls' *They all Ran Wild: The Animals and Plants that Plague Australia* (1969), which mainly focused on rabbit plagues, had become regarded as a classic of Australian history. Second, Crosby's broad comparative approach may not have been appreciated by Australian specialists. Indeed there is more space in *Ecological Imperialism* devoted to New Zealand than to Australia.[2] Third, Australia's environmental history may be too complex for Crosby's explanations. Some examples which are difficult to reconcile with Crosby's arguments include the fact that rabbit introductions initially failed and it took 80 years before they became pests and that European settlement led to increased koala and kangaroo populations and the replacement of grasslands by forests of indigenous trees (Barr and Cary 1992: 13–18; Flannery 1994: 212–5, 218–21; Griffiths 1992: 15; Rolls 1994: 23–33).

This chapter focuses on this third objection to Crosby's argument. It presents a bioregional case study of the clearance and settlement of the high-rainfall forests of Australia's Pacific coast. Here European farming methods led to *extreme* environmental degradation. However, in this case it was Australian plants and animals, rather than exotics, which grasped the opportunity presented. Indeed so enormous was the resilience of the Australian plants and animals, that in some cases European farming failed. In presenting this case study, it is not the intention to reject Crosby, but rather to argue for a modification of his argument.

Australia's high-rainfall forests

At the beginning of European settlement large areas of dense high-rainfall forest extended along Australia's Pacific Rim from Northern Queensland to Victoria and occupied much of Tasmania.[3] Predominantly wet sclerophyll (eucalyptus) forests with some rain-forests, the high-rainfall forests grew on the coastal fringe, rarely extending more than 150 miles inland. The topography covered by these forests included the narrow coastal plains, steeply gullied hill country, plateaus and tablelands, the gorges of the Great Escarpment and the Tasmanian Tiers, and the slopes of the Great Dividing Range. These forests received annual rainfall of at least 35 inches (and in some cases over 100 inches).

Despite a wide variation in types (usually based on climate, see Figgis 1989; Ashton and Attiwill 1994; Busby and Brown 1994; Webb and Tracey 1994), some common features of the dense high-rainfall forests were notable. They were dense and lush, in marked contrast to the far more open, "park-like" forests of the drier plains. In the high-rainfall forests the tightly packed trees were tall, generally 100 to 300 feet high, enormous in bulk and sometimes threw out massive buttress roots.[4] Beneath the main trees grew a very dense understorey (or scrub) of small trees, shrubs, ferns and vines, but no useful grasses.[5] As one pioneer described it,

> the scrub itself was, generally speaking, a dense growth of many kinds of trees – hazel, musk, blackwood, wattle, gum, saplings, etc., etc., – growing so thickly together as to present the appearance of a forest of bare poles, with foliage at the top and a ruck of undergrowth and rubbish in the bottom; while all through it grew a forest of very large eucalypt trees
>
> (SGPA 1972: 20–1)

These forests had developed through a long and complex process. When Australia broke away from Gondwanaland about 45 million years ago most of eastern Australia was covered in dense rainforests. However, northwards drift and periodic Ice Ages causing increasing aridity and more frequent bushfires led to a contraction and fragmentation of rainforests. The arrival of Aborigines about 100,000 years ago and their use of fire further exacerbated the trend. As rainforests retreated to sheltered sites they were supplanted by hardy, fire resistant eucalypts. By 1788 the Pacific coast was a sea of dense eucalypt forests with a scattering of rainforest islands (Flannery 1994: 224–36).

However, given the right conditions, rainforests could recolonize eucalypt forests. Rainforest trees have the ability to reproduce under a dense canopy, which eucalypts do not (and this is now seen as the chief difference between the two).[6] Recent archaeological studies in south-west Tasmania have indicated that about 10,000 years ago climatic warming led to rainforest replacing grasslands. As a result game diminished and Aborigines abandoned these areas. Flannery and Rolls have argued that European settlement and the cessation of Aboriginal burning practices have allowed the expansion of rainforests in New South Wales (Flannery 1994: 218–21; Rolls 1994: 23–4).[7] Forestry research in the commercially valuable Mountain Ash (*Eucalyptus regnans*) forests of Victoria has shown that the Mountain Ash must have severe fires to reproduce. If there are no fires, the Mountain Ash will die after 400 years and be replaced by rainforest trees from the understorey (Griffiths 1992: 58–63). Europeans saw the forests as ancient and static, little recognizing their capacity for change and adaptation.

The "Wet Frontier"

Initially settlers preferred the drier inland plains, with their abundant and valuable grasses, light tree coverage and absence of dense understorey. Up to the 1870s clearance and settlement of the forests was confined to a few small areas on the Pacific coast around Sydney and Hobart. However, in the 1870s, the availability of cheap land under the various Selection Acts of each colony, a boom in dairy prices and prolonged droughts in the inland encouraged increased settlement. Between 1880 and 1910 expansion into this new "Wet Frontier" reached its peak, with "rushes" of settlers into what were (sometimes erroneously) believed to be fertile forests. An example of one such rush occurred in 1886 at Beech Forest in the Otway Ranges of Victoria. A release of 200,000 acres for selection quickly attracted 1,500 applicants, with the best blocks having up to 10 applicants each (McIntosh 1988: 15; for a more detailed coverage of the expansion of the "Wet Frontier" see Frost 1997).

Settlement required immediate clearance of the dense forests. European farming, whether the growing of crops or pasture, could not take place in a forest. Trees shaded out European farm plants, got in the way of ploughs and livestock and harbored pests. Efficient, commercial farming required the removal of the forest environment. In framing the Selection Acts, colonial governments aimed to encourage cultivation, which they regarded as true farming and attempted to limit speculators, graziers and timber-cutters. Accordingly they demanded settlers live on their selections, cultivate a reasonable proportion and make improvements. Rigidly enforced, these conditions encouraged the rapid clearance of forests.

Indeed clearance (and even the planting of exotic trees) was counted and valued as part of the compulsory improvements.

Clearance methods

Economics and government policy required settlers to destroy the forest cover quickly and cheaply. This was achieved through the use of fire, using a slash-and-burn method either derived from North America or various European island colonies in the Caribbean Sea and Indian Ocean, though exactly how and by whom it was introduced is still unclear. In the wetter months the dense understorey was slashed with axes and brush-hooks. Small trees were chopped down and the larger ones simply killed by "ring-barking" (removing a band or ring of bark from the base of the tree). By not cutting down large trees or removing stumps a large area could be quickly cleared. Skilled axemen could rapidly clear large areas of small trees and understorey by using the "drive" or "nicking." The small trees were partially cut, then a large tree at the top of a slope was felled so it drove into the smaller trees, breaking them off at the cuts.

The roughly slashed forest was left to dry for a few months. Falling leaves, bark and branches from the dying ring-barked trees added to the slashed understorey. Towards the end of the drier months the dried vegetation was set alight. Settlers hoped for a "good burn" which would destroy as much of the timber, foliage and stumps as possible. Unfortunately sometimes a "bad burn" due to insufficient drying or the onset of early rains, resulted in too little destruction. After the burn varying quantities of timber still remained. These were laboriously "picked up," cut into smaller pieces, restacked and burnt, a process which could take weeks, even months. After the burns all that remained of the forest were the dead trunks and stumps of the larger trees and thick beds of ash. European farming could now commence. Grass or maize seed was sown directly into the mineral-rich ash, live-stock were introduced, houses, sheds and fencing erected.

Clearance destroyed vast expanses of forests very quickly. No records of the area cleared were kept, but in some regions it has been possible to estimate the extent. The "Great Forest" of South Gippsland which covered 1.2 million acres, was almost completely gone by 1910 (calculated from dimensions in SGPA 1972: 16). Similarly of the 180,000 acres of sub-tropical rainforest in the "Big Scrub" of Northern New South Wales, only 1,000 acres survived (Figgis 1989: 142). On the Atherton Tableland of Northern Queensland 183,000 acres out of 190,000 acres of rainforest were cleared (Figgis 1989: 31).

Progress on the Wet Frontier, especially in the first few years, was greatly affected by the environmental disturbance caused by forest clearance. Rainfall decreased. Topsoil was lost and floods became more severe. Crops were badly damaged by increasingly frequent frosts. Plant and animal pests became major problems. It is the pests that I am concerned with here and these can be divided into four groupings: forest regrowth, insects, plant-eating mammals and birds, and predators. Following Crosby's argument these pest should have been opportunistic exotics. Instead the opportunists were mainly indigenous.

Forest regrowth

The high-rainfall forests were well adapted to disturbance and fire. The eucalypt forests were prone to regular large-scale fires and some eucalypts, such as the mountain ash, would only reproduce after a severe fire. The rainforests were less prone or resilient to major fires, but had developed to cope with localized disturbances in their canopies due to storms or the collapse of aged trees. In all the high-rainfall forests, ecological disturbance, whether small or large, was quickly repaired by very fast growing "pioneer plants" (also known as "colonizing plants"). Triggered by the heat of a bushfire or increased light levels, the seed of the pioneer plants, which may have lain dormant for decades, germinated and grew rapidly, forming a new canopy.[8] Typically pioneer plants were short-lived, perhaps 20 to 40 years, but in that time the more slowly growing trees could become established under their protection (even young eucalypts, which would not grow under a full canopy, benefited from some protection).

In destroying the forests with fire, the settlers were unknowingly mimicking a natural process from which the forests were well adapted to recovering. They quickly found that, "the undergrowth flourished after the first fire" (Holland 1929: 158). Dogwood (*Cassinia aculeata*), was an "unsightly stick that sprawled around aimlessly . . . though not much in evidence in the virgin scrub, it came up sometimes after a burn almost like a crop of wheat" (SGPA 1972: 24). Other prolific pioneer plants included hazel pomaderris, blanketwood, blackwood wattle, pencilwood, wiregrass, native bracken, stinging trees, lawyer vines, stinkweed and sword grass (for Victoria see: Collett 1994: 139; Houghton 1984: 10; Legg 1992: 160; SGPA 1972: 24–30, 111; Wilde 1988: 47; for Tasmania see: Skemp 1952: 70, 82; Stokes 1969: 132; for New South Wales see: Henderson 1980: 449; McFarlane 1980: 4 and for Queensland see: Birtles 1978: 25, 34; Bryde 1921: 65–7, 94–5).

After the long and labor-intensive clearance of the forests for crops and pasture, settlers found that, "without constant attention a new growth of scrub soon makes headway, and if neglected, covers the land with more impenetrable thickets than before" (VRC 1899–1901: 7).

Insects

The high-rainfall forests were home to enormous numbers of insects. Indeed, trees and plants had developed efficient methods of survival, such as rapid growth and the generation of immense numbers of seeds, in order to cope with the armies of seed- and leaf-eating insects. Many high-rainfall forest plants contained toxins in their new growth in order to protect themselves against insects. In contrast, introduced plants had no such defence, a phenomenon noted by settlers as early as the 1820s (Cunningham 1966: 106; Williams 1993: 34). In a pattern repeated throughout the newly established settlements in the high-rainfall forests, within two or three years of clearance, crops were attacked by plagues of insects and in particular, caterpillars.

F. Elms, a settler in South Gippsland, recorded, "the grasshopper . . . regularly every Autumn devoured and laid bare the grass paddocks" (SGPA 1972: 38). Albert Nicholas had purchased and sown the finest quality seed of English rye-grass. Within three months it was eight inches high, "but later on the caterpillars came in millions, and not a green blade of grass was to be seen after them" (South Gippsland 1972: 96; and for similar stories see Hartnell 1974: 48–9). Frank Dodd found that after nine months of farming the destruction of pasture by caterpillars forced him to sell all his cattle for less than he had paid for them (SGPA 1972: 136). And another South Gippsland settler, T.J. Coverdale, recalled:

the scourge of caterpillars was very bad, recurring for several years, just at the season when the cattle should be topped off [fattened]. I have seen a beautifully green paddock eaten out and left bare in 48 hours. And I have

seen the caterpillars so thick against a big log that had
stopped their march, that you could easily have taken a
shovel and filled a barrow in short time. After these came
the Winter grubs that ate off the grass below the ground,
necessitating sowing most of the land again.

(SGPA 1972: 114–5)

In West Gippsland one family suffered from caterpillar plagues
for six consecutive years (Wilde 1988: 62). On the Atherton
Tableland selection commenced in 1882 and in 1884 and 1886
maize crops were destroyed by caterpillars (Birtles 1982: 42).
Similar attacks were recorded in the Heytesbury Forest, which
was to the west of the Otways (Fletcher 1985: 148), North-
West Tasmania (Stokes 1969: 132, 136) and Central Gippsland
(Adams 1978: 56).

Crop-eating birds and mammals

New clearings and their crops also provided a tempting food
supply for forest birds and mammals. In South Gippsland, "the
scrub surrounding the little clearings was alive with wallabies that
wrought great damage to the farmers' grass" (Holland 1929: 158).
"In a small clearing they would eat the grass out. At dusk they
would emerge from the scrub on all sides and feed there till
daylight, then disappear into the bush" (SGPA 1972: 34). In
the Otways the native bush rat was a major destroyer of crops
(*Colac Herald* 1886). In Northern Tasmania settlers were limited
to growing potatoes,

for there was little hope of doing much in the way of
wheat and oat growing, on small patches of land sur-
rounded by scrub which harboured opossums, wallabies,
bandicoots, and other vermin, that ate down the cereals as
fast as they grew.

(Fenton 1964: 57)

In Northern New South Wales and Southern Queensland, clearance led to plagues of birds (cockatoo, parrot and lorikeet) and
mammals (bandicoot, flying fox, wallaby and brushpossum) feasting
on newly planted crops (Frith 1977: 12; Pfeffer 1991: 45; Sorenson
1911: 191). In the Clarence River Valley of New South Wales,

The maize that was planted in the day would be visited by bandicoots at night ... When the plants appeared above ground the paddymelons [wallabies] and native companions [large birds] came on the scene. The former devoured the growing maize like cattle and as their visits were at night they were difficult customers to deal with. The native companions ... were very destructive and one of those birds would soon destroy an acre of maize. ... [When] the maize began to cob ... the cockatoos, parrots, redbills and opossums took up the running. ... The cockatoos preferred the maize when the grain was soft and one bite from their strong bills was sufficient to leave the grain exposed. With some hundreds in a field it is easy to understand what destruction would take place even in a couple of minutes as once the husk protecting the grain is cut through the first showers of rain will speedily destroy the whole cob or ear.

(McFarlane 1980: 46–7)

On the Atherton Tableland, Alf Davis noted in his diary,

Bandicoots brought [dug] the seed up and wallabies would eat off the young grass. All paddocks had to be wire-netted in ... When the corn [maize] was about ripe the white cockatoos would come in flocks to eat it. They took a lot of your time keeping off it. One year we had a plague of white tail rats. You could go around of a night with a hurricane lamp and a stick knocking them off the corn cobs.

(Allen 1990: 20; see also Birtles 1982: 52)

Predators

The introduction of European livestock provided an increased food supply for native predators which still lurked in the uncleared forest. In South Gippsland eagles and dingoes indirectly forced farmers to abandon sheep. Sheep, especially the lambs, could only be protected at night by being locked in high-fenced yards. However, in the wet climate the yards were perpetually muddy and the sheep contracted foot rot (SGPA 1972: 114, 261). In Southern Queensland dingoes, hawks and tiger cats (spotted tail quolls) feasted on introduced poultry (Pfeffer 1991: 45).

179

While Tasmania had no dingoes, it had a wide range of native carnivores, including the thylacine (Tasmanian Tiger or marsupial wolf), Tasmanian devil and native cats (quolls).[9] All of these lived in dense scrub, but tended to hunt nocturnally in lightly treed clearings. When Europeans first arrived in Tasmania the carnivores were scarce. However, as settlers cleared forests and introduced livestock they increased the hunting habitat and food supply of these animals and their numbers multiplied. Most damaging was the elusive, wolf-like thylacine, which quickly developed a taste for sheep. In 1886 it was claimed that these animals killed 50,000 sheep annually, and on one property 700 out of 2,000 sheep were taken in one year (Guiler 1985: 18–19).

Exotics

In comparison, exotic weeds and pests were underachievers. Inkweed was probably the most successful (Birtles 1982: 52). In South Gippsland, J. Western noted that the thistle was only a pest for a few years, whereas forest regrowth was more difficult to get rid of (SGPA 1972: 314). Ragwort and blackberries were not a nuisance until after World War I (Collett 1994: 212–3). For a long period settlers thought that South Gippsland was too wet for the rabbit. It was only after severe fires in 1898 that the rabbit penetrated the region (SGPA 1972: 197). It was not till 1904 that rabbits became a problem in Morwell in Central Gippsland (Legg 1992: 165). On the Atherton Tableland the tropical climate kept the rabbit out altogether and the European rat did not devastate crops until 1897, 15 years after the area was settled (Birtles 1982: 55).

Secondary clearance

Forest clearance unleashed plagues of indigenous pests. To survive, settlers had to put aside the tasks of farm establishment and engage in what I term "secondary clearance." The plants and animals of the forests had to be cleared time and time again and nothing could be done to combat insect plagues. The costs were crippling. Mary Fullerton recalled of her youth in Gippsland, "I heard the wise ones say later that the Government charged them a pound an acre for the land, and nature added an extraction of forty" (Fullerton 1921: 43).

In South Gippsland, T.J. Coverdale found that,

After two or three years, a great deal of the scrub began to come again, especially on clearings that had been lightly stocked. The swordgrass was the worst trouble, and it might cost anything from five to thirty shillings an acre to hack it out with mattocks. On well-stocked clearings the second growth did not trouble much at first, but practically the whole of the land had to be gone over again sooner or later for this purpose.

(SGPA 1972: 111)

The initial clearing cost 25 to 40 shillings per acre, so secondary clearance could cost nearly as much. The high cost was because secondary clearance was often more difficult and time-consuming than the first. There were no large trees to drive into the new growth, nor were there large masses of tinder-dry vegetation to aid in burning. Some pioneer plants had to be dug out rather than burnt or cut.

Not surprisingly many pioneer plants had developed defence mechanisms against further disturbances. Dogwood leaves contained a powerful irritant and swordgrass leaves caused severe cuts (SGPA 1972: 24–5). In Tasmania stinkwood regrowth poisoned grazing cattle (Skemp 1952: 82). On the Atherton Tableland a common pioneer plant was the infamous Queensland Stinging Tree, which made secondary clearance an appalling task. Charles Bryde was laid up in bed for a week after accepting a contract to clear a patch,

There must be a frightfully deadly poison in the plant. The bare inhalation of the smell of the fresh-cut stalks makes you vomit, and brings blood from the nose in a few minutes, while the least touch on any part by the bush causes agonising pain, which lasts for weeks sometimes.

(Bryde 1921: 95)

The burden of secondary clearance fell heavily on those selectors with little capital. They were less likely to have sufficient livestock to keep regrowth manageable, or afford to pay for the additional labor. Many worked elsewhere as seasonal workers in order to make payments on their selection. In their absence the forest reclaimed their clearings. On marginal farming land, secondary clearance costs tipped the balance towards abandonment. One estimate for South Gippsland was that out of 450,000 acres cleared by the 1920s, 150,000 acres were abandoned and a further 160,000 acres neglected and overgrown (Webb 1966: 183). In the valleys of East Gippsland 135 selections covering 50,000 acres were abandoned and only those selectors on the river flats survived (Woodgate *et al.* 1994: 46).[10] In the early 20th century governments reallocated abandoned lands for Closer, Empire and Soldier Settlement schemes[11] creating a second round of clearance, regrowth and failure (Legg 1992: 168–70).

In some regions land was saved from abandonment by the use of "clearing leases." The term is misleading, for the land had often already been cleared, perhaps "maintenance lease" is more accurate. Newcomers were leased farms at generous rates, often paying little or no rent for the first four or five years. In turn they were required to control regrowth and perhaps even continue clearing. While such arrangements provided little income to the land-owners, it did prevent their assets from reverting to forest (Birtles 1982: 39–41, 53; Fenton 1964: 58; Wilde 1988: 65).

A variety of costly practices were developed to cope with crop-eating birds and mammals. On the Atherton Tableland, selectors lit and tended fires all night in order to keep flying foxes out of orchards (Bryde 1921: 99), and others spent their nights in their fields clubbing white-tailed rats (Allen 1990: 20). The necessity of being close to their crops at night led to the abandonment of an experimental village settlement, where it had been intended that the selectors live close together in a village and walked to their holdings (Allen 1990: 4). In the Heytesbury Forest wallaby damage led farmers to build wire-netting fences, combine in shooting drives, keep dogs, set snares, and employ children to chase them off (Fletcher 1985: 277). In South Gippsland three trappers caught 1,500 wallabies in one winter (Hartnell 1974: 48), and in Central Gippsland selectors combined to kill large numbers of wallabies in special drives (Adams 1978: 20).

In Tasmania, the Van Diemen's Land Company offered a bounty for thylacines which was twice that for wild dogs and between 1840 and 1910 employed a special thylacine trapper, known as the "tiger man." At its Woolnorth property on 10 out of 35 days in winter 1897 all work was abandoned as all hands were sent out into the scrub to capture or scare away thylacines stalking the flocks (Guiler 1985: 15–28, 95–7).

Secondary clearance of the thylacines was very difficult and expensive. Nocturnal and adept at using the scrub as cover, thylacines were rarely seen. Shooting parties and drives were ineffective. Thylacines were large enough to kill or frighten off most dogs. Poisoned baits failed as the thylacine only eats what it has killed. Only skilled trappers could hope to catch them and their efforts had little effect on numbers. Rather trappers probably just "harvested" surplus numbers without reducing the core population (in much the same way as rabbit-trapping had little effect). Instead the disappearance of the thylacine came about without human intervention. Around 1905 their numbers were devastated by a distemper-like epidemic (Guiler 1985: 28).

As settlers quickly realized that the bird and animal pests lived in the scrub, clearing as much of the scrub as possible was an effective way of reducing their damage. This is probably one of the major reasons why settlers engaged in excessive clearing and did not leave patches of forest undisturbed to protect watercourses or as woodlots. Settlers also lobbied strongly for government State Forests and reserves to be opened for settlement on the grounds that they harbored animals which ate their crops (Adams 1978: 111; Collett 1994: 129; Henderson 1980: 449; NSW 1908: 679).

A modified Crosby thesis

European settlement in the high-rainfall forests led to increased numbers of plant and animal pests. However, these were indigenous, not exotic. The Australian high-rainfall forests were not weak and fragile, as so often portrayed. Rather they were resilient, highly adaptable ecosystems. They had survived and adapted to Ice Ages, climatic change, increased fire frequency and aboriginal land-use patterns. The plants and animals were well adapted to environmental disturbance, particularly fire. Indeed, environmental disturbance was usually the trigger for reproduction.

The response of the Australian biota threatened to overwhelm the settlers. Having engaged in the monumental task of clearing the forest once, they found they had to clear the plants and animals again and again. On marginal land the cost was too great and farms were abandoned. On better land the settlers persevered.

This secondary clearance created the opportunity for exotic plants and animals to establish themselves and often eventually become pests. Time and time again the settlers cleared the land. Realizing that the standing forest harbored further pests, the settlers strove to clear all remnants. In order to tame the wilderness, exotic plants and animals were introduced and nurtured. Ragwort and blackberries, which were to be the great scourges of the Wet Frontier after World War I, were first grown as garden plants. When they initially began to spread the settlers were unconcerned, it was a sign of their success in "Europeanizing" the landscape.

In the twentieth century, the exotics became the great pests. However, this was mainly because so many resources had been devoted to fighting indigenous plants and animals. That ongoing battle gave the exotics their opportunity.

Notes

1 For example, Crosby was not included in the bibliography of Tim Flannery's controversial *The Future Eaters: An Ecological History of the Australasian Lands and People* (1994). Yet Flannery's central thesis, that the arrival of Aborigines in prehistoric Australia, Maoris in New Zealand and Europeans in Australia initiated environmental crises and extinctions is very close to Crosby's arguments. Crosby is also not mentioned in the bibliography of two major environmental histories – Bolton 1992, and Barr and Cary 1992.

2 Australian historians concerned with broad comparative history have tended to be far more appreciative of Crosby. Some examples are Jones *et al* 1993: 173, and Grove 1995: 78.

3 Dense high-rainfall forests also occurred in south west Western Australia. However, as their clearance for agriculture mainly took place after World War I they are not considered here.

4 Only the Californian Redwood (which also grows in high-rainfall forests) is taller than the Mountain Ash.

5 New settlers were often confused by the common description of these immense forests as scrub (SGPA 1972: 263). At first the term scrub only applied to the understorey, but over time came to be applied to the whole forest.

6 Botanically, eucalypt forests, no matter how wet they may be, are not classified as rainforests. Rainforests are characterized by closed canopies usually consisting of a wide variety of tree species. Eucalypt forests have a more open canopy consisting almost entirely of eucalypts, though the understorey may contain many rainforests species. All rainforest trees can reproduce under the canopy, eucalypts need a disturbance in the canopy, typically caused by fire. In Australia the same high-rainfall environment suits rainforest or eucalypts.

7 This is an area which needs further study. Some of the contemporary accounts on which these arguments were based may be unreliable or open to other interpretations.

8 Pomaderris seed remains viable after 100 years and young Mountain Ash grows at over six feet a year (Ashton and Attiwill 1994: 176, 182).

9 Thylacines and Tasmanian devils had inhabited the mainland, but at the time of European settlement were extinct. The commonly held (though entirely unconvincing) explanation of their extinction there is

that they were unable to cope with the Aboriginal introduction of dingoes *c*.5,000 years ago. However, in Tasmania the rapid spread of feral dogs in the nineteenth century appeared to have little impact upon thylacines and devils.

10 Further research needs to be done into these regions where farming was almost totally abandoned. Unfortunately as settlers left, records were lost or dispersed and with little population today there is no impetus for published histories or historical societies. As always history is written by the victors.

11 Following the success of dairying and irrigated crops on small farms in the 1890s, governments developed policies of Closer Settlement – purchasing large estates, sub-dividing them equally and selling them on credit to family farmers. Unfortunately the temptation was to reduce costs by using poorer quality government-owned forest land rather than buying cleared farmland. After World War I these schemes were extended to returned soldiers and British immigrants (Empire Settlers), with disastrous results.

References

Adams, J. (1978) *So Tall the Trees: A Centenary History of the Southern Districts of The Shire of Narracan*. Trafalgar: Shire of Narracan.

Allen, Meryl (ed.) (1990) *Yungaburra District Centenary, 1890 to 1990: The Pioneers Speak*. Yungaburra: Centenary Committee.

Ashton, D.H. and Attiwill, P.M. (1994) [1981] "Tall open-forests," in R.H. Grove, (ed.), *Australian Vegetation*: pp. 157–96. Cambridge: Cambridge University Press.

Barr, Neil and Cary, John (1992) *Greening a Brown Land: The Australian Search for Sustainable Land Use*. Melbourne: MacMillan.

Birtles, Terry (1978) *Changing Perceptions and Response to the Atherton–Evelyn Rainforest Environment, 1880–1920*. Townsville: James Cook University.

Birtles, Terry (1982) "Trees to burn: settlement in the Atherton–Evelyn Rainforest, 1880–1900," *North Australia Research Bulletin* 8: 31–86.

Bolton, G.C. (1992) *Spoils and Spoilers: A History of Australians Shaping their Environment*. Sydney: Allen and Unwin.

Bryde, C.W. (1921) *From Chart House to Bush Hut: Being the Record of a Sailor's 7 Years in the Queensland Bush*. Melbourne: Champion.

Busby, J.R. and Brown, M.J. (1994) [1981] "Southern rainforests." in R.H. Grove, (ed.), *Australian Vegetation*: pp. 131–156. Cambridge: Cambridge University Press.

Colac Herald, (1886) 25 May. A ride through the Gellibrand Forest.

Collett, Barry (1994) *Wednesdays Closest to the Full Moon: A History of South Gippsland*. Melbourne: Melbourne University Press.

Crosby, Alfred W. (1986) *Ecological Imperialism: The Biological Expansion of Europe, 900–1900*. Cambridge: Cambridge University Press.

Cunningham, Peter (1966) [1827] *Two Years in New South Wales*. Sydney: Angus & Robertson.

Fenton, James (1964) [1827] *Bush Life in Tasmania Fifty Years Ago*. Devonport: Richmond.

Figgis, Penny (ed.) (1989) *Rainforests of Australia*. Sydney: Ure Smith.

Flannery, Tim (1994) *The Future Eaters: An Ecological History of Australasian Lands and People*. Sydney: Reed.

Fletcher, Jack (1985) *The Infiltrators: A History of the Heytesbury 1840–1920*. Cobden: Shire of Heytesbury.

Frith, Harry (1977) "The destruction of The Big Scrub." in *Rainforests*: pp. 7–12. Sydney: NSW National Parks and Wildlife Service.

Frost, Warwick (1997) "Farmers, government and the environment: the settlement of Australia's 'Wet Frontier', 1870–1920," *Australian Economic History Review* 37 (1): 19–38.

Fullerton, Mary (1921) *Bark House Days*. Melbourne: Endacott.

Griffiths, Tom (1992) *Secrets of the Forest: Discovering History in Melbourne's Ash Range*. Sydney: Allen & Unwin.

Grove, Richard H. (1995) *Green Imperialism: Colonial Expansion, Tropical Island Edens and the Origins of Environmentalism, 1600–1860*. Cambridge: Cambridge University Press.

Guiler, Eric (1985) *Thylacine: The Tragedy of the Tasmanian Tiger*. Melbourne: Oxford.

Hartnell, Ross (1974) *Pack-Tracks to Pastures: A History of Poowong District*. Poowong: Centenary Committee.

Henderson, Krimhilde (1980) *Farms and forests on the Dorrigo: an historical-ecological study of land use conflict in Northern New South Wales*. PhD Thesis: University of California, Berkeley.

Holland, J.E. (1929) "Korumburra District in the early days," *The Victorian Historical Magazine* XIII: 154–63.

Houghton, Norm (1984) *Beech Forest: A Century on the Ridge*. Beech Forest: Centenary Committee.

Legg, Stephen (1992) *Heart of the Valley: A History of the Morwell Municipality*. Morwell: City of Morwell.

Jones, Eric, Frost, Lionel and White, Colin (1993) *Coming Full Circle: An Economic History of the Pacific Rim*. Melbourne: Oxford University Press.

McFarlane, John (1980) *A History of the Clarence River District 1837–1915*. Maclean: Clarence Press. (MS written c1910–1915).

McIntosh, Ida (1988) *Forest, Lake and Plain: The History of Colac, 1888–1988*. Shire of Cloac, Melbourne.

NSW, Royal Commission of Inquiry on Forestry (1908) "Minutes Part II," *NSW Parliamentary Papers 1908 (1)*.

Pfeffer, C.K. (1991) *The Fassifern Story: A History of Boonah Shire and Surroundings to 1989*. Boonah: Shire Council.

Rolls, Eric (1969) *They All Ran Wild: The Animals and Plants that Plague Australia*. Sydney.

—— (1994) "More a new planet than a new continent," in Stephen Dovers (ed.) *Australian Environmental History: Essays and Cases*: 22–36. Melbourne: Oxford University Press.

Skemp, John Rowland (1952) *Memories of Myrtle Bank: The Bush-Farming Experiences of Rowland and Samuel Skemp in North-Eastern Tasmania 1883–1948*. Melbourne: Melbourne University Press.

Sorenson, Edward (1911) *Life in the Australian Backblocks*. London: Whitcomb & Tombs.

SGPA (South Gippsland Pioneers' Association) (1972) [1920] *The Land of the Lyre Bird: A Story of Early Settlement in the Great Forest of South Gippsland*. Korumburra: Shire of Korumburra.

Stokes, H.J.W. (1969) *North-West Tasmania 1858–1910: The Establishment of an Agricultural Community*. PhD Thesis: ANU.

VRC (Victoria, Royal Commission on State Forests and Timber Reserves) 1899–1901. First Progress Report. The Otway Forest: its resources, management and control. *Victorian Parliamentary Papers 1899–1900 (4)*.

Webb, Leonard (1966) "The rape of the forests," in A.J. Marshall, (ed.), *The Great Extermination: A Guide to Anglo-Australian Cupidity, Wickedness and Waste*: pp. 156–205. Melbourne: Heinnemann.

Webb, L.G. and Tracey, J.G. (1994) [1981] "The rainforests of northern Australia," in R.H. Grove (ed.), *Australian Vegetation*: pp. 87–130. Cambridge: Cambridge University Press.

Wilde, Sally (1988) *Forests Old Pastures New: A History of Warragul*. Warragul: Shire of Warragul.

Williams, Geoff (1993) *Hidden Rainforests: Subtropical Rainforests and Their Invertebrate Biodiversity*. Sydney: New South Wales University Press.

Woodgate, P.W. *et al.* (1994) *A Study of the Old-Growth Forests of East Gippsland*. Melbourne: Department of Conservation and Natural Resources.

9

ECONOMIC MOTIVATIONS FOR CHINA–UNITED STATES RAPPROACHMENT IN 1971

Lori Warner

Introduction

The U.S. trade embargo, imposed on the People's Republic of China (PRC) in 1950, was eventually dismantled by Richard Nixon in 1971. While the motivation for both the imposition of this embargo and for its eventual demise are widely considered to be *political* in nature, this chapter argues that *economics* also played a significant role in both countries' decisions to seek rapproachment.

The chapter begins with a brief history of the embargo, followed by an overview of China's traditional adherence to policies of self-reliance and a discussion of the economic motivations for its willingness to negotiate with the U.S. in ending the embargo. The various economic incentives for U.S. interest in renewing trade relations with the PRC follow, and a summary is then offered.

A brief history of the West's embargo against mainland China

In the spring of 1949, a few weeks after the Communist coup in Czechoslovakia, the U.S. Congress passed the Export Control Act. While *wartime* control over U.S. exports and their destination was, from the Spanish–American War of 1898 until the end of World War II, given to the President of the United States, the Export Control Act was the first comprehensive *peacetime* system of export controls. This Act established the Commodity Control List (also called the Positive List) which continues to this day to dictate U.S. trade policy with Communist countries. The Act gave the President the power to regulate the export and re-export of U.S.-origin goods, regardless of their destination, if protection of the country's national security warranted it. In early 1950, even before the Korean War had begun, China was placed in the same country group as the Soviet Union, with both facing severe restrictions on their import of U.S.-produced goods.

But trade controls, unilaterally imposed, have inherent problems of enforcement. Recognizing this, the United States early on sought international cooperation in restricting trade with China. In 1949, the U.S. and 13 of its NATO allies, plus Japan, had formed the Paris Coordinating Committee (COCOM), agreeing to withhold a wide array of strategic goods from the USSR and eastern Europe. In March 1950, the U.S. persuaded COCOM to apply the same strategic list of controls against Communist China.

China officially entered the Korean War by sending its army (200,000 "volunteers") across the Yalu River in November 1950. In response to this action, President Truman placed China in Group Z (the most restrictive of the Commodity Control List groups), which meant that any direct or indirect exports to China required written authorization from the Department of Commerce. In addition, U.S.-registered ships and planes were prohibited from calling at Chinese ports or carrying any China-bound cargo. The following month, the Treasury Department also blocked all assets owned by citizens of mainland China and prohibited all *imports* from that country. The infamous "China differential" was in place: China was receiving harsher treatment with respect to trade with the United States than were the countries in the Soviet bloc.

In 1951, the U.S. pursued yet another strategy for gaining international support in its economic warfare against China. In October, Representative Laurie Battle sponsored the Mutual Defense Assistance Control Act, commonly referred to as the "Battle Act," which sought to enlist the cooperation of other friendly countries not already a part of COCOM. The Act cited a long list of items (similar to the COCOM list) to be banned from Communist recipients and stated that no aid was to go to any country unless it too embargoed these goods in its trade with China (Lee 1972: 45).

In February 1951, the United Nations adopted the U.S. draft resolution charging China with having engaged in aggression in

Korea, and on May 17 recommended that every UN member apply a strategic embargo on Communist China and North Korea covering such goods as arms and ammunition, atomic energy materials, petroleum, transportation materials of strategic value, and various items useful in the production of implements of war. Soon after, some 45 governments notified the UN that they were applying the embargo. In the autumn of 1952, following the UN resolution, the COCOM nations formed the China Committee (CHINCOM) to coordinate their embargo against China. The China restrictions were much harsher than those imposed on the Soviet bloc, and by the end of the Korean War, over 400 categories of goods (twice as many as applied to the Soviet bloc) were restricted (Lee 1972: 44). The "China differential" had widened, and its adoption was expanding to include more and more of the free world.

Surprisingly, the embargo did not significantly diminish the total volume of China's trade with the outside world. By 1954, trade had already reattained its pre-embargo level, and it continued to grow at unprecedented rates for the remainder of the decade. What did change, however, was the composition of China's trading partners. As shown in Table 9.1, China's trade with Communist countries increased from approximately 29 percent of its total trade volume in

Table 9.1 China's trade with Communist and non-Communist countries, 1950–74 (millions of U.S. $)

Year	Communist countries ($)	Non-Communist countries ($)	Percent of trade with Communist countries
1950	350	860	28.9
1952	1,315	575	69.5
1954	1,735	615	73.8
1956	2,055	1,065	65.8
1958	2,380	1,385	63.2
1960	2,620	1,370	65.6
1962	1,410	1,265	53.7
1964	1,100	2,120	34.1
1966	1,090	3,155	25.6
1968	840	2,945	22.1
1970	860	3,480	19.8
1972	1,275	4,725	21.2
1974	2,435	11,645	17.2

Source: CIA 1976–77.

1950 to 74 percent in 1954 due, in a large part, to the West's trade embargo.

After the Korean Armistice, many Western countries immediately began negotiating with the Chinese on trade issues. As early as 1953, Japan and western Europe, for example, began allowing private traders to travel to China, and many of these missions resulted in unofficial agreements to trade in non-strategic, and even some strategic, goods (Lee 1972: 46). Then, on 30 May 1957, the United Kingdom announced that it would unilaterally abandon the "China differential" and base trade controls on "clear strategic grounds." Anything else, it said, would be economic warfare. While the U.S. officially vowed to keep the "differential," a sizable group in the Senate began advocating renewed trade with Communist China. President Eisenhower gave a press conference after the UK announcement in which he stated that he, too, saw no advantage to the U.S. in maintaining the "differential." In that speech, Eisenhower emphasized the economic advantages of trading with China, stating that " . . . the Yankee is a very fine trader and got to be a great country by trade" (Lee 1972: 47). Unfortunately, the political environment in the U.S. at this time was hostile toward U.S. overtures to any Communist country, and another 18 years would pass before the U.S. began reconciling with China. Over the next four years, most of the other COCOM countries also abandoned the "China differential," despite vigorous U.S. protest. By 1967, non-Communist countries had increased their trade with the PRC to 77 percent of China's total trade volume, while an isolated U.S. attempted unilaterally to enforce its statutes against the Chinese, frequently stepping on the toes of its allies in the process.

China's policies of self-reliance and modernization

China's foreign trade has never represented a significant portion of its GNP (the measure used frequently to gauge the importance of trade to a country). One China expert, John C. Hsu, for example, estimates that in the years between 1956 and 1977, China's foreign trade (imports plus exports) amounted to not more than four percent of its national product – well below that of other large developing countries (Hsu 1989: 1). Similarly, Richard Batsavage and A.H. Usack, in their report to Congress in 1972, estimated Chinese exports alone to be only two percent of China's GNP at that time (Batsavage and Usack 1972: 337). While

foreign trade was never significant according to traditional measures, it was nevertheless critically important to China at different
times in its development. For example, grain imports during the
acute agricultural crisis of 1960–1 helped prevent widespread
starvation, especially in cities, and imports of machinery, transport
equipment, complete plants and other capital goods hastened
China's modernization and technological progress, adding greatly
to its economic growth, particularly in the 1950s and again in the
early 1970s.

Changing trade policies in China, as well as changes in the
commodity composition of its trade and in its trading partners,
have, since the PRC's inception, reflected both shifting political
relations with foreign countries and shifting economic needs in
different phases of China's development process. Both China's
political relationship with other countries and its own economic
needs, on the other hand, were themselves strongly influenced by
its internal political climate.

It is important to bear in mind that Nixon's trip to China, and
the subsequent dismantling of the 21-year-old trade embargo, was
not a unilateral move – China's attitude, too, had to undergo
considerable change to allow it to be receptive to Nixon's overtures. Arthur Dudden, a renowned China expert, aptly described
the events of the early 1970s as follows: "Warily, the two angry
giants inched toward each other to reduce the tension between
them" (Dudden 1992: 265).

China's long-held affinity for self-reliance has been the subject
of countless analyses. The country's vast resource endowment and
its traditional belief in the flawless superiority of its civilization
have both been explored as explanations for its historic reluctance
to become a world trader (Eckstein 1977: 244). The country's
need for self-reliance as a *Communist* country has been examined, as
has the role played by Mao's personal history (Howe 1978: 134;
Hsu 1989: 1). Others have argued that greater emphasis should be
placed on how the actions of foreign powers have influenced the
extent of Communist China's isolation (Friedman 1975: 10–11).
The ever-changing political climate in post-revolution China,
however, has received the lion's share of attention when discussing
that country's choices regarding self-reliance (Heymann 1975:
Appendix I). While each of these examinations of China's notorious
insistence on self-reliance is relevant to the events surrounding the
reconciliation of China and the U.S. in the early 1970s, the last is
especially pertinent to this analysis.

Since the early 1950s, the evolution of China's development and its willingness to conduct foreign trade had been marked by sharp oscillations between two groups – the *radicals*, or so-called "Maoist ideologists," and the *moderates*, or the "conservative Liuist pragmatists," as this group was also called in the late 1960s. This somewhat oversimplified dichotomy is based, first and foremost, on each group's view of the appropriate level for China's trade with the West. (Table 9.2 reproduces an especially useful summary by Hans Heymann of the struggle between these two groups and the effect of that struggle on China's development and on its technology acquisition policy.) The radicals took a highly ideological stand, viewing economic relations with capitalist countries in terms of traditional Marxist theory. They believed that large-scale imports of foreign goods undermined the revolutionary will of the masses, rekindling a sense of inferiority caused by a century of humiliation at the hands of the West. The moderates, on the other hand, held a more pragmatic attitude. While mindful of the past, they were more willing to trade with the capitalists in order to transform China into a modern industrial state as quickly as possible. According to the moderates, China had little hope of moving from a weak, vulnerable, developing country without the import of technologically advanced investment goods from the West.

The Cultural Revolution (1966–9), with its extreme ethnocentricity, marked perhaps the peak of China's drive for self reliance. During this social upheaval, even the few remaining economic ties with the overseas Chinese were broken, leaving the mainland in a state of economic autarky. The effects of the Cultural Revolution upon government institutions in China were somewhat uneven. Some ministries, like those responsible for nuclear development and advanced scientific research, were almost untouched, while others, like the Ministry of Foreign Trade, were devastated. The Red Guards occupied the offices of the foreign ministry, destroyed the files, and brought China's international relations to a complete standstill during most of 1966 (Pye 1978: 315; Fairbanks 1992: 397).

Following the Cultural Revolution, China's policy-makers once again began to weigh the long-touted benefits of self-reliance against the more pragmatic benefits from trade, and out of this ongoing debate a new foreign policy, apparently made at the highest levels, was devised. As shown in Table 9.2 of Heymann (1975: 16–17), the post-Cultural Revolution era was characterized

Table 9.2 Phases in China's development and their reflections in technology acquisition, 1949–74

PERIOD I: RECONSTRUCTION

Development phase
- Rehabilitation of war-torn economy
- Heavy influx of Soviet industrial equipment

Technology acquisition
- 70% of trade with Soviet Bloc; USSR the main source of military technology and training (Korean War)

PERIOD II: FIRST FIVE–YEAR PLAN "LEANING TO ONE SIDE"

Development phase
- Maximum rate of fixed capital formation
- Priority for development of basic industry
- Forced draft industrialization, large-scale centrally planned integrated plants, Soviet style
- Acceptance of principle of developing local industry to serve local needs and using local resources, but mostly lip service in practice

Technology acquisition
- Massive Soviet aid in the form of complete plants and industrial systems
- Soviet support targeted on heavy industry sector

PERIOD III: 1958–1960 – GREAT LEAP FORWARD

Development phase
- Rejection of Stalinist model of industrialization in favor of Maoist mass mobilization and mass participation
- Proliferation of small-scale, inefficient local enterprises with "backyard" technologies
- Nurturing of local initiative and regional self-sufficiency

Technology acquisition
- Soviet turn-key projects begin to phase down in the face of mounting Sino-Soviet tension and Chinese resistance to foreign expertise
- Sudden withdrawal of Soviet assistance in Summer 1960 wrecks havoc

---

PERIOD IV: 1961–1965 – GREAT CRISIS AND READJUSTMENT

Development phase
- Economic crisis forces a shift of priority to agriculture
  – Return to Liuist approach: centralized planning by professionals at national and provincial levels and return to economic rationality (many Great Leap plants closed)
- Rural industrialization pushed vigorously

Technology acquisition
- Technology import resumes on a small scale; few package plants; stress on self-reliance; technology source shifted to Western Europe and to Japan

---

PERIOD V: 1966–1969 – CULTURAL REVOLUTION	
Development phase	*Technology acquisition*
• Reversion to Maoist principles, pitting masses against technical and managerial elites	• Imports of foreign technology drastically curtailed, some plant purchases canceled, foreign contracts ruptured
• Worship of nativism and renewed pitting of "red' against "expert"	
• Destruction of party bureaucracy, sporadic economic disruption and some absolute decline in industrial output	

PERIOD VI: 1970–1974 POST-CULTURAL REVOLUTION	
Development phase	*Technology acquisition*
• Return to economic rationality; new wave of expansion	• Return to more vigorous technology import policy; emphasis on complete plants, diversification of sources, more liberal interpretation of self-reliance
• Shift in planning and decision-making to regional and provincial levels, and further development of decentralized industrial plants in outlying regions	
• Use of more advanced industrial centers to spread industrial systems into the hinterland	

Source: Heymann 1975: 16–17.

by a clear ascendancy of the pragmatists or moderates, with a new wave of expansion and a return to more vigorous technology import policies.

China's economic motivations for rapprochement

The explanations typically given for China's willingness to negotiate with the United States in the early 1970s are *political* in nature. However, as it emerged from the Cultural Revolution, China faced far more problems than just the need for an ally in its escalating conflict with the Soviets and a desire to gain international respectability. Economic growth had stagnated during the Cultural Revolution, foreign trade all but ceased, and several of China's key industries were in dire need of modernization.

In centrally planned economies, decisions concerning both the direction of the country's development and the role that foreign trade will play in that development, can change with a rapidity beyond anything experienced in a capitalist economy. Following the Cultural Revolution, China underwent just such a reorientation in its economic development, with dramatic repercussions for its trade with both Communist and non-Communist countries. As discussed above, the decision had been made to actively pursue trade with technologically-advanced nations, and plainly the United States would be an obvious choice for such economic relations. Perhaps the best way of determining how valuable a trading partner the United States would have appeared to the Chinese in the late 1960s is to compare the leading *imports* of the PRC and the leading *exports* of the U.S. at that time. In other words, did China in the early 1970s demonstrate a need for the types of commodities that the U.S. was then supplying to the international market? Such a comparison is shown in Table 9.3 (parts a,b, and c) and Table 9.4. What follows is a discussion of a few of those sectors where Chinese import needs were most likely to be met by U.S. comparative advantage.

The hypothesis that China was motivated by economic need in its negotiations with the United States also gains support by looking at how important a trading partner the United States eventually became for China *after* the embargo was removed. This can be ascertained by examining U.S. exports to China in

Table 9.3(a) Commodity composition of China's imports, 1966 and 1970 (percentage of total imports)

Commodity category	1966 (%)	1970 (%)
Food, beverages and tobacco	27.1	19.2
Crude materials, inedibles:	6.4	11.3
of which, textile fibers	8.0	5.4
Mineral fuels and lubricants	0.2	0.2
Animal and vegetable oils and fat	0.2	0.3
Chemicals:	12.6	15.5
of which, chemical fertilizers	7.1	7.5
Manufactured goods:	18.7	33.3
of which, metals and metal manufacturers	16.2	29.1
Machinery and transport equipment	19.1	15.1
Miscellaneous manufactures	2.4	1.3
Other	33.3	3.4

Source: Derived from data in the *Reports to Congress* by the U.S. Mutual Defense Assistance Control Administrator. Published by the U.S. Department of Commerce, 1973.

196

Table 9.3(b) The PRC's leading imports, 1969 and 1970 (millions of U.S. $)

Commodity	Percentage of total imports
Grain	13.5 ($540m total)
Chemicals:	16.0 ($640m total)
of which, fertilizer	10.8
Machinery and equipment	15.8 ($635m total)
Iron and steel	16.6 ($665m total)
Nonferrous metals	10.8 ($435m total)

Source: Derived from figures given in *People's Republic of China: An Economic Assessment* 1972: 353.

the years immediately following the Shanghai Communique. This is shown in Tables 9.5 and 9.6. Despite the various problems emanating from both sides of the Pacific (which are elaborated below), trade between the two countries blossomed after 1972, and often in just those areas that one would have predicted from examining pre-rapproachment trade patterns.

Technology and capital

As mentioned above, fluctuations in China's domestic production of certain goods undoubtedly impacted its need for specific imports at different times. China's machine-building industry is an obvious example of the country's overall economic plan influencing its interest in trading with the U.S. The Great Leap Forward had encouraged the widespread construction of many small, locally controlled, machine-building plants, but the decentralized planning and control of these small factories had, in many cases,

Table 9.3(c) The PRC's leading imports from the West, 1967 (percent of total imports from the West)

Commodity	Percentage
Cereals and preparations	18.3
Chemical fertilizers	5.4
Machinery and transport machinery	13.7
Ferrous and non-ferrous metals	23.2

Source: Feng-hwa Mah 1971: 199.

Table 9.4 Commodity composition of U.S. exports, 1969 and 1970
(percentage of total exports)

Exports	1969	1970
Food and animals:	10.00	10.20
of which grains and preparations	5.60	5.90
Crude materials (except fuel):	9.50	10.80
of which textile fibers	11.79	11.79
of which iron scrap	9.70	9.70
Mineral fuels and related materials	3.00	3.70
Chemicals:	9.00	9.00
of which manufactured fertilizers	.58	4.60
Machinery and transport equipment	43.70	42.00
of which transport equipment	38.00	34.60
Other manufactured goods	18.70	17.90
Firearms of war and ammunition	1.90	1.90
Other	3.20	4.20

Source: USBC 1970: 779–80; 1974: 786–7

encouraged haphazard location, poor construction, and shoddy production. Further, the small plants diverted scarce raw materials from China's modern industrial sector. The machine-building industry retrenched with the rest of the economy from 1961–3 and investment programs were narrowed to essential industries, with new emphasis given to the production of agricultural machinery, petroleum production, and military goods. Considerable dislocation again occured in the machine-building industry during the political turbulence of the Cultural Revolution. Despite these disruptions, however, China achieved substantial increases in its machine-building capacity in the late 1960s as orderly economic planning was re-established and the country engaged in a wide-ranging campaign to construct hundreds of small-, medium- and large-scale industrial projects throughout its remote interior regions. The fourth five-year plan, which began in 1971, included increased support for machine-building targeted at agriculture and basic industries such as mining, petroleum, chemicals, and electric power (Payne 1982: 249).

At the same time that China was expanding production capacity in its capital goods industry, it began a renewed push for modernization

Table 9.5 Commodity composition of China's imports from the U.S., 1974 (millions of U.S. $)

SITC nomenclature	Amount	% of total imports of goods	Other suppliers (% of total)
Wheat (041)	$291	30.6	Canada (42) Australia (23)
Corn (044)	121	100.0	
Beverages and tobacco (1)	3	75.0	Canada (25)
Oilseeds (22)	157	100.0	
Cotton (263)	205	96.6	East Africa (3.3)
Synthetic fibers (266)	2	2.1	Japan (86.3)
Iron and steel scrap (282)	14	100.0	
Animal and vegetable oils and fats (4)	8	25.0	Canada (18.7) Norway (37.5)
Chemicals (5)	509	.2	Japan (61) West Germany (13.9)
Organic chemicals (512)	5	4.0	Japan (40.1) West Germany (28.7)
Steel and iron (67)	3	.3	Japan (67) West Germany (21.8)
Non-electric machinery (71)	44	8.0	Japan (47.7) West Germany (14)
Electrical machinery (72)	7	7.0	Japan (44) West Germany (14)
Aircraft (734)	60	38.9	USSR (42) UK (16.2)
Technical instruments (86)	2	4.0	Belgium/Luxembourg (38) Japan (24)
TOTAL	$1,431 million*		

Source: Numbers taken from CIA 1975: 15.

Note:
* This represents 26.2% of China's total imports of $5451m for 1974.

which quickly exhausted its own machine-building capabilities. The spectacular opening of China that occurred in the late 1970s is generally thought to have begun following Chou En-lai's "Four Modernizations" speech in 1975. Surprisingly, the "Four

Table 9.6 Commodity composition of China's exports to the U.S., 1974 (millions of U.S. $)

Commodities	Amount of total ($)	% of total exports of goods	Other recipients (% of total)
Food and live animals	13	1.19	Hong Kong (55) Singapore (23)
Beverages and tobacco	3	6.80	Hong Kong (41) Singapore (18)
Crude materials (not fuels) of which, animal materials	16 10	2.77 62.50	Japan (45) Hong Kong (11)
Chemicals of which, rosins and turpentine	18 8	7.20 44.44	Japan (23) Hong Kong (18)
Manufactures of which, cotton fabrics of which, non-ferrous metals	43 26 11	4.80 60.04 25.50	Hong Kong (31) Japan (15)
Misc. manufactured articles of which, works of art	19 8	3.50 42.00	Japan (31) Hong Kong (20)
TOTAL	$175 million*		

Source: Numbers compiled from CIA 1975: 15.

Note:
* This represents 4.42% of China's total exports of $3,954m for 1974.

Modernizations' had been mentioned by name in another speech by Chou in 1964, at which time he outlined a thorough revamping of agriculture, industry, national defense, and science and technology. By 1969, Mao was willing to listen and had consolidated sufficient political power to begin the processes of modernization. Despite the ongoing revolutionary and anti-imperialist rhetoric of Jiang Qing and other radical leaders of the Cultural Revolution, Mao held sway and negotiations with the West were undertaken (Spence 1990: 629).

Several sectors of China's economy required immediate attention. Agriculture, which had responded well to the investments and new policies instituted in the 1960s, was approaching a point where further growth required both machinery and fertilizer supplies on a larger scale than could be provided domestically. Established industries like transport, iron and steel, and coal all required modernization, without which any one of these could seriously constrain the entire industrial sector. In addition, the remarkable growth of China's oil and petrochemical industries demanded a technological sophistication beyond anything that China could produce at that stage of its own development (Howe 1978: xxxi). Oil-recovery and processing is an especially capital-intense process, and China's so-called "Petroleum Group" is known to have actively lobbied for increased importation of advanced Western technology. In addition, aircraft, trucks, ships, dredgers, mining equipment, and general construction machinery were also mentioned frequently as China's top priorities for importation in the early 1970s.

In keeping with the drive for increased domestic production, at this time China was also importing so-called "turn-key" production plants or comprehensive equipment packages, complete with the technical data and advisory assistance to set them up. While much of the technology imports from the Soviet Union prior to 1960 came in the form of complete plants, the Chinese resorted to this form of acquisition only on a modest scale in the post-Soviet period. After the Cultural Revolution, however, plant acquisitions were expanded significantly. Between January 1972 and May 1974, for example, a total of 149 complete plants were imported by mainland China, as shown in Table 9.7. In 1973 alone, China negotiated contracts to import 37 plants (valued at $1,259 million) from the West (Batsavage and Davie 1978: 738).

China's renewed interest in capital imports is dramatically reflected in the trade figures for this period. In their report to the Joint Economic Committee of Congress, Richard Batsavage and John Davie reported a 12 percent increase in China's total

Table 9.7 PRC purchases of complete plants (by country). Contracts concluded January 1972 through May 1974

Country	Cost (US millions $)	Share percentage
Japan	1,029	44
France	540	23
West Germany	293	13
United States	208	8
Italy	103	4
Netherlands	90	4
USSR	25	1
Other	54	3

Source: Heymann 1975: 30.

import of capital goods in 1971, the year of Nixon's historic visit. Between 1971 and 1974, capital imports rose almost 200 percent (see Table 9.8). Obviously, China was relying heavily on imports of capital goods, predominantly from the West, in its drive for modernization following the Cultural Revolution.

In the 1950s, the import of foreign capital had accounted for an astonishing 40 percent of China's fixed investment. This ratio declined dramatically in the 1960s, but in the early 1970s imported capital had increased to approximately 10 percent of China's yearly additions to its capital stock. Given the comparative advantage of the U.S. in just those capital-intense products which the PRC

Table 9.8 Commodity composition of China's imports, 1970–4 (millions of U.S. $)

Commodity	1970	1971	1972	1973	1974
Foodstuffs of which:	395	320	510	1,080	1,600
grain	210	215	345	840	1,180
sugar	80	70	135	135	175
oilseeds	0	0	10	65	160
Consumer durables	15	15	20	40	45
of which, watches	5	5	5	20	20
Industrial supplies of which:	1,460	1,555	1,875	3,380	4,125
natural fibers	95	125	215	450	520
synthetic fibers	15	15	25	35	95
synthetic fabrics	45	40	40	110	170
paper and paper board	15	10	20	35	100
rubber	80	60	70	170	165
petroleum and products	NA	NA	NA	75	105
fertilizers, manufact.	140	135	145	210	220
plastic materials	30	20	35	50	125
metalliferous ores	NA	NA	NA	110	125
iron and steel	405	465	510	930	1,210
metal products	NA	NA	NA	85	125
Capital goods of which:	375	420	445	725	1,650
machinery	195	215	210	310	770
transport equipment	160	185	215	390	835
precision instruments	15	10	15	40	50
TOTAL	2,245	2,310	2,850	5,225	7,420

Source: Batsavage and Davie 1978: 738.

needed for its modernization, there would be an obvious interest on the part of the Chinese in renewing economic relations with the U.S.

Not surprisingly, the U.S. in the early 1970s was a significant source of high-tech *capital*. In 1971, for example, the U.S. was exporting 26 percent of the world's non-electric machinery, 30.1 percent of its transport equipment, and 24.5 percent of its electric machinery (*USBC 1974*: 715). Capital exports were also an important part of this country's total exports. The year before Nixon's visit, for example, "machinery and transport equipment' comprised 44.7 percent of total U.S. exports. In terms of its ability to meet China's specific needs for capital, in 1971 the U.S. exported $180 million worth of "agricultural equipment," while "tractors and parts" added another $695 million. Together these categories represented 9.97 percent of all U.S. exports of non-electrical machinery that year (*USBC 1974*: 797). Domestic production of oil-drilling equipment – another area where the U.S. was a significant supplier of the type of capital China desperately needed – totaled $962 million in 1971 (10.9 percent of total U.S. output of non-electric machinery). The same year, the U.S. produced $2,673 million in mining machinery and construction machinery (except tractors), while production of textile machinery (another type of capital of particular interest to the Chinese) totaled $672 million. Transportation equipment was considered critical to China's modernization in the early 1970s, and the U.S. was a significant supplier of railway vehicles, automobiles, trucks, and aircraft (as well as parts for all of these).

Once trade opened, some of the anticipated trade between China and the U.S. in capital goods came to pass. According to the CIA's *People's Republic of China: International Trade Handbook* (1975), a widely-cited source of US–China trade statistics, China's importation of "machinery and equipment" from the United States increased 87 percent (from $860 million to $1,610 million) between 1973 and 1974 alone. "Aircraft and parts" represented China's fourth largest import from the U.S. in 1973, comprising 8.4 percent of total U.S. exports to China that year (see Table 9.9). More importantly, U.S. aircraft and parts represented almost 39 percent of China's total imports of these goods by 1974. In addition, as shown in Table 9.7, the U.S. became the fourth largest exporter of complete plants to the PRC between 1972 and 1974.

Yet, three years after the trade embargo had been removed, the U.S. was providing only eight percent of China's imports of non-electric machinery; seven percent of its electric machinery; four

Table 9.9 Commodity composition of U.S. exports to China, 1973–4 (percentage of total U.S. exports)

Commodity	1973	1974
Wheat	41.5	28.6
Corn	19.1	11.7
Cotton	13.6	22.7
Aircraft and parts	8.4	9.3
Soybeans	7.5	16.9
Iron and steel scrap	3.3	1.6
Fertilizer	0.6	negligible
Telecommunication equipment	0.6	0.1
Other	5.4	9.2

Source: Avery and Clark 1975: 513, Table 4.

percent of its technical instruments; and none of its trucks or ships (see Table 9.5). Even U.S.–Chinese trade in aircraft was not as robust as one would have expected given China's need and U.S. expertise in this industry. The reason, of course, was that various types of aircraft were among those goods included on both the Commodity Control List and the COCOM list of strategic goods which the U.S. and its NATO allies had agreed not to export to Communist countries. The Chinese were also known to have wanted certain other transportation equipment, earth-moving equipment, and measuring and controlling instruments which were not listed among those categories allowed by Nixon's order relaxing trade barriers on exports to China 10 June 1971. Thus, while China did import some of the goods it required for modernization from the U.S., for the most part it continued to look to Japan and Western Europe as its main sources of industrial plants and equipment. Still, in 1969, China could have reasonably expected to import much of its needed technology from the world's leading industrialized country – the United States – once political relations were re-established.

Agriculture

While China's land mass is approximately the same size as the continental U.S., only 11 percent can be cultivated as farmland, compared to 22 percent in the U.S. (Groen and Kilpatrick 1978: 608). Feeding one-fourth of the world's population on seven percent of the world's arable land has been a continuous struggle for the PRC, and agriculture has always been a critical sector of the Chinese economy.

The severe food shortages associated with three successive years of poor harvests (caused by bad weather and the mismanagement associated with the Great Leap Forward) necessitated huge imports of grains from China's trading partners in the early 1960s. China went from a net exporter of grains (mostly rice) in 1960 to a net importer of grains (mostly wheat) in 1961 (Surls 1978: 655). While grain imports were first undertaken on an emergency basis, they soon became a normal part of the country's food supply, and huge imports of grains continued intermittently throughout the decade. Several reasons can be given for this. While China was considered very efficient in *rice* production (concentrated south of the Yangtze River), it had low productivity in *wheat*, the second most important grain grown in China. Furthermore, when China began its policy of "putting agriculture first" in 1962, emphasis was placed on rice production, with the result that wheat output did not re-attain the levels of the 1960s until 1976 (Groen and Kilpatrick 1978: 614). Also, because of poor transportation facilities, it was often less costly to ship wheat from abroad (say from Vancouver to Shanghai) than overland from China's remote surplus-producing province of Szechwan (Eckstein 1977: 236). Last, relentless population growth during this period required increased imports of cereals, fertilizers and other food-related raw products (Heymann 1975: 33). In the two years prior to Nixon's visit, yearly grain imports represented an average of 13.5 percent of China's total imports. The slow growth in China's grain output, coupled with a population increase of approximately 15 million people a year during the late 1960s, meant that grain imports would, in all likelihood, have been expected to continue at significant levels indefinitely.

As the world's principal "breadbasket" in the early 1970s, the U.S. would have been regarded as a potential low-cost supplier of grains to the PRC. As shown in Table 9.4, the U.S. exported $2,127 million in grains in 1969 ($2,956 in 1970), which represented 5.6 percent of total U.S. exports that year (5.9 percent in 1970). *Wheat* production in the U.S. represented 13 percent of the world's wheat output in 1970; its export of wheat represented 36.8 percent of world's total wheat exports. U.S. exports of *corn* (another important Chinese import), represented 50.5 percent of world corn exports (*USBC 1972*: 605). The U.S. also supplied 28.5 percent of the world's exports of unmanufactured *tobacco*. U.S. exports of *soybeans* represented a full 93.5 percent of world exports of soybeans in 1971. *Rice* was another of America's important farm exports (representing 23.8 percent of world rice exports), but China, of course, was itself an exporter of rice in the early 1970s. Undoubtedly, the United States, as one of the world's most efficient producers of agricultural products, would have to be considered a prized trading partner for China in 1971.

In the case of agricultural products, China's optimistic expectations concerning potential imports from the U.S. were fully realized. By 1973, *wheat* represented 41.5 percent of total U.S. exports to China, as shown in Table 9.9. The United States had become China's second largest supplier of wheat by 1974, supplying 30.6 percent of China's total import of this much-needed grain, as shown in Table 9.5. *Corn* represented 11.7 percent of total U.S. exports to China in 1974 and accounted for 100 percent of China's corn imports. By 1974, over half of China's total grain imports were coming from the United States, putting the U.S. ahead of both Canada and Australia. While in the early 1970s grains were far and away China's most important agricultural import from the U.S., other farm products were also exchanged between the countries. *Soybeans* represented 16.9 percent of total U.S. exports to China by 1974, while a full 75 percent of China's *beverages and tobacco* and 100 percent of its *oilseeds* came from the United States that year, as shown in Tables 9.5 and 9.9. In 1974, over 80 percent of U.S. exports to China were agricultural products.

Fertilizer

In the 1960s, China began to move away from the Soviet model of economic development. Using agricultural exports to earn the foreign exchange needed to import the capital required by heavy industry had begun to fail in the late 1950s prompting a reorientation of domestic investment funds, and, consequently, a change in the composition of China's imports. With the agricultural and economic crises of the late 1960s, China accelerated the redirection in its development strategy, with a much higher priority being placed on agricultural production and the improvement of those industries that supported agriculture. These included the machine-building industry mentioned above, and to an even greater extent, the fertilizer industry. In addition, the high yields of the miracle strains of wheat, rice, and other

206

grains that had been introduced throughout much of China could not be sustained without large inputs of fertilizer. While the PRC produced enormous amounts of natural and chemical fertilizers for domestic use, it was still heavily dependent on foreign sources for chemical fertilizer at the time the trade embargo was removed. China's annual import of chemical *fertilizers* rose from about one million tons in the early 1960s to more than seven million tons in the early 1970s (Eckstein 1977: 251).

During the mid-1960s large foreign fertilizer plants were imported by China to serve as models for the domestic heavy-machinery manufacturing sector. With the Cultural Revolution, however, came development policies favoring small chemical fertilizer plants, and hundreds were built throughout the country while the large-plant program was sharply curtailed. Following the Revolution, China found itself again in transition; while clearly needing fertilizer imports, it was increasingly intent upon becoming self-sufficient in an industry critical to feeding its people.

The U.S. at the same time, was a net exporter of manufactured fertilizer and would unquestionably have been seen as a valued supplier of a much-needed import for China when trade talks got underway. However, once trade between China and the U.S. did begin in earnest in the early 1970s, China did not experience the expected imports of fertilizer from the U.S., with fertilizer exports representing only 0.6 percent of total U.S. exports to China in 1973 (see Table 9.9). In part, this was a result of China's renewed attempts beginning around this same time to reduce its dependence on imported fertilizer (Eckstein 1977: 256). After a poor harvest of 1972, the Chinese leadership decided that the domestic programs were still not supplying enough fertilizer, and in a more moderate political climate, purchased 13 of the world's largest, most technically advanced ammonia–urea complexes over the next three years (Groen and Kilpatrick 1978: 614–15). Consequently, China's imports of manufactured fertilizers fell approximately 84 percent between 1974 and 1975 (Avery and Clarke 1978: 739; Eckstein 1977: 256).

Textiles and metals

Textiles have represented a significant export for the PRC since its inception. Textile exports were sustained at high levels throughout the agriculture crisis years (1960–2), for example, and played a crucial role at that time in supplying the foreign-exchange earnings required to finance China's grain purchases abroad. Throughout the latter 1960s and into the early 1970s, textile exports stabilized at approximately 20–5 percent of China's total exports. While the lion's share of China's textiles were made of silk (which it produced in abundance), *cotton* yarn, material, and clothing were also popular Chinese exports. The U.S., as a major exporter of raw cotton (an intermediate good used to produce textiles), would surely have been deemed an important trading partner for the PRC. In 1969, for example, the U.S. was producing approximately 20 percent of the world's cotton and exporting about 25 percent of its domestic output (USBC 1970: 602). As shown in Table 9.5, almost a quarter of U.S. exports to China were cotton in 1974. More importantly, this represented approximately 97 percent of China's total cotton imports that year (CIA 1975: 15).

Following the Cultural Revolution, when China was becoming increasingly outward looking with respect to trade, it still pursued many of the import-substitution policies begun during the Revolution. In particular, China sought to substitute the less costly semi-manufactures for imported end-items (or final goods) in the capital-goods industry (Eckstein 1977: 249). In particular, *metals* (iron and steel and non-ferrous metals) began to play a more important part in China's imports as it began to manufacture its own machinery and military wares. The U.S., in 1970, produced 37 percent of the world's aluminium, 24 percent of its copper, 20 percent of its iron, and 46 percent of the world's steel ingots. That year the U.S. exported $358 million in copper, $358 in aluminium, and $447 million in iron and steel scrap. The U.S. would undoubtedly have been considered a potential supplier of these metals for use as intermediate goods in China's machine-building industries.

While iron and steel were not major U.S. exports to China at the start of trade, such exports did represent 3.3 percent of total U.S. exports to China by 1972. On the other hand, 100 percent of China's imports of scrap iron and steel came from the U.S. in 1974, totaling $14 million that year alone (Eckstein 1977: 252).

The U.S. as an export destination

The dominant theme in China's trade relations in the 1950s and 1960s was a search for *export markets* to earn foreign exchange for its grain and technologically-advanced capital imports. While the

U.S. was clearly more important to China as a potential source of these imports, its large prosperous market must have been inviting to Chinese planners in the late 1960s. Once trade opened, the U.S. did purchase significant amounts of tin, bristles, feathers and down, works of art and antiques, raw silk, and rosin, as discussed in some detail below. However, China seems to have offered little the American consumer needed in the early 1970s, and China suffered large trade deficits with the U.S. throughout the early 1970s. In terms of economic motivations for China's rapprochement with the U.S., therefore, it was as a consumer of agricultural products and advanced technology for modernization that China would have welcomed Nixon in July 1971. And Chinese expectations concerning potential trade with the U.S. were well justified. Chinese–American trade flourished once Nixon began dismantling the embargo, as shown in Table 9.10. From virtually nothing in 1970, two-way trade skyrocketed to almost $1 billion in 1974. This seems especially significant in light of the myriad of impediments to trade which lingered between the two countries. The remaining antagonism which the Chinese felt towards the U.S. "two China" policy, its inability to win full diplomatic recognition from the U.S., the continued tariff discrimination, and the inability of the PRC to utilize Export-Import Bank facilities are all seen as dulling Chinese enthusiasm for trade with the U.S. after the removal of the trade embargo (Avery and Clarke 1978: 742; Barnett 1981: 509; Howe 1978: xxxii). The U.S. was perhaps equally hesitant to fully accept a long-time enemy. Yet trade between the two persevered, and by 1974 the U.S. was China's second largest trading partner, after Japan.

Table 9.10 China–U.S. trade, 1971–5 (in millions of U.S. dollars)

Year	*Total U.S./ China trade*	*China's exports*	*China's imports*	*China's trade balance with U.S.*
1971	5.0	5.0	–	+5.0
1972	95.5	32.4	63.5	−31.1
1973	805.1	64.9	740.2	−675.3
1974	933.8	114.7	819.1	−704.4
1975	462.0	158.3	303.6	−145.3

Source: Chinese Economy Post-Mao 1978.

Economic motivations for U.S. reconciliation with China

In his 12th day in office, President Nixon instructed Henry Kissinger to begin exploring the possibilities for reconciliation with the PRC. The process of opening trade between the two countries began in July 1969, when American tourists in Hong Kong and elsewhere were allowed to bring back $100 worth of goods from their travels to Communist China, and ended on June 1971 with Nixon lifting the 21-year embargo against Chinese goods. The "China differential" had ended – China had been given equal status with the Soviet Union with respect to U.S. exports.

Explanations as to what occasioned the dramatic change in U.S. trade policy with China in the early 1970s have always been *political* in nature, not *economic*. However, as argued below, there were certainly many compelling economic motivations for Nixon's trip as well.

China as a market for U.S. exports

Foreigners have long cast a greedy eye on the huge market represented by China, and that country's history is replete with intriguing episodes of foreign trade triumphs and disasters. In the late 1960s, American business showed a keen interest in the potentiality for a new market of about 760-million consumers, few of whom possessed washing machines, electric refrigerators, automobiles, or other "American necessities of life", as one analyst so aptly put it in *China and U.S. Foreign Policy* (CQI 1973: 6). In a 1970 study prepared for the National Committee on U.S.–China Relations, Robert F. Dernberger, a University of Michigan economics professor, offered the much-quoted prediction that under favorable conditions for growth and under the same terms that apply to U.S.–Soviet trade, China's purchases of American goods might reach $900 million by 1980, an amount equal to about two percent of the 1970 level of American exports (CQI 1973: 15). Within only two years after Nixon's trip to China, U.S. exports to the PRC had already reached $819 million (see Table 9.10).

In 1970, China's total foreign trade was approximately $4.3 billion a year, divided roughly equally between imports and exports. In contrast, U.S. exports totaled $43.2 billion in 1970, while imports came to $40 billion (CQI 1973: 60). Obviously,

Communist China was neither a huge buyer nor seller on the world market. But as a *potential* world trader, it loomed large. While China's population represented an admittedly poor group of consumers in the early 1970s, their sheer number led many analysts, even then, to predict rapid increases in the economic influence of the country. As elaborated below, policy makers and entrepreneurs alike recognized the potential trade that might develop between the two nations.

The American embargo was fundamentally a political act meant to economically cripple Communist China. While the embargo is now widely seen as having had little impact on China's international trade or on that country's economic growth, many observers have noted that it did have the effect of depriving U.S. businesspersons of Chinese trade contracts to the advantage of other industrialized states (Cahill 1973: 133). Just as China undoubtedly recognized specific areas of U.S. comparative advantage that could prove beneficial to its development, so too did the American producers of these goods realize the potential demand represented by the Chinese market. As discussed above, agricultural goods (wheat, corn, soybeans and cotton), capital goods (for oil-production, mining, and transportation), manufacturing goods (such as fertilizer), and natural resources (iron, steel, and coal) were all widely expected to become important U.S. exports once the embargo was removed.

Not only was there an intense interest in the Chinese market on the part of U.S. businesspersons, but they frequently voiced a sense of urgency in prodding U.S. interactions with the PRC. As shown in Table 9.11, Japan, Great Britain, and West Germany (and to a lesser extent, Italy and the Netherlands) had all experienced significant increases in their exports to China between 1962 and 1969. (Canada, also, which established diplomatic relations with Peking in 1970, was especially successful in selling vast quantities of wheat to China.) As increased pressure began to mount from America's business community, policy-makers themselves began making statements which touted the buying potential represented by the large Chinese market. The general mood was that the U.S. didn't want to be left further behind in China's economic opening to the West following the Cultural Revolution.

China as a supplier of U.S. imports

As a market for U.S. products China was undoubtedly an enticing prospect in the early 1970s. The possibility of large U.S. imports

Table 9.11 Commodity composition of China's exports by sector of origin, 1970–5 (millions of U.S. $)

Sectors of origin	1970	1971	1972	1973	1974	1975
Agriculture	980	1,160	1,470	2,175	2,585	2,855
Of which:						
Live animals	65	90	110	135	195	215
Meat and fish	150	185	225	335	335	415
Grain	110	95	155	445	715	720
Fruit and vegetables	170	155	180	245	315	360
Tea and spices	–	–	–	–	100	100
Oilseeds	65	65	70	110	135	140
Natural textile fiber	100	120	205	330	190	250
Crude animal material	115	105	115	170	200	230
Extractive	115	130	165	240	705	1,095
Of which:						
Crude animals	–	–	–	–	105	120
Coal	–	–	–	–	115	130
Crude oil	0	0	0	30	425	760
Manufacturing	1,005	1,210	1,515	2,660	3,370	3,225
Of which:						
Chemicals	105	130	160	255	400	300
Textile yarn and fabric	340	325	460	855	940	1,065
Iron and steel	40	65	65	120	170	86
Non-ferrous metals	25	45	30	60	75	120
Machinery and transport equipment	90	120	125	215	255	340
Clothing	155	155	190	354	360	345
Handicrafts and light manufacturing	–	–	–	–	220	190

Source: Batsavage and Davie 1978: 737.

of Chinese goods, on the other hand, was unlikely to have exerted much pressure on policy makers to negotiate with the PRC. The country's cheap and extensive labor resources and the high quality of its raw materials gave China a comparative advantage in some areas of interest to the United States but, for the most part, these needs were met by other low-cost producers. As shown in Table 9.12, China's top four exports in 1970 were textiles, yarn and fabrics (16.22 percent of its total exports), fruit and vegetables (8.11 percent), clothing (7.3 percent), and meat and fish (7.15 percent). While one does see occasional reference to hog bristles and tung oil as specific goods which American consumers had difficulty getting from elsewhere during the embargo, most of

Table 9.12 Growth of exports to China by selected nations, 1962–9 (millions of U.S. $)

Exporting nation	1962	1969	Percentage increase
Japan	39	411	954
West Germany	31	171	451
Italy	19	64	237
Netherlands	4	28	600
United Kingdom	24	141	488

Source: 1962 figures from 1966: 281.

China's other exports were readily available on the international market.

Once trade opened between the countries, Chinese exports slowly trickled into the United States. To a large extent, the profile of U.S. imports from China in the early 1970s shows America's intention to use that country for supplying its own manufacturing sector – imports from China, in other words, had low value-added. These goods included cotton fabrics, crude animal materials, non-ferrous metals, rosin and turpentine, loose precious and semiprecious stones, dressed fur skins, and albumins and starches, to name a few. The CIA's *People's Republic of China: International Trade Handbook (1975)*, also lists U.S. imports of small amounts of clothing and footwear, household wares, travel goods, fireworks, works of art and antiques, porcelain, bicycles, essential oils, and spices, edible nuts, and fish (see Table 9.6).

U.S. tariffs, of course, played an important role in determining the composition and magnitude of imports from China. Since 1922, the United States had vigorously promoted free trade throughout the world by extending the *most-favored-nation (MFN) status* to all of its trading partners. In direct response to the Korean War, Congress, in 1951, terminated these tariff concessions to all Communist nations, including the PRC. In his 1973 book entitled, *The China Trade and US Tariffs*, Harry Cahill evaluates the potential importance that American most-favored nation tariff concessions to other countries would have for Chinese–American trade. He reports that many Chinese exports to the U.S. entered duty free (e.g., raw silk, essential oils, spices, and antiques) or with duties identical to those paid by MFNs (nuts, for example, were assessed the same duties whether supplied from the "free world" or Communist sources). Chinese metals, chemicals, and materials of animal origin (e.g., hog bristles) were given a higher tariff than the same goods from MFNs, but their quality was higher and U.S. manufacturers were willing to pay the higher price. Luxury goods imported from China (e.g., jewelry, oriental rugs, and cashmere) also faced higher duties, but the height of the duty was not of crucial importance to the user (Cahill 1973: 69). Consumer goods and housewares that did not require advanced technology would seem to offer China a natural comparative advantage. These were, in fact, exported to the U.S. despite sizeable tariffs (e.g., handbags and flatware, athletic footwear, hand tools, sports equipment, toys, floor covering, paper articles, kitchen utensils, glassware and earthenware).

On the other hand, several of China's leading exports faced high tariffs which significantly curtailed their export to the United States. For example, silk fabrics were taxed at an *ad valorem* rate of 60 percent compared to a MFN rate of 11 percent, and U.S. imports of Chinese silk fabrics were minimal. Similarly, the existing capacity of China's textile industry, its expanding share of free-world textile markets, and the steadily increasing American consumption of textiles would make these promising exports. However, the high tariffs which Chinese textiles faced in the U.S. market (up to four-to-one against China) meant less was actually traded than one might have expected once the embargo was removed. Other less important Chinese exports, such as precious stones, faced high tariff walls and trade was hampered as a result.

By the early 1970s the U.S. had clearly lost any comparative advantage in the production of textiles, and textile imports from developing countries were generating significant political debate over appropriate trade restrictions. Partly in response to pressure from southern textile products in the late 1960s, the Nixon administration was threatening to impose import quotas on Japanese textiles unless Japan voluntarily adopted "reasonable" quotas on its own. A potential new supplier of textiles (namely China) may have given the U.S. bargaining power with the Japanese during these ongoing negotiations over the so-called "voluntary export restraints".

The quality of Chinese exports does not seem to have been an impediment to trade with the U.S. While tastes were notoriously exacting in both American and western European markets, goods from mainland China were widely accepted (Cahill 1973: 132). In general, however, Chinese exports to the U.S. were minimal, and it would be difficult to make a case for Nixon's opening trade with the Chinese to enable Americans to purchase their products.

The U.S. trade deficit and unemployment

In 1970, the United States experienced its first merchandise trade deficit in 50 years, with prospects of an even larger deficit in 1971. As early as 1967, the Federal Reserve proclaimed that the country was faced with an intolerable deficit in its balance of payments and that it was in the midst of the worst financial crisis it had had since 1931. When Nixon began dismantling the embargo on Chinese trade, it was obvious to policy-makers on both sides of the Pacific that the U.S. had far more goods to offer China than it would import from them. A substantial U.S. trade surplus with the PRC was clearly anticipated, and as discussed above, did in fact occur once trade began. While it is unlikely that this favorable trade balance was a critical motivation for Nixon's reconciliation with Communist China, several analysts have suggested that it may have played a role in moving the U.S. into a more receptive position in the negotiations.

Another factor contributing to Nixon's willingness to open trade talks with China was the gradual increase in structural unemployment which the U.S. had suffered since World War II. The anticipated increase in exports to the PRC was seen as a potential stimulus for the domestic economy which would ease unemployment. While economists generally agree that a country's unemployment rate is affected only slightly by changing trade patterns in the short run, and not at all in the long run, this reasoning may have had some appeal to policy makers at the time.

Additional evidence of the importance of economic motivations for rapproachment

When looking for evidence that economic considerations were, in fact, important to both China and the U.S., one must somehow ascertain what policy-makers on both sides were thinking when negotiations between the two began. This is obviously easier to do with respect to the Americans' perspective.

President Nixon, a politician first and foremost, plainly recognized the economic significance of his overtures to Communist China, as evidenced in many of his public statements in the late

1960s and early 1970s. On 6 September 1969, in a speech to the Sixth Annual Assembly of the Organization of African Unity, he extolled the many benefits of increased trade. In that speech, he stated, " . . . in 1969 [w]e took a series of steps towards dismantling trade barriers and assuring fair treatment for our own industry and agriculture in world commerce. I submitted new trade legislation which proposed specific steps toward easing economic relations between the United States and Communist China".

Economic motivations were specifically referenced again on 6 July 1971, when President Nixon acknowledged the economic importance of the PRC. In a briefing on domestic policy to Midwestern new media executives in Kansas City, Nixon stressed the importance of mainland China as a potential market for world trade:

> And 800 million Chinese are going to be, inevitably, an enormous economic power, with all that that means in terms of what they could be in other areas if they move in that direction. *That is the reason why I felt that it was essential that this Administration take the first steps toward ending the isolation of Mainland China from the world community* [emphasis added].

Later, in the same speech he reiterated,

> What we have done is simply opened the door – opened the door for travel, opened the door for trade . . . What we see as we look ahead 5 years, 10 years, perhaps it is 15, but in any event, within our time, we see five great economic super powers: The United States, western Europe, the Soviet Union, Mainland China, and, of course, Japan . . .
>
> (CQ1 1980: 322)

It is clear from this and other public pronouncements, both by Nixon and others in his administration, that the economic potential of China was an important motivation for U.S. overtures to the PRC.

Both before and after Nixon's 1971 visit to mainland China, many groups, both domestic and foreign, worked (often behind the scenes) to influence U.S. policy on China. One analyst argued

216

that there was not one but several "China Lobbies," including several focusing specifically on the economic issues surrounding rapprochement. Among those seeking to influence the alignment of forces in the 1971 "China campaign" was the American Farm Bureau Federation, which urged the government to authorize the sale of U.S. grains and other farm products to Communist China. Federation President, William J. Kuhfuss, wrote to President Nixon on June 8 requesting the removal of cargo preference and part-cargo restrictions on sales to Communist countries. Mr Nixon on June 10 announced that farm products and fertilizer would be included among commodities for which export sales could be made to Communist China under general license (CQ1 1971: 33).

Another influential lobby in the China debate was the Emergency Committee for American Trade, ECAT. In the late 1960s and early 1970s, ECAT was recognized as the leading organization working to advance the interests of multinational corporations in the United States. Donald Kendall, Chair of ECAT and CEO of PepsiCo Inc., stated in April 1971 that Nixon's initial moves toward opening trade with the PRC was very good news to him and to the institutions he represented (*China and US Foreign Policy* 1971: 33). Other groups registering as lobbies for closer economic ties with the PRC were clearly representing U.S. business interests. These included, among others, the Committee for New China Policy and the National Committee on U.S.–China Relations Inc.: the latter was established in 1966 and chaired by Alexander Eckstein, Professor of Economics at the University of Michigan. Among the many commercial interests in the U.S. which lobbied actively for renewed trade with the PRC were: Chase Manhattan Bank, General Motors, Monsanto, Xerox, Pan American World Airways, Trans World Airlines, United Air Lines and the Boeing Company (Wilson 1977: 324). Arthur Stahnke, in his influential book, *China's Trade with the West: A Political and Economic Analysis*, offers an extensive list of quotations from U.S. officials and business executives as to the exigency of opening the Chinese market to the U.S. (Stahnke 1973: 67). President Nixon would obviously have been aware of the increasing pressure from American business to open trade with China – pressure, mentioned earlier, that took on an increased sense of urgency as other western countries rushed to take advantage of China's opening to the West.

In 1971 both the House and Senate held extensive hearings on the China question. In both cases, testimony was solicited from economists and other China experts concerning the economic implications of rapproachment with the PRC. As mentioned above, for example, Professor Robert Dernberger in his testimony before the House's National Committee on US–China Relations said, in a widely reported statement, that China's purchases of American goods might reach $900 million by 1980. Fully aware of China's needs at that time, he added, "Under favorable conditions, China might by 1980 buy up the $650 million in U.S. minerals, industrial equipment and machinery." As discussed earlier, the U.S. was not expected to import much from China. Dernberger acknowledged this saying, 'Chinese sales to the United States might reach $250 million in raw and processed agricultural products and other items' (*China and U.S. Foreign Policy*, 1971: 33).

Similarly, on 29 June 1971, Professor Stanley Lubman offered the following testimony before the Senate Foreign Relations Committee hearings on China:

> The resumption of trade between the United States and China should continue to be encouraged. Trade offers some economic advantages to each nation; it promises to increase the knowledge each country has of the other, it would symbolize the intent of the two nations to improve their relations, and it would begin to create the economic links which form part of the very substance of normal international relations.

In the same speech he added, " . . . I again emphasize my strong belief that the China trade has proven profitable and challenging to Western traders, and that it promises to prove so to Americans as well" (*China and U.S. Foreign Policy* 1971: 81).

In September 1970, the House Foreign Affairs Subcommittee on Asian and Pacific Affairs, another committee charged with investigating rapproachment, issued seven policy recommendations at the end of its meetings. The first concerned U.S. travel to the PRC. The second read,

> The time has now come for the United States to take major steps in the trade field. The small steps taken during the past year, opening the first small crack in the two decade-old embargo on trade with mainland China, have been desirable steps in the right direction. But now the United States should go much further and

move to end the embargo on China trade, putting United
States–China trade on the same basis as trade with the
Soviet Union and other countries . . . The change in U.S.
trade policy is long overdue . . .

(*China and U.S. Foreign Policy* 1971: 75).

Professor Fred Greene of Williams College, an Asian expert and
a Johnson Administration State Department official, offered the
following testimony at the 1970 House hearings mentioned
above.

Can they [the Chinese] do without very close and sustained relations with the non-Communist industrialized
world? The answer is "No." They have given this answer
themselves. When they switched off from the Russians, in
economic relations, they immediately switched on with
the West Europeans and the Japanese, particularly in
trade. The central question really becomes: If the Russians
are to be excluded, do the Chinese contain the Americans
in a sort of perpetual condition of isolation, and continue
to deal with the Japanese and West Europeans? Or will
this be an insufficient basis for them to conduct the kinds
of economic development that they will need and desire
in the future. This must be a matter of grave concern to
their long-range planners. The United States is obviously
a better prospect, in terms of resources for the long future.

(*China and U.S. Foreign Policy*, 1971: 59).

Further evidence of the importance of economic motivations in
rapprochment, both for the Americans and the Chinese, is found
within the Shanghai Communique itself. This document was issued
jointly by both countries at Shanghai on 27 February 1972 at the
conclusion of President Nixon's trip to the PRC. It states,

Both sides view bilateral trade as another area from which
mutual benefit can be derived and agreed that economic
relations based on equality and mutual benefit are in the
interest of the peoples of the two countries. They agree to
facilitate the progressive development of trade between
their two countries.

(Wilson 1977: 324)

It is important to bear in mind that the first steps taken towards rapprochement with China involved the removal of *trade* restrictions. In April 1970 Nixon authorized the selective licensing of goods for export to the PRC. This occurred three months before Henry Kissinger began secret meetings with Premier Chou En-Lai in Peking and preceded even the easing of travel restriction to Communist China. In August, the U.S. again made overtures to China, this time with the removal of certain restrictions on American oil companies so that foreign ships could use American-owned bunkering facilities on voyages to and from mainland China's ports. These initial steps towards reconciliation were taken almost two years before Nixon's historic trip to Peking. While it is generally argued that the elimination of trade restrictions was merely an *economic* means to a *political* end, given the obvious advantages to both countries from opening trade, and the attention given those advantages by policy makers, the economic motivations, I argue, were plainly an end in themselves.

Summary

While the prevalence of political motivations for both Communist China and the United States' seeking an end to the 21-year-old embargo cannot be denied, economics unquestionably played a significant role in the rapprochement as well. In the early 1970s, the specific needs of the PRC were surprisingly well matched with the comparative advantage of the U.S. The Chinese were intent on modernization and the ascendancy of the "moderates" meant the PRC had recently become receptive to imports of Western technology. In addition, China's growing population required grain imports which the U.S. could supply in abundance at low cost. Within two years of Nixon's visit, the U.S. had become China's second largest trading partner, despite the myriad ongoing political problems between the two countries. It is clear that the potential for such robust economic interaction must have been uppermost in the minds of the Chinese when negotiations were broached.

Nixon's historic trip to China in 1971 reflected a change in U.S. policy towards China that contrasted sharply with two decades of unrelieved hostility towards the Peking government. The Shanghai Communique, which resulted from Nixon's visit, has been called the most significant foreign policy document of Nixon's tenure, not only for the political breakthroughs it represented, but for the economic opportunity it afforded U.S. businesses (Cahill 1973: 14). While trade with China represented only a small fraction of total U.S. trade in the early 1970s, it was the potential of this huge market, and the desire not to be left behind by its rivals, that I argue motivated the Americans to instigate the negotiations. While today, few question the importance of the economic relationship that the U.S. has with the PRC, many see it as a relatively recent development. This chapter argues that the mutual benefits to trade were clearly discernable in the early 1970s and were, in fact, important considerations in both countries' desire for rapprochement.

References

Avery, Martha and Clarke, William (1975) "The Sino-American Commercial Relationship," in *China: A Reassessment of the Economy*, Joint Economic Committee, U.S. Congress. Washington DC: U.S. Government Printing Office.

Batsavage, Richard E. and Usack, A.H. (1972) "The International Trade of the People's Republic of China," in *People's Republic of China: An Economic Assessment*. Washington, D.C: U.S. Government Printing Office. 335–70.

Batsavage, Richard E. and Davie, John L. (1978) "China's International Trade and Finance," *Chinese Economy Post-Mao: A Compendium of Papers* (1978), submitted to the Joint Economic Committee of the U.S. Department of Commerce. Washington DC: U.S. Government Printing Office.

Cahill, Harry A. (1973) *The China Trade and U.S. Tariffs*. New York: Praeger Publishers, Inc.

CIA (1975) *People's Republic of China: International Trade Handbook*. Washington DC: U.S. Government Printing Office.

CIA (1977) "China: International Trade, 1976–77," Washington, DC: CIA, National Foreign Assessment Center.

CQI (*Congressional Quarterly* Inc.) (1980) *China: U.S. Policy Since 1945*. Washington, D.C: U.S. Government Printing Office.

CQI (*Congressional Quarterly* Inc.) (1971) *China and U.S. Foreign Policy*. Washington, DC: U.S. Government Printing Office.

CQI (*Congressional Quarterly* Inc.) (1973) *China and U.S. Foreign Policy* 2nd edn. Washington, DC: U.S. Government Printing Office.

Chinese Economy Post-Mao: A Compendium of Papers (1978) Volume 1, *Policy and Performance*. U.S. Department of Commerce, Joint Economic Committee, 95th Congress, 2nd session. Washington DC: U.S. Government Printing Office.

Doak, Barnett A. (1981) *China's Economy in Global Perspective*. Washington, DC: The Brookings Institution.

Dudden, Arthur (1992) *The American Pacific: From the Old China Trade to the Present*. New York: Oxford University Press.

Eckstein, Alexander (ed.) (1972) *China Trade Prospects and United States Policy*. New York: Praeger Publishers.

Eckstein, Alexander (1966) *Communist China's Economic Growth and Foreign Trade: Implications for U.S. Policy*. New York: McGraw-Hill Book Company.

—— (1977) *China's Economic Revolution*. Cambridge: Cambridge University Press.

Fairbanks, John King (1992) *China: A New History*. Cambridge, MA: The Belknap Press of Harvard University Press.

Freidman, Edward (1975) "The International Political Economy and Chinese Politics," in Bryant Garth (ed.) *China's Changing Role in the World Economy*, pp. 1–14. New York: Praeger Publishers.

Groen, Henry J. and Kilpatrick, James A. (1978) "China's Agricultural Production," *Chinese Economy Post Mao: A Compendium of Papers*, submitted to the Joint Economic Committee, Congress of the United States, Washington DC: U.S. Government Printing Office: pp. 607–62.

Heymann, Hans Jr. (1975) "'Self-Reliance' Revisited: China's Technology Dilemma," in Bryant Garth (ed.), *China's Changing Role in the World Economy*, pp. 15–35. New York: Praeger Publishers.

Howe, Christopher (1978) *China's Economy: A Basic Guide*. New York: Basic Books, Inc., Publishers.

Hsu, John C. (1989) *China's Foreign Trade Reforms: Impact on Growth and Stability*. Cambridge: Cambridge University Press.

Lee, Oliver M. (1972) "U.S. Trade Policy Toward China: From Economic Warfare to Summit Diplomacy," in Arthur A. Stahnke (ed.), *China's Trade with the West: A Political and Economic Analysis*, pp. 33–87. New York: Praeger Publishers.

Mah, Feng-hwa (1971) *The Foreign Trade of Mainland China*. Chicago: Aldine–Atherton Publishing, Inc.

Payne, Douglas (1982) "Sino-Japanese Trade: Does it Hold Lessons For American Traders?" in David Buxbaum, Cassondra Joseph and Paul Reynolds (eds). *China Trade: Prospects and Perspectives*. New York: Praeger Publishers: pp. 249–75.

People's Republic of China: An Economic Assessment (1972) Washington DC: Joint Economic Committee, U.S. Congress, 92nd Congress, 2nd session.

Prybyla, Jan S. (1978) *The Chinese Economy: Problems and Policies*. South Carolina: University of South Carolina Press.

Pye, Lucian W. (1978) *China: An Introduction*. Boston: Little, Brown and Company.

Reports to Congress (1973) U.S. Mutual Defense Assistance Control Administrator. U.S. Department of Commerce.

Spence, Jonathan (1990) *The Search For Modern China*. New York: W.W. Norton and Company.

Stahnke, Arthur A. (ed.) (1973) *China's Trade with the West: A Political and Economic Analysis*. New York: Praeger Publishers.

Surls, Frederick (1978) "China's Grain Trade," in *Chinese Economy Post-Mao: A Compendium of Papers*, submitted to the Joint Economic Committee, Congress of the U.S.: Washington DC: U.S. Government Printing Office. 653–70.

USBC (U.S. Bureau of the Census) (1970), *Statistical Abstract of the United States: 1970* (91st Annual Edition). Washington, DC.

USBC (U.S. Bureau of the Census) (1974) *Statistical Abstract of the United States)* (95th Annual Edition). Washington, DC: U.S. Government Printing Office.

Wilson, Richard (1977) "Mao Tse-tung in the Scales of History: a Preliminary Assessment," organized by the *China Quarterly*. Cambridge: Cambridge University Press.

10

MIGRATION AND PERCEPTIONS OF IDENTITY

The case of Singapore and Malaysian
perceptions of the Australian identity,
1966–96

Kevin Blackburn

Introduction

One of the largest migrations in the Pacific was the exodus of
millions of people from the poverty and turmoil of the provinces
of southern China from the mid-nineteenth to the mid-twentieth
centuries (Wang 1978: 9). Most of this population movement was
into Southeast Asia. By the late 1960s, it was estimated that there
were between 11 and 13 million Overseas Chinese in Southeast
Asia (FitzGerald 1972: 192). In conjunction with a similar movement of people from India, this process was responsible for producing the multiracial and multicultural societies of the independent
states of Malaysia and Singapore. In the late 1960s, the population
of Malaysia was around 53 percent Malay (the indigenous people),
35 percent Chinese, and 11 percent Indian (Comber 1983: 89).
Singapore's population was about 74 percent Chinese, 14 percent
Malay, and 8 percent Indian (Ee 1961; Saw 1969: 41).

An open immigration policy was adopted by the British colonial
administration in the economic exploitation of the Malayan peninsular. The Chinese were brought into Malaya and Singapore by the
British to mine the large deposits of tin, and the Indians worked on
the rubber plantations. In contrast, Australia, as a self-governing
dominion in the British Empire, administered throughout much of
the time of these major migration movements in the Pacific an
immigration policy that was designed to forge an Anglo-Saxon

identity by preventing the entry of non-white migrants into Australia and encouraging British migrants – the White Australia Policy (Brawley 1995a; Yarwood 1964; and Yarwood 1968). In Australia, after an initial influx of Chinese during the gold rush period of the mid-nineteenth century (in 1861 Asians were estimated to comprise 3.5 percent of the population), colonial governments erected what one historian called the "great white walls" restricting the entry of non-whites (Price 1974). The White Australia Policy reduced the percentage of the population of Asian ancestry to 0.4 percent by 1947. In the late 1960s, the consequences of the White Australia Policy were still present despite it being liberalized to allow the entry of a small number of Asians. One and a half percent of the people were indigenous and less than one percent were Asian. The rest of the population was from a European background which was dominated by people of British and Irish ancestry. In 1978, Australians of British and Irish descent were almost 77 percent of the population (Inglis *et al.* 1994; Price 1984: 13).

However, when the multiracial societies of Malaysia and Singapore assumed independence in the 1950s and 1960s, they, like many other Asian countries, had little sympathy for an immigration policy that had discriminated against Asians, and its concomitant national identity that had isolated Australia from Asia (Rivett 1975: 97–128). Australian governments were aware of these feelings and conscious that their immigration policy was harming Australia's relations with the newly independent countries of Asia which had arisen after the European empires had been dismantled (Brawley 1995a: 320; 1995b; Viviani 1992). The diplomatic historian, Neville Meaney, has described Australian governments as engaged in a process of divesting Australia of the image of a white society and promoting it as a multicultural and multiracial one, partly as a result of having to live with a new Asia which American and European imperial power had exited. Australia now had to treat the new nations of Southeast Asia as equals and improve relations with them (Meaney 1995: 171–89). Australia began to move away from the identity created by the White Australia Policy and embrace a different identity, a multiracial and multicultural identity, similar to its neighbors, in what it now saw as its region – Southeast Asia. The beginnings of this shift in the identity projected to Southeast Asia date from 1966 when the White Australia Policy was liberalized to admit well qualified Asians.

There is a need to investigate how successfully the new identity that Australia has projected as a multiracial and multicultural country, claiming to be part of Asia, has replaced in the minds of many people in the region the former image of a predominantly Anglo-Saxon and Celtic country that practiced racial discrimination against non-whites. In undertaking this investigation it would be best to look at the perceptions of the Australian identity in the two nations, Singapore and Malaysia, which were not only among the countries most affected by the population movements in the Pacific from which Australia sought to insulate itself, but also which claim to know Australia better than the rest of Southeast Asia. This study is an analysis of how Malaysian and Singapore public opinion leaders, i.e., government leaders and newspapers, have perceived Australians and their national identity.

Malaysian and Singapore knowledge of Australia

Malaysia and Singapore have been described by the foreign editor of the *Australian*, Greg Sheridan as countries that "above all Asian nations, they know Australia" (*Australian*, 21 April 1994: 15). He also believes that "probably no two Asian leaders know and understand Australia better than Lee Kuan Yew and Malaysian Prime Minister Dr Mahathir." Sheridan detailed the reasons why Singaporeans and Malaysians would know Australia and Australians well. He listed various connections, such as long-standing defense arrangements, their common British colonial experience, their shared World War II experiences, and the presence of Australian soldiers in Singapore and Malaysia intermittently for the past 50 years. Other reasons which he cited to prove that the people of these countries knew more about Australians and their identity than other Southeast Asian countries included the fact that they share similar legal and political systems, and that English is widely spoken in Malaysia and the most widely used language in Singapore (*Australian*, 13 December 1995: 17). Sheridan affirmed a statement by Lee Kuan Yew, the Prime Minister of Singapore from 1959 to 1990, that these two former British colonies in Southeast Asia are Australia's "old friends" in the region (*Australian*, 15 January 1996: 11).

Perhaps one of the most significant reasons why Singapore and Malaysia would know more about Australia than other countries in the region is that since the 1950s, 120,000 Malaysians and over 30,000 Singaporeans have gone to universities in Australia.

Malaysians and Singaporeans studying at Australian universities seem to provide one of the strongest connections between the countries. In 1994, there were 7,739 full fee-paying students from Singapore in Australia compared to 4,000 each in the United States and Britain. In 1994, Singapore leaders who had been educated at Australian universities included the President, Ong Teng Cheong, and his wife; Deputy Prime Minister, Dr Tony Tan, Communications Minister, Mah Bow Tan; Labour Minister, Dr Lee Boon Yang; and Trade and Industry Minister, Yeo Cheow Tong (Martin 1995: 40–1). Also, there have been strong links between the countries through migration. By 1993, 76,961 Malaysians and 25,804 Singaporeans had migrated to Australia, and most still had family and business connections with their home countries (*Straits Times* 16 October 1993: 18; and *Straits Times* 10 August 1994: 10). The majority of these migrants are well-educated professionals, many of whom had studied in Australia (Ramachandran and Arudsothy 1992).

Images of itself that Australia projected in Southeast Asia (1960s–80s)

The first major shift away from the White Australia Policy came in March 1966 when the Holt Government (1966–7) liberalized the policy by allowing skilled non-whites to be admitted into Australia. However, the reforms meant that while unskilled Europeans could enter, unskilled Asians could not. In an interview with the Singapore *Straits Times* in April 1967, Prime Minister Harold Holt began to talk of Australia as an Asian power and also to sell a new image of Australia. He made public exact figures on how many Asians had been admitted to Australia. He remarked that 30,000 Asians had been admitted to Australia since World War II out of a total of 2,500,000 migrants. Holt revealed that in recent years 6,200 Asians had taken out citizenship after five years on same basis as other people, and that "any Asian who marries an Australian enters this country with full citizenship." He commented on the consequences of the recent changes in immigration policy and the growing trade relationship between Australia and Asian countries (in 1966 Japan had replaced Britain as Australia's largest export market). He said that "I am sure this will lead to a larger entry of Asians into the community life of Australia." However, he added that, bearing in mind divided Australian public opinion on non-white immigration at the time, "it is well recognised by Asian governments that there are limits to the extent that this can be done" (*Straits Times* 5 April 1967: 10).

The initial move away from the image of the Anglo-Celtic Australian identity usually projected to Asia was made in January 1971, when Prime Minister John Gorton (1968–71) first proposed that Australia become a multiracial society like Singapore. Gorton, in Singapore to attend the Commonwealth Heads of Government Meeting, was besieged with criticism of Australia's racial policies by Singapore's press and citizens (*Straits Times* 9 January 1971: 10; 19 January 1971: 5). The Labor Premier of South Australia Don Dunstan had even written a well publicized letter to the Prime Minister of Singapore calling for an end to the White Australia immigration Policy (*Straits Times* 13 January 1971: 24). Gorton attempted to ease a furore that had been created in Singapore and Malaysia when the comments of an Australian immigration official Vance Dickie were reported. Dickie had clearly stated on the BBC that non-white immigration was not encouraged. He said: "Let's be perfectly honest about the whole situation. As far as Australia is concerned down through the years we have believed that in the interests of the Australian people it would be best if we developed our race with people of European background" (*Straits Times* 8 January 1971: 10). On the day after reporting the story, the *Straits Times* ran an editorial in which it sarcastically described Australia as "Whiter than White," and commented that Prime Minister Gorton would have to show reason why in Australia's immigration policy "colour is everything" (9 January 1971: 10). The *Sin Chew Jit Poh*, a major Malaysian Chinese newspaper, was even more outraged. It commented in its editorial for 11 January that Australia was "trying to make itself a white continent," and added that Prime Minister Gorton would have to explain this in what it called "multi-racial Singapore" (*Mirror of Opinion* 11 January 1971: E3). The *Sin Chew Jit Poh* prophetically mentioned that "bearing in mind Australia's inseparable relations with Asia and particularly Southeast Asia, Australia will one day realize that Asia is more important to her than her ties of consanguinity with Europe and the U.S." (*Mirror of Opinion* 11 January 1971: E4)

Before a gathering of the Singapore alumni from Australian universities on 18 January, Gorton outlined that Australia, far from being a racially homogenous country that restricted the entry of non-whites, was becoming a multiracial society modeled on Singapore:

You are a lucky State. You are able, quite properly, to call yourself a multi-racial society and get the good feeling that comes from being able to say that. And if one replies and says yes, that you are 90 per cent Chinese or 85 per cent Chinese and therefore Singapore is homogenous as we will keep Australia homogeneous, that nevertheless enables you to say you are a multi-racial society. Well, we are moving a little bit that way.

. . . I think that if we gradually build up inside Australia a proportion of people who are not of white skin, then as that is gradually done, so there will be a complete lack of consciousness of difference between the races. And if this can be done as I think it can, then that may provide the world with the first truly multi-racial society with no tensions of any kind possible between any of the races within it.

At any rate, this is our ideal.

(Rivett 1975: 31–2)

When he returned to Australia, Gorton was asked in an interview to reaffirm this commitment, which he did (Rivett 1975: 32).

However, Dickie's message, not Gorton's, was more consistent with the image that had been projected of Australia's national identity by immigration ministers prior to Gorton's *volte-face* in Singapore in January 1971. In 1960, the then Immigration Minister, Alexander Downer had maintained that he did "not believe that Australians, certainly not at this stage of their development, either desire or are ready for, an East–West potpourri." He went on to add that there was no evidence Australia was part of Asia because "our population with the exception of a fractional percentage is European," and that "in a more particular sense, of course, this is still a British country" (London 1970: 208–9). In December 1966, two years after stepping down from the Immigration portfolio and several months after the well publicized March 1966 liberalization of immigration to allow skilled Asians to enter, Downer in a speech on "The Influence of Immigration on Australia's National Character" expressed the notion that Australia could afford to relax the White Australia Policy, but "not to the extent of changing its Anglo-European basis" (London 1970: 98; see also White 1981). Even during July 1969, Billy Snedden, then Immigration Minister, remarked that "we must have a single culture" and "if migration implied multiculture activities within

Australian society, then it was not the type Australia wanted" because "we should have a mono-culture with everyone living the same way" (Foster and Stockley 1984: 46).

After Gorton's ground-breaking announcement in Singapore, there was an ever-growing number of statements that echoed Gorton's words. In May 1972, Don Chipp, Minister for Customs in the McMahon Government (1971–2), said he envisaged that, in the 1980s, Australia would be a multiracial society. "I believe that we have now, to a small degree, a multi-racial society," he commented; "but as years go on we'll have one that works not one that brings problems." Gorton, who was not in the McMahon Government, argued that Chipp's statement was entirely consistent with government policy since 1966. He argued that "Australia is already a multiracial, or non-racial society, in the sense that there is now a considerable number of non-European Australians and no tension had been created as a result" (Rivett 1975: 32).

Finally in 1973, the White Australia Policy was completely abolished by Al Grassby, the first Immigration Minister in the Whitlam Government (1972–5), and no distinction was made on colour. After 1973, a points system was introduced whereby migrants were allowed to enter after they had accumulated enough points, which were given for qualities such as education, skills, family in Australia, age, etc. The intake of Asian migrants into Australia slowly reflected the changes in immigration policy. In the late 1960s, Asians comprised only three percent of the migrants coming into Australia. In 1970–1 the percentage of the intake who were Asians reached 5.4 percent, and in 1975 it was at 11 percent (Ramachandran and Arudsothy 1992: 34). In June 1973, Grassby went on a three-day tour of Jakarta, Singapore, and Kuala Lumpur with the announcement that Australia was taking steps to dismantle the "wall of isolation which has hampered its relations with Asian countries" by removing the discriminatory immigration policy and restrictions on visas to Asians visiting Australia (*Straits Times* 12 June 1973: 2; 13 June 1973: 7). It was not lost on Singapore public opinion that Grassby's tour to tell Southeast Asia of the abolition of the White Australia Policy came at the same time as Prime Minister Whitlam proposed an Asian power bloc in the wake of the United States' disengagement from the region after Vietnam. The *Straits Times* subtly expressed its cynicism when, after a polite editorial, it gave prominence to a very critical letter which remarked that "Mr

Whitlam leads the country which for years discriminated against Asians," and that his proposal for an Asian bloc was the result of Whitlam "feeling a compelling urge to carry the whiteman's burden in post-Vietnam Asia" with Australia leading the bloc (*Straits Times* 11 March 1973: 7).

In 1973, Grassby, as well as dismantling what remained of the White Australia Policy after the 1966 liberalization, introduced the notion of Australia as a multicultural country (Foster and Stockley 1984: 61–7). This concept gave recognition to the rising political power (in terms of numbers of voters) of migrants from non-British and non-Irish backgrounds, such as the large Greek, Italian, and Yugoslav communities, as well as many other smaller non-Anglo-Celtic migrant communities (Castles *et al.* 1993: 60). Non-Anglo-Celtic migrants had constituted over a third of Australia's massive post-war immigration intake. Previously, migrants from non-British countries were expected to assimilate into the Australian Anglo-Celtic identity. The large immigration programme had significantly added to Australia's population increase from 7.4 million in 1945 to 14 million in 1975 (Foster and Stockley, 1984: 62). By 1971, one in five Australians was born overseas (Castles *et al.* 1993: 62). This massive post-war immigration programme itself was designed to populate Australia with Europeans to prevent an Asian power from taking over the continent, as had almost happened with Japan during World War II. Many of these European migrants were unskilled or had a low level of skills; the emphasis was then on race, not skills (Castles *et al.* 1993: 9, 45). The Fraser Government (1975–83) recognized the new cultural diversity created by the non-Anglo-Celtic migrants, and gave its endorsement to the idea of the Australian identity being a multicultural one. In May 1978, Prime Minister Fraser said "the Government accepts that it is now essential to give significant further encouragement to develop a multicultural attitude in Australia" (Foster and Stockley 1984: 71). The idea was also embraced with enthusiasm by the Hawke Government (1983–91), which endorsed the idea of multiculturalism as a national ideology (Castles *et al.* 1993: 71–9).

Australia's growing multiracialism was also increasingly projected into Southeast Asia by Australian governments. In 1982–83, Asians comprised 34 percent of all Australian migrants. Vietnamese refugees alone accounted for 10 percent of the intake (Ramachandran and Arudsothy 1992: 34). The Foreign Affairs Department's own literature for its representatives in Asia and elsewhere highlighted that in 1991–2, of the 107,000 migrants who arrived in Australia, 21 percent were from Southeast Asia and 20 percent were from Northeast Asia (ADFAT 1993a: 3). Australia's immigration intake began to reflect two world demographic features. The difference in living standards between Europe and Australia was not high enough to attract large numbers of European migrants, as it had been when Europe was recovering from World War II. Secondly, the intake of Asian migrants was moving more closely towards the proportion of the world's population that was Asian – two-thirds. By the early 1980s, two percent of Australia's population was from an Asian background. According to the 1986 census, the percentage of Asian-born Australians was 3.4 percent. By 1991 this had grown to 4.1 percent. The 1996 census revealed that 4.8 percent of Australians were Asian-born (Inglis *et al.* 1994; Shu *et al.* 1994; *Straits Times*, 17 July 1997: 7). During 1983 and 1984, the Hawke Government's Foreign Minister, Bill Hayden (1983–88) on several occasions expressed his belief in a "Eurasian" future for Australia (Betts 1988: 159). In an interview for *Asiaweek*, a magazine which is widely read and circulated throughout Southeast Asia, he was unequivocal:

> We're an anomaly as a European country in this part of the world. There's already a large and growing Asian population in Australia and it is inevitable in my view that Australia will become a Eurasian country over the next century or two. Australian Asians and Europeans will marry another and a new race will emerge; I happen to think that's desirable. That means we are becoming part of the mainstream of the region.
>
> (*Asiaweek*, 19 August 1983: 7)

Singapore and Malaysian impressions of the Australian identity (1960s–80s)

In contrast to the multicultural view that Australia has had of itself since the 1970s, the image of an Anglo-Celtic Australia of the 1960s has remained firmly etched into Malaysian and Singapore impressions of the country. In April 1970, in his seminal work, *The Malay Dilemma*, the future Prime Minister of Malaysia, Dr Mahathir Bin Mohamad (1981 to present) outlined what he and many Malaysians perceived to be the identity of Australians. He noted that "the international personality of the

Australian has been established" and that "the Australians themselves wish to retain this identity." Mahathir described how "the
whole immigration, administration, and educational policy is
designed to permanently retain the identity of the Australian as
a basically white, English-speaking person whose customs are
British and whose religion is Christianity." He mentioned how
new immigrants from different backgrounds had to conform to
that identity:

> We know that the first settlers in Australia were of
> British extraction. Subsequently there were settlers of
> other European extraction. But by the time other races
> came the Australian was recognizable as an international
> personality. He was English speaking, practised basically
> English customs, and followed the Christian faith. He
> accepted his link with the British Crown, and even
> when his country became independent he maintained
> this link. The establishment of this identity meant that
> settlers who came later from other European and even
> Asian countries had to conform to this identity. Failure
> to conform would mean failure to obtain legal status as an
> Australian.
>
> (Mahathir 1970: 122–3)

Perceptions of Australia's national identity in the Malay
language press, and those held by Malay opinion-leaders were
overwhelmingly influenced by knowledge of the White Australia
Policy and Australia's racial policies, in particular its treatment of
the Australian Aborigines. In 1966, an editorial in the Malay
paper in the Jawi script *Utusan Melayu* described Australia as
being of the "same skin colour" as Ian Smith's white-minority
rule in Rhodesia, and it implied that it too was a country whereby
white settlers were able to dominate the indigenous population
and exclude non-whites from the country (*Daily Highlights of the
Chinese, Malay, and Tamil Press* 11 January 1996: D4). In 1970,
Mahathir, while on a visit to Monash University in Melbourne,
vehemently denounced Australian racial policies. It was reported
that in 1975, Mahathir had remarked that "Malaysia did not
indulge in genocide to solve its race problem as the Australians
did with their Aborigines in the past" (*Far Eastern Economic Review*
25 September 1981: 11). According to sources in the Malaysian
government, Mahathir himself had trouble with Australia's

restrictions on the entry of non-whites when an official invitation to visit Australia in 1968 was hastily withdrawn after he lost his parliamentary seat in 1969 (*Straits Times* 29 September 1981: 15).

Malaysian and Singapore perceptions of the Australian identity in the 1960s and 1970s were partly shaped by race relations in their own countries. Malaysia was strongly divided along communal lines (Ratnam 1965: 210–13). In 1969, race riots in Kuala Lumpur between the Malays and Chinese had resulted in hundreds of deaths. Singapore had also experienced racial riots between Malays and Chinese in 1964. In the aftermath of this racial tension, in both Malaysia and Singapore, strong government measures and restrictions on freedoms were thought necessary in order to build successful multiracial nation states (Bedlington 1978; Comber 1983). Malaysian and Singaporean leaders, such as Mahathir, believed that Australia, also an immigrant society, was not experiencing these problems because it had long had an immigration policy based on racial discrimination and homogeneity. Claims that Australia was a multiracial society were thus particularly irksome to Malaysians and Singaporeans because they were experiencing the real problems of creating multiracial nations. Malaysian and Singaporean leaders were frequently lectured to and criticized by journalists and academics in Australia for the restrictions on freedom that the Malaysian and Singapore governments felt were necessary in order to maintain racial harmony (see Searle 1996: 57). Malaysians and Singaporeans thus kept a critical eye on developments in Australian immigration policy.

The immigration reforms of 1966 and 1973, which were designed to improve Australia's image and end the isolation of the White Australia Policy, were perceived, in Malaysian and Singapore public opinion, as not having substantially reversed the discrimination against Asians. When it was announced in March 1966 that the White Australia Policy was to be liberalized, the Chinese major daily the *Nanyang Siang Pau* saw through the superficial changes and retorted that there was still a color bar because ordinary laborers were still not welcome. The Chinese newspaper called for an influx of migrants from Asia similar to the numbers that were part of the large-scale planned immigration scheme from Europe during the early post-war period, which inevitably would have implications for Australia's national identity, if it wanted to prove that it was truly non-discriminatory in its immigration policy (*Daily Highlights of the Chinese, Malay, and Tamil Press* 12 March 1966: D5). In 1967, the Singapore *Straits*

Times, in an editorial dealing with immigration policy in Australia entitled "At it Again," expressed its skepticism about the reforms of 1966 when it commented "there is a residual element of official discrimination" (6 April 1967: 10). The editorial remarked "it is much harder" for an Asian to get into Australia than a European, and that many Australians still "suffer" from "racial prejudice" which "is a form of cultural backwardness that cannot be eradicated – and often is made worse – by external pressure."

The official abolition of the White Australia Policy in 1973 was viewed with some degree of hope, but also a certain measure of disbelief in Singapore and Malaysia. The *Tamil Nesan* of Malaysia expressed its hope that the Australian identity as a predominantly European nation would be altered so that it would become more a part of Asia with increased Asian migration:

> Although geographically, Australia and New Zealand are close to South East Asia, their "White immigration policy" has alienated them from other countries in this region. The Asian countries have all along looked upon Australia and New Zealand as part of Western influence, but after the introduction of new policies by the two Governments, there is no doubt that the new-found concern and enthusiasm towards the Asian countries will grow.
>
> (*Mirror of Opinion*, 26 June 1973: E6)

The *Straits Times* was more skeptical, and highlighted that Grassby in Jakarta had "emphasised that Australia would not open its doors to Asian immigrants but would select prospective immigrants on their merits, as it does with Europeans" (12 June 1973: 2).

This skepticism about the new immigration policy pervaded the highest levels of government. At a Commonwealth Heads of Government Conference in August 1973, Lee Kuan Yew noted that under the new policy there may be few Asian migrants able to get into Australia. He commented that "Australia does not want our hewers of wood or our drawers of water. No they want our doctors and skilled men" (Rivett 1975: 112; *Straits Times* 5 August 1973: 4). Singapore's Minister for Health and Home Affairs, Chua Sian Chin believed that there were still restrictions on Asians entering Australia even after the White Australia Policy had been abolished. He said that "only Asians with professional or semi-professional skills are allowed in," but "this restriction, how-ever, does not apply to the people of European stock." Chua described how "in Singapore, we can see planeloads of Italians, Greeks, Turks and other Europeans on their way to Australia," and "many of these are in working class occupations, some are even peasants." He concluded by stating that the point that he and Prime Minister Lee were making was that "we do not see planeloads of workers and peasants from the overpopulated countries of Asia in transit to Australia" (*Straits Times* 12 August 1973: 3).

Malaysian leaders expressed sentiments similar to those of Singapore's. In September 1981 Dr Mahathir, the Prime Minister of Malaysia, voiced the same complaint when he said that Australia's immigration policy, which required "all kinds of qualifications" for people wanting to migrate "hurt us a bit because you tend to take the best of Malaysians." He remarked that "we would like unemployed Malaysians who want to work as labourers to go to Australia and settle down there" because "they, too, would like to go. But they are taking away doctors, lawyers, engineers . . . " (*Sunday Times* 27 September 1981: 3).

Malaysian and Singapore opinion tended to remain skeptical of Australia's willingness to admit Asian migrants. This was parti-cularly the case in the 1970s when both countries pressured a reluctant Australia to admit significant numbers of Vietnamese refugees who were landing on peninsular Malaysia. In May 1975 on American television, Prime Minister Lee Kuan Yew ridiculed Whitlam when Lee voiced his suspicion that the days of White Australia may not be over. Lee commented on where the thou-sands of Vietnamese refugees waiting off Singapore in a flotilla of boats could go to settle. He said that "there's the great wealthy continent of Australia, and they have a very sympathetic Prime Minister who believes the White Australia policy is most deplor-able and damnable, and here is his chance" (Viviani 1980: 14). On 6 May 1975 in Kingston Jamaica, Lee Kuan Yew repeated his observation that Australia only took professionals and highly skilled Asians (*Mirror of Opinion* 7 May 1975: N3). In Malaysia and Singapore, the Chinese newspapers the *Sin Chew Jit Poh* and the *Nanyang Siang Pau,* as well as the Tamil newspapers *Tamil Malar* and *Tamil Murasu,* added to Prime Minister Lee's comment by raising the issue of whether Australia's immigration policy still did restrict the entry of Asians, especially in the case of the Vietnamese refugees (*Mirror of Opinion* 10 May 1975: N3, N4, E, E3). To put pressure on the Australian government, authorities in Malaysia and Singapore either refused to allow some of the Vietnamese boat people to land or helped them to refuel and buy maps and compasses so that they could sail on to Australia. The embarrassing appearance of these boats on the northern Australia coast forced the Australian government to ask Southeast Asian governments to hold refugees until they could be processed by Australian immigration authorities. In 1978, Australia accepted that it would take 9,000 a year mainly from the Vietnamese camps in Malaysia, Singapore, and Indonesia (Viviani and Lawe-Davies 1980: 9; Viviani 1984; *Mirror of Opinion* 5 December 1977: N4; and *Mirror of Opinion* 10 December 1977: N2–4).

The diplomatic wrangle over taking Vietnamese refugees reinforced the existing stereotype of a White Australia rather than fostering the multicultural and multiracial image that Australia wanted Asian countries to accept. In February 1984, when Prime Minister Hawke visited Singapore, the Malay language newspaper of Singapore, the *Berita Harian* could still remark on Australia's "image as the 'European territory' in Asia" (*Mirror of Opinion* 15 February 1984: 6). In the 1980s, these images were readily evoked by debates in Australia on race and immigration. In 1984 and again in 1988, the Liberal-led opposition parties in Australia raised the prospect of reducing the intake of Asian migrants. This was described by some Southeast Asian leaders as an example of the anti-Asian sentiments in Australia (Kelly 1992: 133). Lee Kuan Yew commented that the proposals "harked back to the days of the country's 'White Australia' policy" (*Straits Times* 21 November 1988: 3; *Far Eastern Economic Review* 1 December 1988: 26). The Singapore-Chinese newspaper, *Lianhe Zaobao* remarked that "in Australia, some people are still prejudiced against Asians, feeling that not too many Asians should be allowed to migrate to Australia so as to preserve the characteristics of the Australians" (*Mirror of Opinion* 19 November 1988: 1).

Images of the Australian identity in Singapore and Malaysia during the 1990s

Over 20 years of projecting a multiracial and multicultural image into Southeast Asia have done little to change the impressions of Australia in Southeast Asia. To publicize Australia Day in 1994 and 1995 in Singapore, the Australian High Commission placed in the national newspaper of the country a speech by Prime Minister Paul Keating (1991–6) affirming Australia as a multicultural country that was seeking to become integrated into Asia (*Straits Times* 23 January 1994: 9). Members of the Keating Government frequently highlighted that Australia was already economically enmeshed into Asia, with Asia taking 60 percent of its exports (ADFAT 1993b). Prime Minister Keating in a 1995 speech to the Perth Chinese Chamber of Commerce, which was aimed at Singaporean, Malaysian, and Indonesian journalists present in Australia, claimed that "Asian culture and Asian values would soon begin to impact on mainstream Australian culture just as earlier waves of European migration had done." Keating rejected the idea of Australia as a melting pot in which migrants gradually lost their culture. He added that "if we need a culinary metaphor for Australia's approach to migrants in our society, a much better one is the Chinese *wok*, in which all ingredients retain their own distinctive identity but become part of a harmonious and balanced whole" (*Straits Times* 16 February 1995: 9).

The Australian Department of Foreign Affairs and Trade's own material, which its High Commissions in Malaysia and Singapore distributed, also stressed this multiracial and multicultural image (ADFAT 1992). A fact sheet disseminated by the High Commissions in late 1993 and early 1994 included the large subtitle: "Australia is a multicultural society being enriched by settlers from 200 nations" (ADFAT 1993a: 1). The Australian Tourist Commission's promotional material distributed in late 1994 at various exhibitions to encourage Singaporean and Malaysian tourists to visit Australia also projected this identity as well (ATC 1994).

Yet still the perception of the old identity of Australia has remained. Felix Soh, the foreign editor of the Singapore *Straits Times,* could still write in August 1995 that "many Asians continue to perceive Australia as a white man country, with white man orientations." He evoked the images that Asians had of Australia during the time of the White Australia Policy. "This policy to seal Australia from Asia hermetically, though now abandoned," Soh wrote, "has left negative psychological residues on both sides, even up to this day" (11 August 1995: 34). This was evident in Malaysia during 1991. In April, there appeared in the Malaysian press several articles by the Perth journalist, Illsa Sharp, stressing Australia as a multicultural nation. She even mentioned that Australia was regarded as the new "Nanyang" by today's Chinese (the old Nanyang being the Southeast Asian countries where millions of Chinese emigrants moved to from the mid-nineteenth to the mid-twentieth centuries) (*New Straits Times* 22

April 1991: 10; Sharp 1994: 276). Despite this public relations effort, in June 1991, the Malaysian television station TV3, as a "pay back" for Australian coverage of Malaysia that the Malaysian government felt was unfair, broadcast a documentary on Australia (Wong 1994: 172–88; *New Straits Times* 2 May 1991: 4). The programme depicted anti-Asian sentiment as being common and part of what the narrator of the series called the "typical white Australian manner." The series stressed that there was deep racism against the indigenous people of Australia and continuing destruction of their culture and families by the dominant white population (*New Straits Times* 19 June 1991: 11; 21 June 1991: 9).

Australia's image may only change when Australia becomes what some prominent Malaysians and Singaporeans have called more "Asianized," which appears to mean a greater percentage of the population being Asian. This has been referred to a number of times in the statements of opinion leaders of Singapore and Malaysia. George Yeo, Singapore's Minister for Information and the Arts and Second Minister for Foreign Affairs, noted in December 1993 at the Pacific Rim Business Collaboration Symposium in Kuala Lumpur that a recent survey showed that the majority of Australians still do not consider themselves as part of Asia. However, Yeo affirmed that Australia will become increasingly a part of Asia as Australian society becomes "more Asianized," presumably through greater numbers of Asian migrants (Yeo 1993: 72). In October 1994, the Singapore journalist Nirmal Ghosh reported that among other factors, "the Asianisation of Australia's population ratio through immigration, and the integration of Asian-born people in Australian politics and government service" would "produce Australians who will be more and more tuned in to Asian ways of thinking" (*Straits Times* 26 October 1994: 27).

In Malaysia, too, there is the impression that Australia will have to become more Asianized to be part of the Southeast Asian region. There is also the feeling that it is still apt to describe Australia, as it was in the 1960s by the Malaysian press, as a "white man's continent." In May 1995, when speaking on Malaysia's proposed East Asian Economic Caucus, which excluded Australia and New Zealand, Dr Mahathir noted that "as Australia becomes more Asianised, certainly in terms of geographical relations but also in terms of outlook, there is no reason why they cannot be a part of EAEC" (*Australian* 15 May 1995: 1). A few days later Mahathir again commented on Australia:

I have always told Australia that if you want to become
Asian, it is not enough for you to declare, "We are
Asians", or to say, "We are near Asia".

It is their decision. If they want to be Asianised they
must become culturally Asian. You should not go around
saying you know better than anyone else. That is not what
Asians do.

We know that they [Australians] have one foot in
Europe still and mentally, they are Europeans.

(Australian 18 May 1995: 1)

On 15 December 1995, at the Association of South East Asian
Nations (ASEAN) summit in Bangkok, Dr Mahathir actually
stated that until enough Asians had settled in Australia, Malaysia
would veto any Australian membership of Southeast Asian economic and political organizations, such as ASEAN. Dr Mahathir
jokingly said that Australians would only be guaranteed to act the
way other Asian countries acted when their population mix had
become 70 percent Asian and 30 percent Caucasian (*Straits Times*
18 December 1995: 25; *Australian* 15 January 1996: 2). In
January 1996, Malaysia's International Trade and Industry
Minister Datuk Seri Rafidah Aziz reaffirmed his point when she
commented on the possibility of Australia joining ASEAN.
Rafidah said that Australia and New Zealand could join "but
the condition is that they have to become Asianised," and that
"the day would come when Australia and New Zealand became
Asianised" (*Straits Times* 19 January 1996: 21).

The Mahathir Government's position has been that the Australian
identity has not changed much since the days of White Australia.
Mahathir himself definitely sees Australia in terms of it being a
white European continent separate from Asia. In his 1995 book *The
Voice of Asia,* which he co-wrote with Shintaro Ishihara, the author of
The Japan that Can Say No, Mahathir even set aside valuable space to
once again reiterate his opinion on Australia and its identity, which
appears to reflect that found in his 1970 book, *The Malay Dilemma*:

In recent years Australia has emphasized its ties with East
Asia, seeking in various ways to associate more closely
with the region. However appropriate geographically it
may be to include Australia as part of Asia, we have never
regarded Australians as fellow Asians, they have always
considered themselves basically European. Consequently, I

tell the Australians this: You can't simply decide to be
Asian. You must have an Asian culture. This means, for a
start, changing your attitude and improving your manners.
Asians don't go around telling others what to do. But don't
think that a change of heart will be enough. When Europe
was rich, you were European; now that Asia is rich you want
to be Asian. You can't change sides just like that.

(Mahathir and Ishihara 1995: 85)

Singapore's Lee Kuan Yew had made a similar observation, that
Australia was culturally isolated from its nearest neighbours in
Asia, but culturally very close to Britain and North America. In
March 1995, when Lee was awarded an honorary Doctorate from
the University of Queensland, he remarked that "an Indonesian, or
Malaysian, or Singaporean who lands in Brisbane or Sydney may
be forgiven for believing that he has landed on an offshore island
in the Atlantic somewhere between America and Britain." Lee
added that such a visitor "would not know he is close to home in
Asia by reading the newspapers and watching the television"
(*Straits Times* 21 March 1995: 2).

There were strong similarities between Singapore and Malaysian
perceptions of Australian society in the 1990s and those expressed
from the 1960s to the 1980s. However the context was different.
In Malaysia, there had been a move away from some of the strong
government measures used to promote a Malay identity for the
country in the aftermath of the 1969 race riots. The economic
progress of the Malay community that was evident by the 1990s
allowed the Malaysian government to relax some of the restrictions
that had been designed to redress the economic backwardness of
the Malay community, which had fostered racial tension in the
1960s. The racial and cultural diversity of Malaysia increasingly
came to feature prominently in the identity projected by the
country (Crouch 1996: 124, 163). Also, in the 1990s, Mahathir
and other Malaysian leaders began to speak of Asian values that
bound different Asian races and cultures together. This talk of an
Asian unity was very much a part of an external political agenda
in which Asian countries asserted themselves in a world order
dominated by the West (Mahathir and Ishihara 1995).

In the 1990s, the Singapore government was also encouraging
its different cultural communities to preserve their "cultural heritage" as part of an Asian mosaic that made up Singapore (Hill and
Lian 1995: 90–112). The idea of existing shared Asian values that

the different ethnic communities could accept was emphasized (Hill and Lian 1995: 188–219). The political stress on an Asian identity as being crucial to Malaysian and Singapore multiracial societies influenced perceptions of Australia. There was also present a political agenda which held that there existed a sense of community of Asian nations because of these shared Asian cultural values. This intellectual climate acted to prevent Australia from being seen as a part of Asia and as a multicultural and multiracial country. Thus, in the 1990s, in order for these countries to perceive Australia as a part of Asia, there needed to be a significant Asian population and a stronger Asian cultural presence in the country.

In this environment, the Keating Government's attempts to move away from the old Anglo-Celtic identity that was rooted in Australia's British colonial past were viewed favourably by Singapore and Malaysia. These efforts were linked with Australia mentally becoming a part of the region by being more Asianized or Asian in cultural background. The Singapore press thoroughly endorsed the Keating Government's attempts to make Australia a republic and remove the Queen of Britain as its head of state (*Straits Times* 22 October 1993: 34; and *Straits Times* 16 Februay 1995: 9). Not only did the Singapore press support the idea of Australia severing its colonial links with the British crown, but also the process of making the Australian identity based less upon the British background of the country. The editor of the *Straits Times* wrote in June 1995 that "in words of [the Australian] Foreign Minister Gareth Evans, [1988–96], it would be a 'very, very overt' commitment to the Asianisation of Australia if the Crown were dropped" (12 June 1995: 28). During the Keating Government, there were signs that Australia was beginning to be perceived as a multiracial country that was part of the Asian region. The Prime Minister of Singapore Goh Chok Tong (1990 to the present), when visiting Australia in September 1994, after surveying all the societies of the Pacific Rim, remarked that "Australia is the most Asianised country of Western origin" (Goh 1994: 13).

However, the old perceptions of Australia, as a white settler-nation that dispossessed its indigenous people and then excluded non-whites through a racist immigration program, are so strongly embedded in the consciousness of Malaysians and Singaporeans that they have been easily evoked. In April 1996, when Bill Hayden, a former Governor-General of Australia (1988–96), remarked that

Australia had nothing to be ashamed of when it came to racism if it was compared to Asian countries such as Malaysia, several public figures and the press in Malaysia were quick to revive the images of White Australia (*New Straits Times* 4 April 1996: 22). They did this in a manner which revealed that Australian governments still have a long way to go in convincing public opinion in Malaysia that there has been a fundamental shift in the Australian identity. In his column in the Malaysian newspaper, the *Star* V.K. Chin commented:

> There is a racial bias which exists in most of the Anglo-Saxons not only in Australia but worldwide. They only differ in degree. In Australia, some of them may be 100 percent racist, others may be 50 per cent.
>
> (6 April 1996: 19)

The President of the Barisan Nasional (the governing coalition of Malaysia) Backbenchers' Club, Ruhanie Ahmad remarked that "those who want to criticise others should look at their own countries before passing judgment on others. Australia has not been treating Asians and other non-White citizens fairly and the plight of its own aborigines is a classic example" (*New Straits Times* 4 April 1996: 4). It was not just members of the government and press that resurrected the old images of Australia. A Member of Parliament who was in the Opposition Democratic Action Party, Karpal Singh said that "Hayden should endeavour to put his own house in order first before commenting on the other countries." He said that "there are certainly cases of racism and anger towards Asians even in Australia and New Zealand." Director of the Just World Trust Dr Chandra Muzaffar, one of the Mahathir Government's staunchest critics, asked "Hayden to investigate the racist attitude of certain members of Australian society towards the Aborigines and Asian community before accusing Malaysia of being a racist nation" (*New Straits Times* 5 April 1996: 2). A Malaysian who had obviously lived in Australia and had knowledge of the isolated incidents of racism against Asians in Australia sent a letter to the *New Straits Times* on his impressions of Australia. He remarked that in Malaysia, "we don't call others derogatory names like the way Australians do. We don't call people 'Wogs' or 'Chins,' or 'Slant Eyes,' or 'Blackies,' or 'Pommies' or whatever." He added that "we don't go round painting slogans on bus shelters such as 'Asians out' or fire-bomb Chinese restaurants" (*New Straits Times* 11 April 1996: 13).

Surveys of the population of Singapore and Malaysia have revealed that the image of a White Australia that discriminates against Asians has been an enduring one. A questionnaire given to Singaporeans intending to migrate to Australia in the 1980s, revealed that 90 percent of them expected to experience racism and discrimination in Australia (Sullivan and Gunasekaran 1994: 25). Surveys of Singapore university students in the early and mid-1990s confirmed this result by obtaining a similar very high response to questions on whether there was racism against Asians in Australia (Blackburn 1997: 17). These studies reflected surveys done in the early 1960s, which revealed that high school and university students of Malaysia (which then included Singapore) were well aware of the White Australia Policy and felt that Australia was a country that isolated itself from Asia and practiced racial discrimination (Jones and Jones 1965: 272–85).

The images associated with the White Australia Policy were strongly reinforced by the race debate that was initiated in Australia by the independent Member of Parliament Pauline Hanson's maiden speech in Federal Parliament during September 1996. In early November 1996, a correspondent writing in a regular column called "Insight: Down Under" for the Malaysian *Sunday Star* noted that in Southeast Asia, Pauline Hanson's remarks on "the danger of Australia being 'swamped' by Asians, her considered argument that multiculturalism should be abolished, and her repeated attacks on funding levels for aborigines have revived memories of the days of the White Australia Policy" (3 November 1996: 23). A report in the Malaysian *New Straits Times* observed that, regarding Australia, "Asia has an historic suspicion when it comes to the issue of racism because of the now-defunct White Australia immigration policy which discriminated in favour of white migrants . . ." (31 October 1996: 12). A letter to the *Star* from a Malaysian who had lived in Australia during the 1988 race debate expressed his view that "the current debate on racism in Australia is a reflection of the deep-rooted racist nature of the majority of white Australia" (21 November 1996: 21). The *New Straits Times* in late November and early December 1996 published a series of feature articles on race relations in Australia which highlighted incidents of racism and intolerance. These newspaper features were reminiscent of the 1991 Malaysian television documentaries on Australia (*New Straits Times* 26, 27 and 28 November 1996, 3 December 1996). They contained many comments from Asians living in Australia who had experienced racism.

In Singapore, the reaction to the rise in support for a white Australian identity by stopping Asian immigration was similar to that in Malaysia. The Singapore *Business Times* expressed its suspicions about Australians when it discussed the opinion polls on the issues that Pauline Hanson had raised. The editor commented that "it is hardly surprising that an opinion survey this week found that most Australians want an immediate freeze on immigration and 53 per cent want the proportion of Asian immigrants cut." He sarcastically commented that "given a choice, most white Australians would probably like to see their country relocated somewhere in the north Atlantic." The editorial stated that these attitudes could mean that Australia "will revert to being an outpost for distant allies as it was in the White Australia years" (*Business Times* 6 November 1996: 17).

The fears of racism against Asians in Australia were heightened by extensive press coverage of cases of harassment and beatings of Asians in Australia that were apparently inspired by the race debate that Pauline Hanson and her supporters had initiated. This reached a high point in Singapore when a Singapore Ministerial Delegation led by Foreign Minister Jayakumar met their Australian counterparts in Canberra in late October and early November 1996. Television coverage of this meeting in Singapore reflected the perception that racism against Asians in Australia was pervasive. On 31 October 1996, at the beginning of the seven o'clock English language news on Singapore state run television, the normally staid news reader Brendan Wong looked tense, as news had come in during the day that several Singapore Armed Forces personnel training in Australia had experienced racial harassment in Rockhampton. He did not start the first story with his prepared script of questions about the ministerial meeting. His first question to the Singapore correspondent live in Australia was, "did you encounter hostility or notice any towards other Asians?" The sense of apprehension and alarm in his voice was clearly noticeable. Wong Shuk Min, the correspondent, replied, "none at all", and then discussed the ministerial meeting. At the press conference after the ministerial meeting, the Singapore ministers, to "save face" for their Australian hosts, politely downplayed the Rockhampton incident as an isolated case. However, media coverage in Singapore of the rise of racism in Australia continued to intensify.

The revival of the ideas behind the White Australia Policy by Pauline Hanson and her supporters in 1996 confirmed long-held suspicions in Singapore and Malaysia that there exists deep-seated racism against Asians in Australia and an even stronger desire of many Australians for a homogenous white Australian identity. Surveying the perceptions of Australia in Singapore and Malaysia in the 30 years after the White Australia Policy began to be dismantled and a new image projected in Southeast Asia, does tend to confirm immigration historian Sean Brawley's point that the White Australia Policy has left an indelible mark upon the minds of Australia's Asian neighbours about the Australian identity (1994: 255). The new identity that Australia has projected as a multicultural and multiracial society has yet to be fully accepted by the people of countries who have a greater claim to such descriptions – Malaysia and Singapore. These perceptions of the Australian identity held in Malaysia and Singapore are the historical legacy of Southeast Asia's and Australia's different reactions to one of the Pacific Rim's largest migrations – the exodus of the Nanyang Chinese.

References

ADFAT (Australian Department of Foreign Affairs and Trade) (1992) *Australia*. Canberra: Australian Department of Foreign Affairs and Trade Overseas Information Branch.

ADFAT (1993a) *Australia: An Introduction*. Canberra: Australian Department of Foreign Affairs and Trade Overseas Information Branch.

ADFAT (1993b) *Australia in Asia: Background Information*. Canberra: Australian Department of Foreign Affairs and Trade.

ATC (Australian Tourist Commission) (1994) *Australia: Land of Dreams*. Singapore: Australian Tourist Commission.

Bedlington, Stanley S. (1978) *Malaysia and Singapore: The Building of New States*. London: Cornell University Press.

Betts, Katharine (1988) *Ideology and Immigration: Australia 1976 to 1987*. Melbourne: Melbourne University Press.

Blackburn, Kevin (1997) "Singapore students open a window on Australia," *Current Affairs Bulletin* 73 (6): 14–19.

Brawley, Sean (1994) "'An Iron Curtain Canberra Style', Asian Perceptions of the White Australia Policy," in Don Grant and Graham Seal (eds) *Australia in the World: Perceptions and Possibilities*. Perth: Black Swan Press.

Brawley, Sean (1995a) *The White Peril: Foreign Relations and Asian Immigration to Australasia and North America, 1919–1978*. Sydney: University of New South Wales Press.

Brawley, Sean (1995b) "The Department of Immigration and the Abolition of the 'White Australia' Policy Reflected Through the Private
Diaries of Sir Peter Heydon," *Australian Journal of Politics and History*
41 (3): 420–434.

Castles, Stephen, Kalantzis, Mary, Cope, Bill and Morrissey, Michael
(1993) *Mistaken Identity: Multiculturalism and the Demise of Nationalism
in Australia*. Sydney: Pluto Press.

Comber, Leon (1983) *13 May 1969: A Historical Survey of Sino-Malay
Relations*. Kuala Lumpur: Heinemann Asia.

Crouch, Harold (1996) *Government and Society in Malaysia*. London: Allen
and Unwin.

Ee, Joyce (1961) "Chinese Migration to Singapore, 1896–1941," *Journal
of South East Asian History* 2 (1): 33–51.

FitzGerald, Stephen (1972) *China and the Overseas Chinese: A Study of
Peking's Changing Policy, 1949–1970*. London: Cambridge University
Press.

Foster, Lois and Stockley, David (1984) *Multiculturalism: The Changing
Australian Paradigm*. Clevedon, Avon: Multilingual Matters.

Goh, Chok Tong (1994) "Integrating Asia in the World Economy,"
Speeches 18 (5): 1–13.

Hill, Michael and Lian, Kwen Fee (1995) *The Politics of National Building
and Citzenship in Singapore*. London: Routledge.

Jones, Gavin and Jones, Margaret (1965) "Australia's Immigration
Policy: Some Malaysian Attitudes," *Australian Outlook* 19: 272–285.

Inglis, Christine, S. Gunasekaran, Sullivan, Gerard, and Wu, Chung-
Tong (eds) (1994) *Asians in Australia: The Dynamics of Migration and
Settlement*. Singapore: Institute of Southeast Asian Studies.

Kelly, Paul (1992) *The End of Certainty: The Story of the 1980s*. Sydney:
Allen and Unwin.

London, H.I. (1970) *Non-White Immigration and the "White Australia"
Policy*. Sydney: Sydney University Press.

Mahathir Bin Mohamad (1970) *The Malay Dilemma*. Singapore: Times.

Mahathir Mohamad and Ishihara, Shintaro (1995) *The Voice of Asia*, trans.
Frank Baldwin. Tokyo: Kodansha.

Martin, Brett (1995) *Australia in Singapore*. Singapore: Australian High
Commission.

Meaney, Neville (1995) "The End of 'White Australia', and Australia's
Changing Perceptions of Asia, 1945–1990," *Australian Journal of
International Affairs* 49 (2): 171–89.

Price, Charles Archibald (1974) *The Great White Walls Are Built: Restrictive Immigration to North America and Australasia 1836–1888*. Canberra:
Australian National University Press.

Price, Charles (1984) "Immigration and Population Policy," in Donald
J. Phillips, and Jim Huston (eds) *Australian Multicultural Society:
Identity, Communication, Decision Making*. Melbourne: Drummond.

Ramachandran, Selakumaran and Arudsothy, Ponniah (1992) "A Socio-Economic Profile of Malaysian Immigrants in Australia," in James E. Coughlan (ed.) *The Diverse Asians: A Profile of Six Asian Communities in Australia*. Brisbane: Centre for the Study of Australia-Asia Relations, Griffith University.

Ratnam, K.J. (1965) *Communalism and the Political Process in Malaya*. Kuala Lumpur: University of Malaya Press.

Rivett, Kenneth (1975) *Australia and the Non-White Migrant*. Melbourne: Melbourne University Press.

Saw, Swee-Hock (1969) "Population Trends in Singapore, 1819–1967," *Journal of South East Asian History* 10 (1): 36–49.

Searle, Peter (1996) "Recalcitrant or Realpolitik? The Politics of culture in Australia's relations with Malaysia," in Richard Robison (ed.) *Pathways to Asia: The Politics of Engagement*. Sydney: Allen and Unwin.

Sharp, Illsa (1994) "Looking Beyond the Wayang: Perceptions and Coverage of Australia in Southeast Asian Media (with special reference to Singapore/Malaysia)," in Don Grant and Graham Seal (eds) *Australia in the World: Perceptions and Possibilities, Papers from Outside Images of Australia Conference, Perth, 1992*. Perth: Black Swan Press.

Shu, Jing, Khoo, Siew Ean, Struik, Andrew and McKenzie, Fiona (1994) *Australia's Population Trends and Prospects 1993*. Canberra: Australia Government Publishing Service.

Sullivan, Gerard and S. Gunasekaran (1994) *Motivations of Migrants From Singapore to Australia, Field Report Series No.28 Social Issues in Southeast Asia*. Singapore: Institute of Southeast Asian Studies.

Viviani, Nancy (1980) *Australian Government Policy on the Entry of Vietnamese Regugees in 1975: Australia–Asia Papers No.1*. Brisbane: Centre for the Study of Australian-Asian Relations, Griffith University.

Viviani, Nancy and Lawe-Davies, Joanna (1980) *Australian Government Policy on the Entry of Vietnamese Refugees 1976 to 1978: Australia-Asia Papers No.2*. Brisbane: Centre for the Study of Australian-Asian Relations, Griffith University.

Viviani, Nancy (1984) *The Long Journey: Vietnamese Migration and Settlement in Australia*. Melbourne: Melbourne University Press.

Viviani, Nancy (ed.) (1992) *The Abolition of the White Australia Policy: The Immigration Reform Movement Revisited*. Brisbane: Centre for Australia–Asia Relations, Griffith University.

Wang, Sing-Wu (1978) *The Organization of Chinese Emigration: 1848–1888: With Special Reference to Chinese Emigration to Australia*. San Francisco: Chinese Materials Center.

White, Richard (1981) *Inventing Australia: Images and Identity 1688–1980*. Sydney: Allen and Unwin.

Wong, Loong (1994) "Touchy Neighbours: Australia's Muddled Relationship with Malaysia," *Southeast Asian Journal of Social Science* 22: 172–88.

Yarwood, A.T. (1964) *Asian Migration to Australia, The Background to Exclusion, 1896–1923*. Melbourne: Melbourne University Press.

Yarwood, A.T. (ed.) (1968) *Attitudes to Non-European Immigration*. Melbourne: Cassell Australia.

Yeo, George Yong-Boon (1993) "Southeast Asia in the Pacific Century," *Speeches* 17 (6): 62–72.

INDEX

Aborigines 173–4, 183, 225, 233, 239, 242–4
Abu-Lughod, Janet L. 58
Acapulco, Mexico 2, 25, 27–30, 33, 51–2, 73
Adams, Edgar 160, 161
Adams, J. 178, 182, 183
agriculture 125, 135, 139–46, 198, 200, 203–6, 209, 211–12, 217–18
agro-ecology of South China and trade 85–105
Ahmad, Ruhanie 243
aircraft 203–4
Alderman, H. 118
Allen, Franklin 55
Allen, Meryl 179, 182
almojarifazgo taxes 27–31
American Farm Bureau Federation 217
American trade dollars 152–67
Americas: island trade 78; silk trade 50–3, 62–3
Amerindians 79
Anatolia 44
Andaya, Leonard Y. 25
Anglo-Celtic identity in Australia 224, 226, 228, 231–2, 242
animals 171–2, 176, 178–80, 182–4, *see also* livestock
Arthur, Chester, president of USA 14, 153
Arudsothy, Ponniah 227, 230, 231
Ashton, D.H. 173
Asia: Australian relations with 225–32, 234–40, 242–6; economic collapse 1–3, 19–20; silk trade 38–45, 47, 52–3, 56–7, 62; Spain and 24–5, 27
Asianization of Australia 239–40, 242
Association of South East Asian Nations (ASEAN) 240
Atherton Tableland, Queensland, Australia 176, 178–82
Atlantic interdependence 19–20
Attiwill, P.M. 173
Australia: ecology 71, 76, 78–9, 82; environmental change 171–84; gold rushes (1848–57) 125–47; Singapore and Malaysia and perceptions of identity 224–46
Avery, Martha 204, 207, 209

Bag, Sailendra Kumar 54
balance scale peso 156
Banaba 76
Bancroft, H.H. 131, 135, 139–40, 142
bandicoots 179
banditry 45, 59–61
Bangladesh 117–18
barley 112–14, 116, 140–1, 144, 146
Barr, Neil 172
Batsavage, Richard E. 191, 201, 202, 212
Battle, Laurie 189
Bauzon, Leslie E. 25, 30, 31, 32

Bazant, Jan 51
Bedlington, Stanley S. 234
Belfanti, Carlo Marco 48
Bentley, Jerry H. 41
Berry, Thomas 129, 138, 145
Besher, A. 2
Betts, Katharine 232
bills of exchange 159
bimetallism 153–4
biological invasion of islands 72–5,
    77–9, 81
birds 176, 178–9, 182–3
Birtles, Terry 177, 178, 179, 180,
    182
blackberries 180, 183
Blackburn, Kevin 19, 224–46
Bland–Allison Act (1878) (USA)
    152–3
Bonner, Nigel 80
boom sectors and economic analysis
    132–3
Borah, Woodrow 51
Borneo 79
Boulnois, L. 41, 42
Brandt, Loren 121–2
Braudel, Fernand 24, 38, 92
Brawley, Sean 225, 246
Bray, F. 111
British East India Company 24, 49,
    61, 88, 92, 97–102, 155, 157
Brouk, B. 112, 113
Brown, M.J. 173
Brownstone, David M. 39
Bryde, Charles W. 177, 181, 182
buckwheat 113–14
Bulliet, Richard W. 57
bullion, silver 98, 100–1, 104,
    155, 160–6
Busby, J.R. 173
Buttrey, T. 156
Byzantine Empire 40–4, 56, 62

Cahill, Harry A. 211, 213, 214,
    215, 221
California gold rushes (1848–57)
    125–47
camels 57–9
Canada 211
Canton 50–2
Canton dollar 157

capital goods 208, 211
caravans 40, 45–6, 57–61
caravansaries 57
Carothers, Neil 165
carp 102
Cary, John 172
cash crops 104, 116, 120
cassava 113–14
Castles, Stephen, et al. 231
caterpillars 177–8
Cayez, Pierre 53
centralization, economic 195
Chamorros 73
Chaudhuri, K.N. 23
Chaunu, Pierre 27, 28, 60, 61
chemicals, China–U.S. trade 197,
    199, 202
Chen, Gao-Hua 47
Chen Guanghui 89
Chin, V.K. 243
China: American trade dollars in
    nineteenth century 152–67;
    economy 4, 24, 79–81; island
    trade 75–6, 78; maritime trade
    and agro-ecology in South
    85–105; Nanyang migration
    224–5, 238, 246; rice imports
    110–11, 121–2; silk trade
    39–49, 51–6, 62; trade 2–3, 19;
    U.S. trade and 188–221
China Committee (CHINCOM)
    190
Chipp, Don 230
chopping 157, 164
Chou En-lai 199, 200, 220
Chua Sian Chin 235, 236
Chuan, Hang-shen 6, 27, 28, 52,
    61
citizenship, Australian 227
Clark, A.H. 78
Clarke, William 204, 207, 209
clearance, forest 174–7, 180–3
clearing leases 182
climate 71
clothing 212
coal 80, 200, 211–12
Coghlan, T.A. 128, 129, 136, 146
Coinage Act (1873) (USA) 152–3,
    165
coinage and silk trade 56

Cole, Arthur Harrison 145
Collett, Barry 177, 180, 183
colonialism 27, 33, 72, 78, 130–1, 171, 224–6, 229, 233, 242
Columbus, Christopher 73
Comber, Leon 224, 234
commercialization of Chinese agriculture 85–6, 97–8, 104–5
commodities 115, 138–9, 192, 196–9, 202, 212
Commodity Control List (U.S.) 189, 204
communism and U.S. trade 189–92, 196, 204, 213, 217
comparative advantage, China–U.S. 211–12, 214, 220
Comstock Lode 152, 158, 161–2, 165–6
Cook, James 7, 72, 74, 75, 79
copper 81
Corden, W.M. 131
corn 205–6, 211
cotton 77, 85–6, 94–101, 104–5, 115–16, 120, 208, 211
Coverdale, T.J. 177–8, 180–1
cowhides 142
crop rotation 85–6, 94–7, 115–16
Crosby, A.W. 74, 78
Crosby, Alfred, *Ecological Imperialism* 16, 171–84
Crouch, Harold 241
Cuddihy, Linda 77
Cultural Revolution (China) (1967–9) 193, 195, 198, 200–2, 207–8, 211
Cunningham, Peter 177
Curtin, Philip D. 60
Cushman, Jennifer 87–8, 89, 91, 93, 94
customs: houses 87, 92–3, 97–8; silk trade 59, 61

Daigle, Douglas 3
Dampier, William 90–1
Davie, John L. 201, 202, 212
Davis, Alf 179
Davis, Horace 144
de los Rios Coronel, Hernando 31
de Morga, Antonio 32–3
de Vries, Jan 7, 92

DeBow, J.D.B. 130, 140
demand: concentrated of islands 72, 75–7, 79–81; cotton 94, 96–100, 104–5; rice 114, 118–19; silk 26, 41, 54, 102–4; silver 51, 80–1, 167; timber 80
Dernberger, Robert F. 18, 210, 218
Dickie, Vance 228, 229
dingoes 179–80
direct/indirect profit in Spain and Philippines 25–6, 29, 31
disease 72–4, 78, 171
Doak, Barnett A. 209
Dodd, Frank 177
Dodson, John 78
Doggett, H. 112
dogwood 176, 181
Downer, Alexander 229
drought 71
Druett, Joan 78
Drummond, J.C. 117
dry rice 113–14
Dudden, Arthur P. 3, 192
Dunstan, Don 228
'Dutch disease' model of economic analysis 131, 139
Dutch East India Company 24, 49, 61

eagles 179
earthquakes 71
Eckstein, Alexander 192, 205, 207, 208, 213, 217
ecology and Pacific Islands 70–82
economy: Asian collapse 1–3, 19–20; Australia in gold rush 130, 146–7; China 4, 24, 79–81, 86, 96–7, 105; island 70, 73, 81; motivations for China–U.S. trade 188, 192–3, 195–221
ecosystems, island 72–3, 75, 81
Edler, Florence M. 46
Ee, Joyce 224
8-reales dollar 156
Eisenhower, Dwight D., president of USA 191
Elms, F. 177
Elvin, Mark 78

embargo, Chinese trade 188–92, 203, 209–11, 215
Emergency Committee for American Trade (ECAT) 217
ENSO (El Niño/Southern Oscillation) 71
environment: change 171–84; history of Pacific islands 70–7, 79
erosion 71, 78
ethnocentricity of Chinese 192–3
eucalypts 172–3, 176
Europe: Australian immigration policy 228–9, 231–6, 240–1; China trade 85, 87, 91–3, 97–105, 191, 204, 219; migration 171–2, 174, 180, 184; silk trade 39, 41, 45–9, 51, 53–4, 56, 60–1; trade 26–7, 161, 166
Evans, Gareth 242
exotics 73–4, 172, 176, 180, 183–4
Export Control Act (U.S.) (1949) 188–9
exports: Australia 227, 238; China 96, 98–103, 105, 191, 200; trade dollars 152–4; U.S.A. 126, 142–6, 188–9, 196, 198, 203, 205–8, 210–11, 215, 217–18, 220

Fairbanks, John K. 99, 193
Fan I-chun 89, 91, 93
Fan, Jin-ming 39, 42, 44, 45, 46, 50, 51, 52
Fang, Hao 41, 42
farming, Europeans in Australia 172, 174–5, 180–1
Federico, Giovanni 49, 61
Fenton, James 178, 182
fertilizers 115, 200, 202, 205–7, 211, 217
Figgis, Penny 173, 176
Fiji 75, 77
fire: environmental change 173–6, 180–1, 183; forest 71
fish pond–mulberry tree ecology 97, 102–5, 115
fisheries 71
Fitzgerald, Stephen 224
Flannery, Tim 78, 172, 173, 174

Fletcher, Jack 178, 182
flour 142, 144
flying foxes 182
Flynn, Dennis O. 1–22, 23–37, 51, 61
Foreign Affairs Subcommittee on Asian and Pacific Affairs 218
forests: high-rainfall in Australia 172–83; island 80–1
Foshan, China 94–5, 99, 104
Foss, Theodore Nicholas 49
Foster, Lois 230, 231
France 48, 53
Franck, Irene M. 39
Frank, Andre Gunder 3
Fraser, Malcolm, prime minister of Australia 231
French Indo-China 110
Friedman, Edward 192
Frith, Harry 178
Frost, Lionel 1–22
Frost, Warwick 16
fruit tree–fish pond ecology 102–3
fruit and vegetables 114, 140, 142, 212
Fukien, China 110, 116
Fullerton, Mary 180
Furuta, K. 116

Garnett, Porter 163, 165
Genoa, Italy 45
geology 70–1, 80
George, Robert Lloyd 2
Gerber, James 12, 13, 125–47
Germany 211, 213
Ghosh, Nirmal 239
Gippsland, Australia 175, 177–82
Giráldez, Arturo 2, 4, 5, 23–34, 51, 161
global economy 1
global trade 3–4, 23–4, 26–7; silk and 38–63
GNP (China) 191
goats 74, 78
Goh Chok Tong 242
gold 160–1, 166; rushes (1848–57) 81, 125–47, 225
Gorton, John 228, 229, 230
grains: China domestic trade 92–3; China–U.S. trade 192, 197, 199,

202, 205–8, 212, 217, 220; rice and 112–14, 116–18; U.S. gold rush 125–6, 140–2, 144, 146–7, *see also by type*
Grassby, Al 230, 231, 235
grasshoppers 177
Great Britain: Australia trade 227; China trade 191, 211, 213; colonialism 224–6, 229, 233, 242; silk 53, 60; trade coins 157–8
Great Leap Forward (China) (1958–60) 194, 197, 205
Greene, Fred 219
Griffiths, Tom 172
Groen, Henry J. 204, 205, 207
Guadalupe Hidalgo, Treaty of (1848) 125
Guam 73, 75, 77
Guangdong, China 73, 85–7, 89–97, 101, 103–5
Guangxi, China 86, 92, 104–5
Guangzhou, China 86, 88, 90–2, 95–7, 99–101, 104
guano 76
Guiler, Eric 180, 182, 183
Gunasekaran, S. 244
gunpowder 38

Hamashita, T. 110
Hamilton, Capt. 90
Hamilton, Earl J. 28, 29
Han dynasty (202BC–220AD) 40, 59
Hanson, Pauline 244, 245, 246
Hargreaves, Edward 128
Hartley, golddigger 128
Hartnell, Ross 177, 182
Hawaii 75, 77
Hawke, Bob, prime minister of Australia 231, 232, 237
Hayami, A. 113–14
Hayden, Bill 232, 242, 243
Hein, Philippe L. 76
Henderson, Krimhilde 177, 183
Hepburn, A. Barton 165
Heymann, Hans, Jr 192, 193, 194–5, 205
Heytesbury Forest, Australia 178
Hill, Michael 241, 242

Hoa, Y. 158
Holland, J.E. 176, 178
Holland 24, 27, 33, 49–51, 60, 92, 211, 213
Holt, Harold 227
homogeneity, racial 228, 234, 246
Hong Kong dollar 157–8
Houghton, Norm 177
Hourani, G.F. 47
Howe, Christopher 192, 201, 209
Hsiao, Liang-lin 121
Hsu, John C. 191, 192
Huang Juzhen 89, 90, 91
Huang, Shansheng 98
Hubbard, C. 156
Hyndman, David 81

ideas exchange and Silk Road 38–9, 55, 62–3
identity, perceptions of Australian 224–46
immigration 135; policy in Australia (1966–96) 224–37, 239, 242, 244–5
imports: Australia and grain 126, 145; China and cotton 94–5, 99–101; China and rice 110–11, 121–2; China and U.S. 192–3, 196–7, 199, 201–3, 205, 207–15; U.S. and Chinese 53–5, 63, 189, 208–9, 211–15
Inalcik, Halil 46
Incas 79
income and rice consumption 117–20, 122
India 43, 94–6, 98–9, 101, 110, 112, 117–18, 224
Indica rices 110
indigenous peoples 72–4, 171
Indonesia 70–1, 117–18
industrialization of China 198, 201, 206
influenza 73, 78, 171
Inglis, Christine *et al.* 225, 232
inkweed 180
insects 176–8, 180
interdependence, global 3
international relations and China 193, 196, 203, 208, 218–19, 221
Inuit 79

iron: ore 80–1; and steel 192, 197, 199–200, 202, 208, 211–12
irrigation 115
Ishihara, Shintaro 240, 241
Islam and silk trade 43–4, 47, 50, 56, 58, 61–2
islands, ecology and Pacific 70–82
Israel, Jonathan I. 31, 33
Italy 46, 48, 55, 211, 213

Jacquard, Joseph 48
Jacquard loom 48, 54–5
Japan: Australia trade 227; China trade 91, 189, 191, 204, 209, 211, 213–14, 219; grains 111–13, 115, 118; island trade 79–82; silk trade 42, 50–5; silver 23, 26; trade coins 158, 162–3
Java 111, 114
Jayakumar, Foreign Minister of Singapore 245
Jiang Qing 200
Jiang, Yu-xiang 43
Jianghan 95, 104–5
Jones, Eric et al. 2
Jones, Gavin and Margaret 244
Juan Fernández Islands 80
junks 88–92, 96
Justinian, emperor 41

Kahn, E. 155
Kangxi emperor 86–7, 89
Keating, Paul 237–8, 242
Kelly, Paul 237
Kendall, Donald 217
Khan, Genghis 44
Khotan, China 41–2
Kilpatrick, James A. 204, 205, 207
King, Carolyn 78
Kishimoto-Nakayama, Mio 86
Kissinger, Henry 210, 220
Kito, H. 114, 115
Kobata, A. 81
Korea 42, 111–13, 115
Korean War 189–91, 213
Kozinga, Ming loyalist 86
Kuhfuss, William J. 217
Kuhn, Dieter 46

Kushans 40
Kwangtung, China 110, 116

La Trobe, Charles Joseph 128
labor: cheap in China 212; gold rushes 129, 135–6, 145–6
lagging sectors and economic analysis 132, 139–42
Larkin, Thomas O. 135
Latham, John 1–22, 110–24
Laughlin, J. Laurence 163, 164, 165
Lawe-Davies, Joanna 237
Lee Boon Yang 227
Lee, H. 112
Lee Kuan Yew 226, 235, 236, 237, 241
Lee, Oliver M. 189, 190, 191
legal tender and trade coins 153–5, 165–6
Legarda, Benito, Jr 27
Legg, Stephen 177, 180, 182
Leggett, William F. 50
Li Diaoyuan 95
Li, Jin-ming 47
Li, Lillian M. 63
Li, Ming-wei 40, 42, 47, 58
Li Shizheng 89–90
Lian, Kwen Fee 241, 242
Linder, Stefan 2
Linderman, Henry 162, 165
Little, Charles 153
Liu, T-j. 115, 116
Liu, Ts'ui-jung 78
Liu, Xinru 43, 44, 62
livestock 72–4, 78, 142, 179–81
living standards 116, 137–8, 232
Lombe brothers 48
London, England 52–3
London, H.I. 229
Lopez, Robert 41, 45
Lubman, Stanley 218
Lucca, Italy 46
luxury goods 61–2, 214
Lynch, John 28, 29
Lyon, France 53, 55

Ma, Debin 5, 38–63
Macao 27, 50
MacDonald, Barrie 76
McDonald, D. 154

Macfarlane, Ian 2
McFarlane, John 177, 179
machinery, China–U.S. trade 192, 197–201, 203, 206–7, 212
McIntosh, Ida 174
McLean, Ian 132
McMahan, prime minister of Australia 230
McNeill, H. William 57, 58, 59, 60, 61
McNeill, John R. 3, 7, 16, 70–82, 99
Maddock, Rodney 132
Magellan, Ferdinand 7, 70, 72–3, 78, 81
Mah Bow Tan 227
Mah, Feng-hwa 197
maize 78, 113–17
Malaysia 111–12; perceptions of Australian identity (1966–96) 224–46
mammals 176, 178–9, 182
Manila, Philippines 2, 4, 24–33, 51–2, 73, 75, 77, 79, 90
manufactured goods 93, 96, 211–13
Mao Zedong 192, 200
Maori 74
Marchak, Patricia 80
Maria Theresa, empress of Austria 156
Maria Theresa thaler 154–6, 166
Marianas 77
market: gold rushes 133, 137, 142–7; rice 115–16, 120, 122; U.S. and trade dollar 158, 162
Marks, Robert B. 3, 9, 10, 85–105
Marquesas 74–5
Marseilles, France 53
Martin, Brett 227
Mason, R.B. 135
Mathatir Bin Mohamad 226, 232–3, 234, 236, 239–41
Matsui, Shichiro 42
Mazumdar, Sucheta 94, 95
Meaney, Neville 225
measurement, standardization 56
meat and fish 212
Melbourne, Australia 130, 133–4, 136–7, 145

merchant trade 26–7, 49–50, 54
mercury 28
Merlin, Mark 75
Merrill, E.D. 73
metals 50–1, 80–1, 197, 202, 207–8, 212
Mexico: silk trade 50–2; silver 90; trade dollars 155–6, 159–63, 165–7
Middle East and silk trade 42–6, 46, 48, 53, 57
Milan, Italy 53
Miller, Sally M. *et al.* 2
millets 111–12, 114, 116–17
milling 141
Ming dynasty (1368–1644) 24, 45, 47, 50–2, 89, 97, 102
mining 80–1
Mizoguchi, T. 114
moderates in China 193, 195
modernization of China 191–5, 198–204, 209, 220
Moerenhout, Jacques Antoine 135
Moluccas 30–3
Monfalcon, Grau y 31, 32
Mongol empire 43–7, 59
monsoons 79, 88–9
Monterey, Ca, USA 131
Morris-Suzuki, Tessa 49, 50
Morse, H.B. 88, 90, 92, 99
most-favored-nations status 213–14
mother-of-pearl 75
mountain ash 174, 176
mulberry trees 97, 102–5, 115–16
multiculturalism 224–6, 229–32, 237–8, 241–2, 244, 246
multiracialism 224–6, 228–31, 234, 237–8, 241–2, 246
Mutual Defence Assistance Control Act (1951) (USA) 189
Muzaffar, Chandra 243

Nagasaki, Japan 50–1, 91
Nan Hai, China 87
Nanyang, China 85, 87–97
NATO and Chinese trade 189, 204
Nauru 76, 82
navigation 56, 60, 75
Neal, L. 110

Neary, J. Peter 131
Needham, Joseph 40, 41, 42, 44, 46, 47, 48
New China Policy Committee 217
New Guinea 81
New Hebrides 75
New South Wales, Australia 125–6, 128, 130, 138–9, 142–3, 175, 178
New York, U.S.A. 54, 145
New Zealand 74, 76, 78, 144
Ng, C-k. 89
Nicholas, Albert 177
Nixon, Richard, president of U.S.A. 17–18, 188, 192, 202, 204, 209–10, 214–17, 219–21
nomads 57–8
North, D. 61
Nunn, Patrick 72

oats 141, 144
Officer, Charles 71
oil 201, 203, 212
oilseeds 206, 212
Ong Teng Cheong 227
opium 76–7, 97, 100–2, 104–5
Opium War (1839–42) 52, 97, 99, 102
Ottoman empire 46–7, 59
Otways, Victoria, Australia 174, 178
Owen, Roger 54

Pacey, Arnold 48
Page, Jake 71
paper making 38, 56
Paris Coordinating Committee (COCOM) 189–91, 204
Pariset, Ernest 55
Parthians 40
Paterson, NJ, USA 53
Paul, Rodman 129
Payne, Douglas 198
Pearl River delta, China 86–7, 94–5, 97, 101–5, 115
pebrine (silkworm disease) 53
peddlars 59–60
Persia 40–4, 46, 48–9, 56, 59
Pfeffer, C.K. 178
Phelan, John L. 32–3

Philip II, of Spain 25
Philippines 78, 117–18; sixteenth and seventeenth century 23–34
phosphates 75–6
pioneer plants 176, 181
piracy 60
plant, manufacturing 192, 198, 201, 204, 207
plantations 77
plants 73–4, 78, 171–2, 176–7, 180, 183–4
political motivations for China–U.S. trade 188, 192, 210, 220
Polk, James Knox, president of U.S.A. 125
Polo, Marco 46
Polynesia 77
Pomeranz, Kenneth 3
Pool, Ian 74
population: China 204–5, 220; consumerism 211; de- 73, 78; effects of gold rushes on 129–31, 133
porcelain 101
port facilities 130–1
Portugal 24, 27, 47, 50–1, 60
potatoes 78, 113–15
predators 176, 179–80
Price, Charles 225
prices: gold rushes and effects on 137–9, 141, 145; silk 59, 61
printing 38, 56
professionals as Australian immigrants 227, 235–6
profitability of Spain in the Pacific 23–34
property rights 130–1, 146
protection costs and silk 59–61
Pursglove, J.W. 112
Pye, Lucian W. 193

Qing dynasty (1644–1911) 45, 86, 89–90
Qu Dajun 87, 94
Quataert, Donald 54
Queensland, Australia 178–9
Queensland stinging tree 181
quicksilver 142, 144

rabbit 172, 180

race: discrimination in Australia 225–6, 228, 231, 233–5, 239, 242–6; riots in Malaysia and Singapore 234, 241
racism 164
radicals in China 193, 195
Rafidah Aziz, Datuk Seri 240
ragwort 180, 183
Rallu, J.-L. 74
Ramachandran, Selakumaran 227, 230, 231
rapproachment, China–U.S. (1971) 188–221
Ratnam, K.J. 234
rats 72, 74, 178, 180, 182
Rawski, T.G. 120, 121
Ray, Haraprasad 43
recognition of trade dollars 156–8, 160
regrowth, forest 176–7
resource effect and economic analysis 132–3
resources, China 192, 211
Reyerson, K. 45
rice: Asian growth 110–22; China–U.S. trade 205–6; trade and agro-ecology of China 86, 93, 95–7, 103–5
ring-barking 175
Rivett, Kenneth 225, 229, 230, 235
Rolls, Eric 172, 174
Roman Empire 40–1, 59
Ross, J. 96
Rossabi, Morris 45, 59
round-grain rice 110
rules of law 130–1, 146
Russia 45, 59

St. Clair, David J. 3, 14, 15, 152–67
San Francisco, CA, USA 54, 125, 127–8, 130–1, 133–9, 141–2, 145, 160–1, 164
sandalwood 75–6
Sassanid Empire 40, 44
Saw, Swee-Hock 224
Schurz, Lyle W. 28
science and silk 49, 54
sea cucumber 75

seal hunting 75, 79–80
Searle, Peter 234
Segal, Gerald 2
Selection Acts, Australia 174, 181–2
self-reliance, China and 191–5, 207
sericulture 39, 41–4, 46, 49–50, 52–6, 62, 103, 115
service sectors and economic analysis 132
settlers, Australian 174–84
Shanghai 100, 122; Communique (1971) 197, 219–21
Sharp, Illsa 238, 239
sheep 142, 171, 179–80
Sheridan, Greg 226
Sherman Silver Purchase Act (1990) (USA) 152
Shi, Z. 116, 117
Shih, Min-hsiung 52
Shineberg, Dorothy 75
shipbuilding 56, 60
Shu, Jing, et al. 232
Siam 89–91, 94, 110
silk: China 2; rice and 115–16, 120; silver and 26–7, 33; trade and agro-ecology of China 86, 97, 99, 101–5; U.S.–China trade 208, 214
Silk Road: modern 52–5; overland 38–47, 49, 56–61; sea route 44, 46–54, 56, 58–62
silk-reeling 48–9, 54–5
silver: bullion 98, 100–1, 104, 155, 160–6; China and 2–4, 23–9, 31–3, 76; China and trade dollar 152–67; island 80–1; silk and 49–52, 62
Simmonds, N.W. 112
Singapore and perceptions of Australian identity (1966–96) 224–46
Singh, Karpal 243
situado 29–33
Skemp, John Rowland 177, 181
skill and Australian immigration policy 227, 229–31, 234–6
slash-and-burn 114–15, 175
smallpox 73, 78, 171

Smith, Adam 23
Smith, Ian 233
smuggling 27–9, 50, 89–90
Sneddon, Billy 229
So, Alvin 100, 101, 102, 103
Soh, Felix 238
Song dynasty (960–1279) 46, 48
Sorenson, Edward 178
sorghum 112, 117
Soule, Frank *et al.* 135
Soviet Union 189–90, 201, 210, 219
soybeans 112, 114, 116, 206, 211
Spain 50, 60, 73, 79; profitability in the Pacific 23–34
Spanish silver dollars 155–7, 162
species, invasion of 72–4, 77, 171–2, 176–80, 182–4
Spence, Jonathan 200
spending effect and economic analysis 132–3
spice trade 24, 30–1
Stahnke, Arthur A. 217
Steensgaard, Niels 58, 59, 61
stinkweed 181
Stockley, David 230, 231
Stokes, H.J.W. 177, 178
Stone, Charles 77
storms 71
subsidiary coins 153, 159, 165–6
Suez Canal 53
sugar cane 77, 85, 94–9, 101, 103–5, 115–16, 120
Sugiyama, Shinya 53
Sullivan, Gerard 244
Surls, Frederick 205
Sutchbury, geologist 128
Sutcliffe, Anthony 3–4
Sutter, John 127, 141
Swaminathan, M.S. 110
sweet potatoes 104, 113–17
swordgrass 181
Sydney, Australia 130
Syria 46
Szechwan, China 205

Taiwan 50, 86, 89
Tan, Tony 227
Tang dynasty (618–960) 43, 59, 62

tariffs, U.S. and Chinese trade 213–14
taro 113
Tasmania 178, 180–2
taxes 27–32, 114, 159, 162
tea 98–9, 101–2, 104–5, 158
technology: island 70, 77; shipping 60; silk 38–9, 41, 44, 46, 48–56, 62, 102; U.S.–China trade 192, 194–204, 208–9
TePaske, John J. 28
textiles 207–8, 212, 214
thistle 180
Thomas, D. 140
throwing, silk 46, 48–9
thylacine 180, 182–3
timber 80
Timmer, C.P. 118
tobacco 114–16, 120, 205–6
tortoiseshell 75
Totman, Conrad 80, 81
Tracey, J.G. 173
trade: Australia 130, 227; China–U.S. 158–9, 161–7, 188–221; environmental change 171; global 3–4; island 75, 79; maritime and agro-ecology of South China 85–105; Pacific 2; silk 38–63
trade coins 154–8; American trade dollars 152–67
transport 56–60, 62, 70, 81, 192, 199–205, 212
treaty port system 52
trees 171–7, 181
Trewartha, geographer 103
tribute trade 28, 47, 50, 89
Truman, Harry S., president of U.S.A. 189
trust and trade dollars 156–8
Tsubouchi, Y. 114
twisting-frame, silk 46, 48
typhoons 71

UN and Chinese trade 189–90
unilateralism 189, 191–2
universities and multiracialism in Australia 226–7, 244
U.S.–China Relations Inc. National Committee 217–18

U.S.A.: Australian immigration policy 228, 241; California gold rushes (1848–57) 125–47; Pacific islands 79; silk 53–6, 63; silver 23–9, 31–2; trade and China 87, 92, 97, 188–221; trade dollars 152–67
Usack, A.H. 191

VanRavensway, Dan 75
Victoria, Australia 125–6, 128, 130, 138–9, 142–3
Vietnam refugees and Australian immigration policy 230–2, 236–7
violence 73, 78
Viraphol, S. 89, 91, 94
Viviani, Nancy 225, 236, 237
volcanoes 70–1
volume of Pacific trade (sixteenth and seventeenth century) 27–8
von Glahn, Richard 3, 26
von Richthofen, Baron Ferdinand 38

wages and gold rushes 133–7
wallabies 178–9, 182
Wang, Gungwu 89
Wang Sing-Wu 224
warehousing 130–1
Warner, Lori 16, 18, 188–221
Warwick, Frost 171–84
water chestnut 113
Watson, David 153
weaving silk 39, 41–2, 44, 46, 48–50, 52–3
Webb, L.G. 173
Webb, Leonard 182
Weeramantry, Christopher 76
weighing, standardization 56
Wen, Jin 39, 42, 44, 45, 46, 50, 51, 52
Werblowsky, R.J. Zwi 39
Wester, Lyndon 80
Western, J. 180

whalers 74
wheat 115–17, 205–6, 211; and gold rushes 125–47
White Australia Policy 225, 227–31, 233–8, 240, 244–6
White, Richard 229
Whitlam, Gough 230–1, 236
Wilbraham, A. 117
Wilde, Sally 177, 178, 182
Willem, John 153, 155, 156, 157, 158, 159, 160, 162, 163, 164, 165, 166
Williams, Geoff 177
Williams, Maslyn 76
Wilson, Richard 217, 219
Wong, Brendan 245
Wong, Loong 239
Wong, R. Bin 3
Wong Shuk Min 245
Woodgate, P.W. et al. 182
Wright, Doris Marion 130
writing 56
Wu, Tai 47
Wu-ti, emperor 40

Xian, China 40, 44
Xu, Xin-Wu 42, 54

yam 113–14
Yan Zhongping 100, 101
Yangtze River, China 39, 44–5, 92, 95, 99, 101, 110, 115–17, 121–2, 205
Yarwood, A.T. 225
Ye Xian'en 90
Yellow River, China 39, 44
Yeo Cheow Tong 227
Yeo, George Yong-Boon 239
Yi, T. 115
yields, 'miracle' 206
Yuan dynasty 47–8

Zanier, Claudier 46, 48, 49
Zhang Chien 40
Zheng Ho 47